AS I RECALL...

Growing Up in the 1950s, 60s, and 70s in Kenmore, NY and Beyond

Antics, Escapades, & Adventures of Gregory Granger Laker:
My Auto-biography, Volume One 1951-1977

BY GREGORY GRANGER LAKER

DORRANCE
PUBLISHING CO
EST. 1920
PITTSBURGH, PENNSYLVANIA 15238

Dorrance Publishing Co
585 Alpha Drive
Pittsburgh, PA 15238
Visit our website at *www.dorrancebookstore.com*

ISBN: 978-1-6366-1142-6
eISBN: 978-1-6366-1735-0

Introduction

Not many people have the patience (or interest) to listen to my stories or to what I have to say. Perhaps by putting it all in writing, it will be easier to read than to listen to my slow (deliberate) speech.

This book is intended to be a part of my (Greg Laker) archives. Hopefully it will give insight into my life as a regular guy, growing up in a middle class family, in suburban Buffalo, NY. By no means am I a professional writer, so expect to read this with the idea the author is taking much artistic license. Don't expect perfect grammar or spelling. I will do my best to keep things in the proper chronology, and to be as accurate as possible. Except for the first chapter, which will take us to age 5 (let's face it – how much of that stuff does anyone remember from their first 5 years?) After that, I will try to go year-by-year chapters... this may help you, the reader, to relate to specific points in time. I will consider this book to be a success if I can get my wife, siblings, children, grandchildren, and maybe a few close friends to read it.

As I write this book, it has been very interesting to exercise my memory and have my mind retrieve information I would otherwise never have had a reason to think about. One thought leads to another, like a chain reaction, and it starts pouring out faster than it can be recorded.

You may read this book and think I am doing a lot of bragging, and it's all about me. After all, isn't that what an autobiography is? There will be many stories I am proud of and some I am not so proud of. Many of the stories include friends and acquaintances I have made through the years. If you are lucky enough to find your name somewhere on the pages, to follow it means you have a warm spot in my heart.

So Kaitlin, Joanna, Carter, Will, Evelyn, Caroline, and Kenley here we go. This is a little bit about what is in your genes. Enjoy!!

Start of writing November 2017 @ age 66
Gregory Granger Laker
grangerlaker@yahoo.com

To those I have offended, please forgive me….
To those who have offended me, I forgive you.

Chapter One
1951-1956

It all started July 8, 1951 at Millard Fillmore Hospital on Delaware Avenue at Gate Circle Buffalo, NY. My parents, James Leo and Amelia Minthorne (Smith) Laker, welcomed their third child into this world – Gregory Granger, 8 lbs. 8 oz. My mother was said to have exclaimed, "He has red hair!" At the time, my mother was 30, Dad was 28, my sister, Amy Clements, was almost 6, and my brother, James Stuart, was 3 ½.

Of course much of what I remember of the first few years is assisted by photos, 8mm family film, and with family stories told over the years. We lived in a typical, two-story wood structure, 1920s vintage home in the Village of Kenmore, bordering the City of Buffalo to the north. The way my mind works, I envision places and buildings from a birds eye view... kind of like Google Earth. Some of the things I remember about our house at 199 Parkwood Ave. were a shared driveway with the Chitley's, a two car garage with a rectangular basketball backboard and hoop (a Laker prerequisite,) super-sized sand box, and a heavy duty "playground worthy" extra tall swing. At some point, around 5 years old, I took a flying leap from that swing which resulted in a sprained wrist which required a trip to Millard Fillmore Hospital for x-rays and a sling. The house itself featured 3 bedrooms, one full bath up, living room, dining room, and kitchen. There was a full basement with a fruit cellar and laundry tubs. The washing machine was a round barrel type with a hand crank ringer (state of the art.) There was also a full-sized walk-up attic with two gables which had a lot of potential. Another fine feature of the house was a full-sized front porch. So, it was a nice modest home in a nice, tree-lined, middle class neighborhood. I think my parents bought this house in the late 40s for $8,000.

As I said, the Chitleys were our shared driveway neighbors. They were an older couple, probably in their late 50's or early 60's at the time, and they had a son, Vern, who was probably in his mid 20's. Naturally, the double driveway became an extended play area for us kids. Vern always had a hot car... seems to me I, somehow, remember a red & black Mercury convertible with a coon tail on the antenna. He would come speeding in and out of the driveway, and my mother would give him hell.

Here is a true story, which must have happened when I was 2 or 3. As the story goes, I was in the kitchen when an electric hot plate fell from the kitchen counter and landed on my face. It more or less branded a coil wound into my face. They say I was healed by the power of Christian Science – prayer. This was the faith my mother and her family were brought up with. A miracle?

Just a note, for the record, sometime in 1955 I had Chicken Pox. Any recollection of this is very vague.

By the time I was 4, there was an activity I distinctly re-member. I had a red, steel framed tricycle with tall rear tires built for speed, and barely noticed uneven cracks in the sidewalks. I was allowed to ride this tricycle around the block (on the sidewalk, of course) by myself. This meant heading east on Parkwood about five doors to Rowley, then south to East Hazeltine, then west (a long block) to Myron, then north back to Parkwood, and back east to 199. This was probably close to a half mile. This would probably be frowned upon these days, but that's the way it was back then.

Speaking of the way things were back then.... another simple thing I remember is the milk man. I think it was Coley's. The milk man would deliver the milk, eggs, and other dairy products right to your insulated tin milk box which hung on the side of your house next to the back door. You would leave your empty, one quart glass bottles in the pass through for exchange.

There were lots of young kids in the immediate neighborhood. Directly across the street was my best friend, Gary Galbreath, who was my age. He had two older sisters, Susan and Barbara, who were more my sister Amy's age, and a much older brother, Donald. Next door to the Galbreath's were the Gates'. Pamela Gates was also my age (Gary, Pam, and I would eventually go through school and graduate from Kenmore West class of 1969) and she had a younger sister, Elaine, younger brother, Allen, older brother, Dennis – close to my brother Jim's age – and an older sister, Linda, who again was more Amy's age. Moving two doors the other direction from the Galbreath's were the Lindhurst's. They had a son, Dennis, who was a year older than me, a son Phillip, a year younger than me, and an even younger daughter, Janice. Suffice to say, this formed a substantial nucleus of friends/playmates. As a group, in fair weather, we would play tag, hopscotch, swim in a 9" inflatable swimming pool, freeze tag, and our favorite, hide & seek (allie-allie-home come free.) We would run and play until the street lights came on, which was the signal to go home.

Like I said though, Gary and I were very tight ,and he always had cool toys. One toy I can clearly remember was his "ride in"

Caterpillar, yellow, pedal powered bulldozer with tracks and lever controls for steering and a front blade. Really cool!

Sometime during the summer of 1956, (around 5 years old) I graduated from my red steel framed tricycle to a hand-me-down 18" 2-wheeler with training wheels… and shortly after, without the training wheels.

Another strange thing I can remember from that time was a reoccurring dream/nightmare. I was thrust into an industrial plant setting complete with molten steel, heavy equipment, and loud noise. Somehow, I always associated it with industry along River Road in the Town of Tonawanda. It made me wonder later about reincarnation. How could this type of information make its way into my young mind?

So, that Fall, 1956, I would start half day (morning) Kindergarten at Washington School. After my Mother took me the first day, it was up to me to walk to and from school. That's the way it was back then. Walk the long block west to Myron, cross Myron to Copley's fix-it shop, then across Parkwood north to Euclid, cross Euclid to Warren, cross Warren to Knowlton, cross Knowlton and go one long block west to Washington School. It was well over a half mile… pretty good for a 5-year-old, and I'm sure sometimes it was with a group of kids… maybe Gary and Pamela. Anyway, Miss Lidy was the teacher, and I liked her. Kindergarten back then was a lot more like what pre-school is today… arts, crafts, counting, skipping, and a nap on your rug.

NOTE: I am happy to say my recently emerged Kindergarten report card will be a part of this book in the photo sections.

Record of Greg Laker

Achievements — S means Satisfactory	1st 2nd and 4th		
1. Can tell own name and father's name.		S	
2. Can tell address.		S	
3. Counts without help to this number.		8 61 100	
4. Ties a bow.		S	
5. Knows right from left.		S	
6. Knows colors.		S	
7. Can name days of week in order.		✓ ✓	
8. Knows age and birthday.		S S	
9. Can copy numbers to 10.		S	
10. Recognizes numbers to 10.		S S	
11. Has learned to write name this way.		S	

Greg

Teacher's message: Parents, please answer on back of card

FIRST QUARTER

Our primary purpose in sending Greg's card home at this time is for you to become thoroughly acquainted with it. Please read the entire card so you can follow through with us at home.

SECOND QUARTER

Greg enjoys talking responsibilities and does so capably. He goes about his work quietly and well and sees a task through to the finish.

THIRD QUARTER

Greg is making satisfactory progress.

FOURTH QUARTER

In what way has this record card been of help to you in understanding your child's progress during his kindergarten year. Please explain.

Parents: Have you visited the kindergarten this quarter? Promoted to first grade.

"The Kindergarten is the link between home and school. It leads the little child from home interests into wider social interests."

S SATISFACTORY PROGRESS   I SHOWING IMPROVEMENT
∨ NEED FOR IMPROVEMENT

Habits — Attitudes — Skills	1st 2nd and 4th		
HEALTH HABITS — Covers cough and sneeze.		I I S	
Has a handkerchief and a pocket for it.		S S S S	
Relaxes during rest period.		S S S S	
Has habits of toilet cleanliness.		S S S S	
PERSONAL HABITS — Dresses promptly with little help. Takes good care of personal belongings and wraps.		S S S	
SOCIAL ATTITUDES — Uses please, thank you, excuse me, pardon me. Has a courteous, gracious attitude towards others.		S S S	
Works and plays well with others.		S S S S	
MOTOR CONTROL — Performs physical activities easily and well. can gallop		I S	
EMOTIONAL HABITS — Shows desirable emotional traits. Depends on self whenever possible.		S S S	
MENTAL HABITS — Shows initiative. Follows directions well. Contributes worth-while ideas to work and play. Is attentive.		I I S	
WORK HABITS — Is neat, capable, busy, quiet. Takes good care of work materials.		I S S	
SPEECH — Speaks plainly.		S	
LANGUAGE — Expresses ideas often and well.		S S S	
NUMBER — Shows a number sense.		S	
MUSIC — Sings on pitch.		S	
Has a good sense of rhythm.			
ART — Expresses ideas well in paint, crayon and other materials.		S S S	
WEIGHT	49¾	—	50½¼
HEIGHT	48¾	—	50¼
DAYS ABSENT	0	0	0
TIMES TARDY	0	0	0

KENMORE PUBLIC SCHOOLS
KENMORE, NEW YORK

KINDERGARTEN
AND JUNIOR PRIMARY
PROGRESS RECORD

School WASHINGTON   Year 19 56–57

Principal Franklin S Johnson

Kindergarten Teacher Fay Leidy

Junior Primary Teacher

To Parents:

The school is interested in the growth of your child, in the development of a healthy, happy, well-adjusted, mentally-alert individual.

Have your child at school on time every day that health permits. School law requires that after an absence or tardiness, a written reason be presented upon the child's return to school.

We invite you to a careful study of this record card. It offers you a suggestive guide by which to work with your school for your child's growth.

The record is sent to you quarterly with a personal message from the teacher concerning your child. After the last marking the card belongs to you permanently.

It is your privilege to observe school sessions at any time. Arrangement for conferences with teacher or principal may be made on such occasions. Often a personal talk will bring about mutual understanding.

CARL W. BAISCH, Superintendent

Chapter Two
1957-1958 (Victoria 2758)

A quick story, which I think happened in the winter of early 1957, so I was still only 5 years old. Dad took my brother Jim and me to Sheridan Park for sledding/tobogganing. Many of the area parks had toboggan ramps or slides which would provide a steep, fast head start down a hill for your toboggan. By the way, Jim and I recently saw a picture of the three of us on a toboggan at the top of one of these slides. It must have been taken that particular day. I think it was from some old Town of Tonawanda literature. Anyway, we also had our sleds and flying saucers. So, I got on my sled, laying down head first. Dad gave me one of those running starts to make sure I had a nice long run. The ride was long, alright, kept on going and going all the way to a creek and splash... in. The "Old Man" came running. I'm sure he could see the outcome developing by the time I was half way down the hill. You need to keep in mind, this was before the time of water resistant clothing... It was 100% wool. So, Jim and Dad fished me out and loaded me into his 1952 Chevy (ESSO company car at the time)... cranked up the heat, stripped me down, and wrapped me in an Army blanket. Needless to say, my mother was not happy, but the tension was cut with a little Nestles hot chocolate.

Here is where it gets a little fuzzy for me, as far as chronology. During the mid-to late-fifties, we took a few family trips. If my sister Amy and my brother Jim ever read this book, they can correct the order of events. After all, they would be the only ones to care. So, I am going first with our trip to Del Ray Beach, Florida. The basis for this choice was it was well documented by the family 8mm film that we were still rolling with the 1948 gray Studebaker with a car top rack. This was before (not long before) the days of the interstate so there was no I-95. We may have been on US 1 or something similar. I think the old Studebaker had to make a couple of pit stops on the way down, but looking back, it must have been the 2nd day of the trip we made it to the "Georgian Lodge" for an overnight. Again, this particular overnight was well documented by the family 8mm films. Mom and Dad must have really splurged for this stop. There was a beautiful, large, concrete swimming pool which was rare in those days, and a real treat for us. The pool was surrounded by palm trees, and there was even shuffleboard. We took full advantage of the facilities… got up the next morning, had some fresh squeezed orange juice, and hit the road for Del Ray Beach. A great family experience.

My father's home town was Mitchell, Indiana. Mitchell was a small town in southern Indiana… maybe about 3,000 in population. The town's biggest industry, by far, was the Carpenter Body Works. They manufacture and mount school bus bodies on truck chassis'. The story goes, my great grandfather, Harry Clements, loaned the money to Ralph Carpenter to start his business.

So, if I have my story straight, Ralph had a cousin, Eulah Carpenter Foddrill, who owned a bungalow in Del Ray Beach and she loaned it to us for a week. It was a beautiful place not far from the beach, complete with palm trees and orange trees. Again, the family 8mm film captured my brother and me attempting to climb the sway backed palm trees. Jim, of course, could climb all the way to the top and knock down some co-conuts... me, not so much. I was still only 5, after all. At that time, Del Ray Beach was still pretty sparse, so we had the ocean pretty much to ourselves. There were fresh water shower heads at the scattered beach entrances. It was the first ocean beach experience for all of us kids. We would take our blow up flotation devices and play in the surf... ride the waves. The 8mm film showed it took me a while to work up the courage to take the plunge. I think Dad gave me the coaxing I needed. This was all before Coppertone, or any other sun screen was popular, so I'm sure there were a few burnt bodies.

That's about all I can remember about that trip... I was only 5, after all. Oh, there *was* something about a shattered glass table?

On my tricycle at 199 Parkwood

In the pool with Pam Gates and other friends

Del Ray Beach

Family photo at Kitty Hawk, NC

That summer, Longfellow school was nearing completion. It was an elementary school designed to be K-3, like many other post war schools, not only in the massive Ken-Ton school district, but around the country. Longfellow school was located on Myron Ave, between Crosby and Nassau, and just across the street from Kenmore Junior High School (grades 7-9.) I was scheduled to start first grade there in September of 1957. The school was about six blocks away from Parkwood, so I would be able to walk with friends, like Gary Galbreath, or ride my new (hand me down) 20" 2-wheeler I graduated into. As it turned out, the Long-fellow school did not get completed on time, so the school district had to go to plan B. Under plan B, the Longfellow kids would have to be absorbed by other elementary schools in the district. This meant that I and many of the Longfellowers had to be bused across Delaware Ave and across Elmwood Ave to Betsy Ross School at Mang and Wilber, right in the middle of Mang Park (still in the Village of Kenmore.) Betsy Ross was also brand new, and similar to Longfellow school. This was the only time in my school years I had to bus to school.

Mrs. Lindberg was my first grade teacher. As I remember, she was older (probably in her 50s) and quite strict. This was when some teachers still carried around a yard stick to use as a pointer and an attention getter. I remember the work sheets being so simple to me. Every class room had the alphabet cards above the chalk board... Aa Bb Cc, and so on. I think it was then I took an interest in the art of lettering. All of these K-3 buildings, like Longfellow and Betsy Ross, had "gymterias"... large rooms that would double as a gymnasium and a cafeteria. You carried your lunch in a lunch box with a thermos, or you bought a lunch for 25 cents. If you bought milk, it was 2 cents for white, or 3 cents for chocolate (no 2% or skim)... ice cream for a nickel.

Gym class was my favorite, and I could sense, even from duck duck goose and relay races, I loved the competition.

So, by the end of the first semester, Longfellow school was complete and, after Christmas break, we headed there... Mrs. Lindberg and all. Another milestone, that spring was the first time I was kissed by a girl. It was Karen Fredo, a classmate. It was at the foot of her driveway on Wardman Ave. near Rowley. I had the funny feeling we were being watched by her father out the front window. Anyway, it "Put a spell on me".

That summer (1958,) I think, was my first trip to Mitchell, Indiana. Mitchell, as I mentioned earlier, was my Father's home town in southern Indiana, maybe 100 miles south of Indianapolis. Driving from Kenmore, the natural half way point was Akron, Ohio, where my father's uncle Carl and aunt Mary Jane (Clements) Christy lived. (By the way, this was still pre-Interstate, so we were traveling Routes 5 & 20 West along the south shore of Lake Erie.) Mary Jane was the sister of my father's mother Marjorie (Clements) Laker. The Christy's were probably in their upper 50s by then. They lived in a charming 20s vintage Dutch colonial home at 94 Kennelworth in an upper middle class neighborhood. Even at age 7, I could sense they were well-traveled. There were things around the house, like small sculptures they had collected from trips to Africa. My recollection is Uncle Carl and Aunt Mary Jane were very easy going and made us feel right at home. As evidenced by our family 8mm film, our cousins Steve (a little older than Jim,) and Valerie (a little older than me,) were also visiting from Bedford, Indiana (near Mitchell) with their parents Dwight and Martha Jane Inman. Martha Jane was my father's younger sister.

By now, I think, Uncle Carl was retired from a career in his business of asphalt paving. They always drove brand new Cadillacs. He would set us kids up on cots with army blankets in the semi-finished basement. We thought it was cool… an adventure for us. Another thing Uncle Carl took pleasure in was measuring and marking each of the kid's heights on a designated doorway jamb. This impressed me so much, I have carried that tradition on to this day.

Also present at that visit were Carl and Mary Jane's son, Jim Harry, and his wife, June. Their son Mike was just a toddler. We probably stayed in Akron a couple of nights, because the Christy's had time to take us for a day trip to their Country Club at Congress Lake. I can remember being loaded in the back seat of their black 1957 Cadillac with my siblings and being impressed by the power windows, A/C, and soft velour interior. Aunt Mary Jane was the driver, and she was a cigarette smoker (probably Lucky Strike or Camel). Meanwhile, Dad was following with Mom in Dad's 1952 Chevy. By the way, Dad was a heavy Camel smoker also, but I never thought much of it at the time. It didn't bother me then.

The Country Club Clubhouse was palatial and the grounds and golf course were beautiful. Congress Lake was large enough to accommodate small motor boats for cruising and fishing.

Now I think of it, my grandmother Marjorie (Nanny) Laker, and great grandmother Carrie Clements (Dad's grandmother), were also there. My great grandmother was always called Mama (pronounced Mamau.) So, after an afternoon at Congress, we would go back to the house and Aunt Mary Jane and the ladies would prepare a nice supper with fresh corn on the cob and burgers Uncle Carl had grilled. We would all gather around the table in their formal dining room a la the Cleavers. Iced tea was the preferred drink, with corn syrup optional.

Now it was onto Mitchell, which was a good day's drive across Ohio, and well into Indiana. Mama and Nanny lived upstairs of the funeral home my great grandfather Harry Clements (Bapa – pronounced Bapau) operated. Harry was deceased by now, and my grandfather, Joseph Laker, was well estranged from Nanny so, unfortunately, I never got to meet either of them.

Of the few things I can remember about that first trip to Mitchell was learning to shoot marbles (early carom play.) I would spend hours on the living room rug practicing, and then going out in the back dirt alley to shoot games with my newly found Mitchell friends. It was competitive, and you could win or lose marbles.

Meanwhile, my cousins Steve and Valerie Inman had returned from Akron to Bedford, which was only about 8 or 10 miles down the road. Bedford was quite a bit bigger than Mitchell... I'm guessing about 10,000 population, at the time. We would go there and play with them... bikes, toys, and other neighbor kids.

Another point of interest near Mitchell was Springmill State Park. It included an historic colonial village with log cabins and other old buildings to tour. There was a lake with swimming and picnic areas. It was a great place for the family to go to spend a day.

I think all together I've made five trips to Mitchell, and I've always enjoyed my time there.

Back in Kenmore, that summer I was starting to get more interested in baseball. My brother Jim was now playing for the Esso Braves and Dad was one of the coaches. Of course, Dad was able to swing the team sponsorship through Esso for uniforms etc. I was the bat boy and I had a uniform, while a few of the players did not - #privileged. I always felt a little uncomfortable about that, but that's the way Dad wanted it. If I do say so myself, I did a fine job keeping the equipment tidy and organized. So, I was spending a lot of time (hours) throwing a rubber ball against the front steps, watching and studying the odd bounces the ball would make and then catching it. When they had time, my brother or Dad would play catch with me.

Somewhere along about this time, my mother signed me up for piano lessons. I had to walk around the block to a lady's house on East Hazeltine. She was a nice lady (maybe my sister Amy would remember her name) but I wasn't into it. I got about as far as chop sticks and Yankee Doodle. Looking back, I wish I had been more patient... I would now love to be able to play a musical instrument. Listening to music has been a lifelong favorite interest of mine.

I was 7-years old, now. That fall, I went into the second grade at Longfellow school. My teacher was a middle-aged, kindly woman, Mrs. Robinson. She was probably my favorite teacher in my elementary years. Among the things we learned about was Winnie the Pooh and Christopher Robin. This delighted my mother because she was a fan. I was really into it, also. My mother had WTP & CR sound tracks on 78 rpm records from her childhood she allowed me to take to school and share with my classmates. The albums included drawings and story lines of WTP & CR, and they were a big hit with Mrs. Robinson and my classmates.

The class of about 20 students was divided into three reading groups. Reading was never one of my strong suits, so I was lucky to be in reading group 2 (borderline the lowly group 3.) So, when it was reading time, which-ever group's turn it was would gather around a round table at the back of the room near the "cloak room" where it was quietest. Eventually, it would be my turn to read from the reading book. I would be sweating bullets... and slowly read, "see Spot run." Of course, the esteemed group 1 was always a book ahead of group 2.

ESSO BRAVES SCHEDULE

6/1	Esso Braves	vs	Jets	at	Phillip Sheridan No. 1
6/15	Esso Braves	vs	Hilburger's	at	Mang 2
6/22	Esso Braves	vs	Mitchell's	at	Mang 3
6/25	Kenmore Klippers	vs	Esso Braves	at	Phillip Sheridan No. 4
6/29	Town Boys Club	vs	Esso Braves	at	Mang 2
7/6	Esso Braves	vs	Town Youth Center	at	Mang 4
7/9	Esso Braves	vs	Jets	at	Phillip Sheridan No. 4
7/13	Crane's	vs	Esso Braves	at	Mang 3
7/16	Esso Braves	vs	Hilburger's	at	Mang 4
7/20	Kenmore Klippers	vs	Esso Braves	at	Phillip Sheridan No. 1
7/27	Esso Braves	vs	Mitchell's	at	Mang 3
8/3	Town Boys Club	vs	Esso Braves	at	Mang 2

Players

Eric Averill	Pitcher	No. 6	Scott Miles	2nd Base	19
Bill Brown	1st Base	7	Garry Miller	Outfielder	18
Sandy Clark	Short Stop	4	Robert Mioducki	Outfielder	9
George Cownie	Catcher	8	Ricky Reddien	Outfielder	10
Allen Eddy	Pitcher	2	Jeff Tubin	Outfielder	3
Jack Etkin	Catcher	20	Jim Ulrich	1st Base	13
Richard Gluckman	Outfielder	15	Jeff Weeks	3rd Base	5
Richard Hartman	2nd Base	16	Greg Yensan	Pitcher	11
James Laker	Outfielder	1	Red McGary	Outfielder	17
Tommy Less	Outfielder	14	Greg Laker	Batboy	21
Don Meidel	Outfielder	12			

Coaches

Coach	Loine Weeks
Coach	Jim Laker
Manager	Lee Miles

Buy at these ESSO STATIONS

Jack's Sheridan	Delaware and Sheridan
Fred Bundy	Sheridan and Belmont
Circle Esso	Military and Merle
Kenwood Service	Kenmore and Military
Plaza Esso	Delaware and Avery
Ken-Lou Esso	Kenmore and Louvaine
Kenmore Kustom	3200 Delaware

Esso Braves

Dad >

Me >

< Jim

Brother Jim and Me

Dennis Lindhurst, Gary Galbreath and me

At Camp Duffield - Dad's '59 Plymouth Fury behind me

Grades 1 through 6 each had three class rooms, so there were three 2nd grades, three 3rd grades etc.. Pretty much the nucleus of students stayed together in the same class 1st through 6th grade. Naturally, you would get to know and be closer to this nucleus of classmates. But, when it came time for gym or recess the common grades would be lumped together. Some of my nucleus of class-mates included: Patty Lenihan, Pam Gates, Danny Webb, Paul Mathias, Jane Hewett, Barbara Hale, Pete Zebrowski, Arthur Ax-lerod, Mike Lippman, Karen Fredo, Jackie Webb*, Bobby Kelley, Bobby Wheaton, Bobby Burwell, Arthur Moran, Mary Rodgers, Dave Koscielniak, Jim Kennedy, Jack Kramer, Becky Abgott, and Ron Sorrento. All of these classmates would go on to be part of the 850+ students who would eventually graduate with me in the Kenmore West class of 1969.

*Here is a good story to end this chapter with. Along about now, I was feeling a new found appreciation for the opposite sex. This was a distraction which would follow me through all of my school years. I had a tendency to day dream. By today's standards I was probably ADD (attention deficit disorder.)

Anyway, Jackie Webb was a cute gal who was part of the nucleus. I had a crush on her, and the feeling was mutual. It was winter with a lot of snow… maybe just before Christmas vacation 1958. Jackie and I were playing with our school mates out back of Longfellow school on the playground. It got later and later and finally, it was just the two of us. We both knew what was on each other's mind, but we were each so shy and awkward. Finally, it happened…the kiss!

SIDE NOTE: Somewhere around this time frame my Mother hosted a birthday party for me at the Glen Casino Amusement Park in Williamsville. I think I had five or six of my friends there. It was a really cool place. The rides, as I remember, were suitable for kids under 10 years old. I wonder if that place still exists.

Chapter Three
1959

Dad worked for ESSO as a sales representative. His territory was Erie and Niagara counties. He would call on all of the ESSO station dealers in that area... I'm guessing there were 25-30, at least. He would train these dealers and their men to promote TBA (tires, batteries, and accessories.) One of his major accounts was at the corner of Main & Delevan, in the city of Buffalo, where they actually had a classroom set up to do some of this training. Here, and at some other key locations, he would occasionally set up major promotional days where there would be prizes and refreshments given to customers. My brother Jim, and later, I, would get paid to dress like a clown and hawk customers in from the street side. We got used to hearing stories about his various dealers and locations from Lockport to Holland. At some point around this time, I remember Dad announcing he had gotten a raise that put him into the five figure range. That wasn't bad iron for those times. He was also provided a company car with gas and an expense account. Sometime that year, they put him in a 1959 Plymouth Fury. It was a hot car... emerald green, big fins in the rear, and some big V8 with a push button automatic transmission. It ran like a Tiger because it drank ESSO EXTRA.

Baseball was still my favorite sport. That spring, Dad took me to my first Buffalo Bison game at Offerman stadium. As we walked through the tunnel to our seats, I could not believe my first look at the bright green grass on the field. It was the most beautiful thing I had ever seen. This is where I really got the feel of the game and how it was supposed to be played… I was hooked. The Bison played in the International League with Rochester, Syracuse, Toronto, Tidewater, Toledo, and Columbus, to name a few. I followed them closely… checking the standings every day in the "Courier Express." The radio broadcasts were done by the infamous Bill Mazur on WGR. Bill would do the road games via ticker tape along with sound effects like the crack of the bat or crowd noise. It was cool. Many of the players we watched went on to the Majors.

Game day would be on Sunday… leaving church at Lafayette Presbyterian… hustling home and changing our clothes. Mom would pack a stack of bologna sandwiches and a thermos full of Kool-Ade in the good old plaid carry case. Dad and I would drive down near Offerman on the east side of Buffalo (black poverty, rough.) On our drive down Michigan Ave, Dad would instruct me to keep my eyes straight ahead… no gawking. We would park in the same front yard of a black gentleman every time. The $5 charge included protection, as well… Dad would explain to me. Sometimes, we might even catch a double header. It was great.

The ESSO Braves were back in action. If I remember correctly, my brother Jim played outfield, first base, and some pitching. Dad was still one of the coaches, along with Mr. Miles and Mr. Loren Weaks (former pro-athlete.) They each had sons on the team, as well. They were competing in the grasshopper division, and I was still batboy, but itching to play.

The Town of Tonawanda Recreational Department ran the baseball leagues in the town for the boys. There was no Little League in the Town of Tonawanda. I think it went something like this: 7, 8, & 9 year olds played in the midget league (doubt that term is still used) …10, 11, & 12 were grasshoppers and 13, 14, & 15 year olds were in the junior league. Midgets played on 60' base path diamonds, and grasshopper and up played on 90' base paths. There were baseball fields spread across the many town parks, including Mang Field, Sheridan Park, Brighton Park, Lincoln Park and Conway Field (now Kenney Field.)

The leagues were very organized; sponsors, scheduling, field maintenance, umpires, and equipment. I remember (as a batboy) making a trip with Dad to the Recreation Department to pick up our gear (provided by the Town.) The Recreation Department, at that time, was located in a small plaza on Colvin Blvd., just south of Brighton Ave., near Conway field where the iconic blue U.S. Navy jet still sits. Anyway, each team got its allotment of bats, balls, wrap around ½ batting helmets, and catcher's equipment. Maybe a couple dozen balls and 10 or 12 bats. The bats were color coded at the bottom of the handle, signifying the length from 28"- 34". As a batboy, I took great pride in meticulously arranging the bats, balls, and other equipment… I had learned by observing the bat boys at the Bison games. It was no doubt the beginning of my natural desire to be organized.

BATBOY SIDE STORY – *The games were very competitive, and the bleachers were always full. There were some loud parents, and not all kids got to play if it was a close game. By the way, not all kids made the team, and there were no girls. There were cuts… you had to make the team. It was before the days of participation trophies. Anyway, one game at Mang 3, it was loud and hectic and I got too close to a batter taking his swings in the on deck circle. Sure enough, I got wacked in the back of the head and it knocked me out, momentarily. There was blood and my mother (in the bleachers) freaked out. One of the other mothers, Joy Cownie, offered to take me across the street to a relative's house to get cleaned up and checked out. I was OK and able to meet the team after the game at Tasty Freeze on Elmwood. Ironically, years later, I would deduce the relative's house we went to was the Browns. Tom Brown (Joy Cownie's nephew) became a good friend of mine in Junior High, and as 9th graders, we would go to his house and have parties when we knew his parents weren't home (out signing the books, no doubt.) Being the tallest 14-year-old of that group of friends, and possessing a "fake" I.D., I would be the one going to a certain known deli on Elmwood to pick up a couple of Genesee beer 6-packs, and a couple of packs of Lark or Terryton cigarettes to fuel the party. There were usually 10 to 12 of us guys and gals partying. The Beatles "Rubber Soul" was popular at the time. Don't think we ever got busted, but I'm getting way ahead of myself.*

Back to 1959 and 199 Parkwood. My mother would occasionally load up my sister Amy, Jim, and me, and go to visit her brother Granger in Manlius (Eagle Village), NY. Mother had two other brothers, Edward and Henry, who predeceased her at a young age. Uncle Granger (Unc) was 9 years older than Mom. He was married to Aunt Maggie Lou, and they had 3 children – Keenan (2 years younger than me), Trent (a year or 2 younger than Keenan), and Jennifer (a year or 2 younger than Trent). It was interesting to stay there a couple of days. My grandmother Smith (mom's mother) would stay at Unc's house for extended periods of time, and I sensed that this caused a little stress between Unc and Aunt Maggie Lou. Gramma Smith was now retired from working as a "house mother" at a Syracuse University women's dormitory. She was in her mid-70s (17 years older than my Dad's mother, Nanny.) Aunt Maggie Lou, I thought, was quite artistic and, by the way, an attractive woman. She was more of the disciplinarian, while Unc was more laid back. Maggie Lou was considerably younger than Unc, and this was her second marriage. Unc was a ham radio operator, and this intrigued my brother and me. We would marvel that he was able to have a conversation with another ham operator, however staticky, halfway around the world. By the way, they were all devout Christian Scientists.

I don't think my Father ever made one of these trips... he would have a "project" going on. Dad was a talented handyman. He could do carpentry, and a certain amount of plumbing and electrical work. My brother Jim told me Dad learned his skills from his grandfather, Harry Clements (Bapa), who not only ran the funeral home, but built beautiful furniture. Dad also painted 199 Parkwood making use of scaffolds and tall ladders.

Well, on one of these trips, during the late 50s, dad stayed home and had a project he wanted to surprise us with. He wanted to finish the large walk up attic into a bedroom for my brother Jim and me. My father had perfectly good intentions, but in his haste, he discarded boxes of some of my mother's family archives. So, when we got home, we (including my mother) were all excited to see the bedroom he had created in the attic, but once my mother realized what had been discarded, she was crushed, to say the least. This may very well be one of the reasons I am so anal about my family archives.

After a while, Jim and I really got to enjoy that bedroom. We hung our pennants and posters. I think Jim, along with our older neighbor, Dennis Gates, took a stab at trying to be ham radio operators… don't think it actually happened. But down in the basement, Dad had one of his greatest projects. It was a custom Lionel train table deluxe. It took up nearly half of our unfinished, full basement… probably the equivalent to 2 ½ ping pong tables. Dad laid track that would go through our fruit cellar, and then back through a series of tunnels and trestles. The operator would need to crawl under the elevated (probably 42" tall) table, and emerge through a trap door in the middle where the various transformers and other controls were. We had engines and train cars from different eras and buildings, landscapes, etc.. As much as Jim and I enjoyed it, looking back, I think my father enjoyed it most of all.

Then, there was Cub Scouts. Pack number 256 met monthly at the Kenmore Methodist Church on Delaware Road in the basement gym. There were five dens, and there were two adult leaders... Mr. David Cownie and Mr. Willis Casselman. Each meeting would start with the pledge of allegiance followed by the Cub Scout pledge: *On my honor, I will do my best to do my duty to God and my country ... and to be square at all times.* When you received a merit badge, your name would be called, and you would cross over a small wooden arched bridge. You would then approach one of the leaders, and he would give you the congratulatory (two finger) Cub Scout hand shake as he presented you with your merit badge. My brother and I were in Den 3. Mr. Willis Casselman's two sons, Richard and David, were in Den 5. This was the first recollection I have of meeting Dave Casselman, who would become a lifelong friend. You'll hear much more about Dave in the chapters to come. It was fun being in Cub Scouts, and you learned a lot of cool stuff on your way to earning these merit badges. The mothers took turns being den mothers and hosting weekly meetings. At the weekly meetings, we would work on merit badge projects, and cover all Cub Scout business. My mother loved taking us to AM&A's (the official store for scouting gear.) It was here you could buy your uniforms, kerchiefs, hats, mess kits, canteens, jack knives, etc.. It was a great family activity.

Another family activity, at that time, was our involvement at the Lafayette Presbyterian Church at the corners of Lafayette, Elmwood, and St. James on the west side of Buffalo. Although my mother was a Christian Scientist, I think she compromised with my father in order to get the family to be involved with church activities. I'm not sure why they chose to drive the 20 minutes into Buffalo when there was a Presbyterian Church in Kenmore, right around the block. We didn't go every Sunday, but we were pretty regular. Lafayette Presbyterian was a huge building, which was cathedral-esque and could accommodate several hundred Congregationalists. It was complete with a bell tower, meeting rooms, a huge kitchen, Sunday school rooms, a second smaller chapel, a gymnasium with stage & projection booth, and even a 4-lane bowling alley in the basement. There were many, many nice families with parents in Mom and Dad's range, and youngsters in ours. I guess this does explain why they made the trip into Buffalo to LPC.

One of those families we met at LPC was the Knights. Bill and Mary Knight had two sons, Jim and Bob. Jim was about my brother Jim's age, and Bob was about a year older than me. Bill and Mary were a little older than my parents, but they really hit it off. Bob and I hit it off, too. Bob was absolutely fearless, and I really looked up to him. I will have much more to say about Bob in the coming chapters (that is, what I dare to say.)

Before I end this chapter, I need to recognize my 3rd grade teacher, Mrs. Ireland. She was older, and a prim and proper teacher probably in her 60s. For some reason, I can't think of anything more remarkable about 3rd grade. Oh! We were starting to learn to write cursive. I think I did just OK that school year.

Chapter Four
1960

1960 was a big year for the Lakers. Our family was upwardly mobile, and about to expand. After some extensive house hunting by my Mother (one of her favorite things to do), they bought a beautiful 4-bedroom Dutch Colonial at 52 Knowlton, just four blocks from Parkwood and only five doors down from Washington School (and playground.) I was lucky enough to get the finished bedroom in the attic with quarter circle windows on each side of the chimney and overlooking the Knowlton Ave. neighborhood. (*History would repeat itself when, years later, I would have a second Knowlton Ave. penthouse suite*).

52 Knowlton also featured a lovely entranceway, large living room, front sunroom, and a fireplace. Dad finished off the basement (a green tile floor, studded up panel walls, and a tile ceiling) and made room for the Lionel train set.

It wasn't long after our move (August 26, 1960), beautiful Wende Elizabeth joined our family. So now, there were four of us kids.

Amy was 15 and a sophomore at Kenmore West. She was always the best student of the group... Honor Society, cheerleading, thespians, etc. She also was rushed and pledged for the prestigious Omega Theta Phi (Theta) sorority, for which she became a member.

Jim was almost 13, and very athletic. He was well-built, fast, and strong (still occasionally roughing me up.) Jim was playing baseball and excelling at swimming. We were all, at one time or another, going to summer "Day Camp" at Kenmore West HS. Jim easily achieved the gold medal (highest award for swimming.) I idolized my brother (always have – still do.) Because of his birthday, December 13, he was classified a (confusing) half year student... so, I think he was somewhere in the eighth grade at Kenmore Junior High School.

I was now in the fourth grade, with Mr. Garling, back at the newly renovated Washington School just down the street. I liked Mr. Garling, and I did pretty well in his class. As a point of reference: I was still in the second reading group, near the edge of the lowly group three. This was pretty much where I hovered throughout my elementary years. Reading was not my strong suit, but math and gym were.

Mr. Alt was our gym teacher, and when it came time for gym, we would march down to the gym with another group of 4th grade boys. By now, the girls had gym separate from the boys, so they were on the other side of the gym divided by an electric folding wall. Mr. Alt was a young stud and gymnast from Buffalo State College... broad shoulders, looked kind of like Superman, but with blonde wavy hair. When it came to physical fitness tests, I was off the charts. I could do sit ups and modified pushups all day long.

Then, there was after school gym – basketball, football, and softball depending what season it was. We competed against the other 4th graders. Football was two-hand touch football on the blacktop playground. Softball was on the blacktop playground diamond, also. Of course, basketball was in the gym.

This is when I really started to think I was getting good (for my age) at throwing and catching. I spent hours throwing rubber balls against the outdoor brick walls and catching them with my "Dick Groat" glove. Same thing goes with shooting hoops. Dad built a real nice rectangular backboard and attached it to the garage roof. By the time I was 11, Dad could no longer beat me at a game of 21 or H-O-R-S-E.

So, it was a great year. We had a new house and new baby sister. That Christmas, Mom had a professional portrait made of the whole family (including 4-month old Wende) posing in front of the fireplace at 52 Knowlton. The portrait was made into a Christmas card, and is definitely an important piece of the Laker archives.)

LAKERS 1960.

< My penthouse

52 Knowlton

Chapter Five
1961

I think it was the summer of 1961 my father finally gave into my begging for a tree house. He built a platform, which was probably 6'x6', it may have been about 7' off the ground with a rope ladder egress. Dad ran a pulley system which reached the back door, so Mom could deliver PB&J sandwiches for lunch so I didn't even need to come down. By the way, it was painted gray. Coincidentally, the same color you would find on any ESSO station garage floor. I had a great view of the Zielbauer's backyard, which backed up to ours on Wardman.

My neighborhood friends, at that time, were Jack Menier and Bill Schull. They were one and two years my senior. Whiffle ball was one of our favorite activities. "Strikeout" and "Homerun Derby" were fun. We would set up different ball parks/fields at our various homes/yards and play for hours. Because I was a little younger, those two would sometimes "ditch" me and go off on their own. I didn't care, because on a good day, Bill would invite us up to hang in his bedroom (junior man cave) which was decorated by cool pennants and posters. He even had the Marilyn Monroe Playboy issue! Mostly, though, it was super hero comic books and such. Bill's bedroom really inspired me to decorate my own room, which I did. As I mentioned earlier, my bedroom at 52 Knowlton was a newly finished room on the 3rd floor with two, quarter round windows overlooking the street... great spot. My comic book of choice, by far, was Dennis the Menace. I would bike to Kiener's and get the most recent edition, along with a supply of penny candy... grape balls, candy pills on adding machine paper, waxed teeth, pretzyl sticks, etc. Kieners had a huge magazine and comic book display. Every quarter, Hank Ketchum (the Dennis the Menace creator) would publish special, longer length, editions which would depict the Mitchell family on vacation. For example,: vacationing in Mexico City, visiting the pyramids and other points of interest. I could go through those comic books like I was in the first reading group. While browsing at Kiener's that summer, I can distinctly remember seeing a Sports Illustrated issue with Roger Maris and Mickey Mantle on the cover. They were New York Yankee teammates in a homerun race chasing Babe Ruth that summer/fall. Maris would eventually hit his record breaking 61st homerun of the season in September to surpass Ruth's 60 homeruns, albeit in a slightly longer season for Maris.

Another incident which happened that summer was a serious automobile accident my father was involved in. Dad was driving Mr. Ebert (Dad's boss) in Mr. Ebert's car on their way to the company picnic. Dad was blinded, momentarily, by sunshine and either hit or got hit by another car. Dad's head hit and broke the windshield. I think Mr. Ebert had a broken ankle and Dad got the worst of it, with two nasty 3" cuts on his forehead, and a chunk off the tip of his nose. Dad was 38 years old at the time. Alcohol was involved.

My brother would sometimes give my father fits. A number of times, I think Jim would now tell you, he earned the wrath of Dad's belt. I would sometimes witness these spankings, and Jim would never even flinch. I think it was the sign of Jim's willpower, which he exhibits to this day. The spankings were not vicious, and not during a heated exchange. Dad would tell Jim to go to his room and wait. The waiting was maybe rougher than the actual spanking itself, and I knew I never wanted to be on the receiving end of the belt.

So, July 4, 1961, Jack Menier and I were invited to go to Bill Schull's family cottage on Lake Erie in Canada near Crystal Beach. Mom was gone somewhere, and Dad was in charge. I asked Dad permission to go to Schull's cottage. The answer was "NO". I was pissed and had a big meltdown. Well, I was about to make the biggest mistake in my young life. I sneaked off and went to the Schull's anyway. Even though there was swimming, fire crackers, and picnicking, I had a miserable time. In the back of my mind, I knew what would be waiting for me when I got home. Remember, there were no cell phones or anything close, so I'm sure my father was very worried about me. It was well after dark when I got home. Of course, there was Dad, sitting on the couch in the living room watching television. He calmly told me to go to my room and wait for him. It was probably the longest 15 minutes of my life. That was the only belt spanking I had, or needed.

At that time (10 years old), I was still rolling on a hand-me-down 20" bike. I was growing like a weed, and was really in need of an upgrade. In the display window at Noah's Ark (Delaware Ave.) was a 26" boys red Raleigh with coaster brakes. I kept my eye on that bike and made continuous hints to the "Old Man" about the bike. Must be the "squeaky wheel gets the grease" saying is true, because somewhere around my birthday, my parents took me down to Noah's Ark and made the deal. I'm sure they made me make a few promises, but I would have promised anything. That was a game changer. I could now really stretch out and cover some new territory around Kenmore. That bike would fly! Eventually, I saved enough money to buy and install a speedometer/odometer. I swear I had that bike up to 50 MPH.

At that time, bikes were a status symbol for kids. One of the most amazing bikes in the neighborhood was owned by Sammy DiBlasi. Sammy's bike resembled Pee Wee Herman's… multi-colored paint scheme, solid body cross bar, lights, horn, fox tail, and, to top it off, a full-sized transistor radio with antenna. By the way, Sammy lived nearby Wolfe Blitzer – now famed CNN reporter.

We would set our bikes up with spoke activated motor noise simulation. This could be achieved with the use of either a baseball card, properly attached with a spring loaded clothes pin, or, to get a richer sound, you would attach a tubular shaped balloon. The faster you went (greater RPM), the louder the noise.

Other popular bike accessories included rear view mirrors, leather saddle bags, bells, and auto axle grease removers… just to name a few.

The longest bike trip I can remember was to Beaver Island State Park (on Grand Island). This was probably about 15 miles each way, and required going over the (only one at the time) high arching Grand Island Bridge. Biking across that bridge and over the raging Niagara River was pretty intimidating. Looking back, I think it may have been the summer of 1962 or 1963. Coasting the down side of that bridge was when I may have seen 50MPH on my speedometer.

Miss Gieger was my teacher when I started the 5th grade that Fall. She was a young teacher… pretty blonde. Despite still being in the 2nd reading group, I did pretty well in her class. Arithmetic and gym were still my favorite subjects. I liked art also… the art teacher would roll his cart into the classroom once a week to do a new project. Music was once a week… same way, unless you were taking an instrument. In that case, you would report to the auditorium for your weekly instruction. I took up drumming for a while… didn't get too far. I never got past the drum pad.

So, gym was still my very favorite. In good weather, Mr. Alt would march the boys out onto the blacktop playground and measure off 50 yards. One-by-one, he would time us with his stop watch and record it on a chart on his clipboard. I wasn't the fastest boy, but probably somewhere around the 90th percentile. But then there was the softball throw! The teacher's parking lot was located in the corner of deep left field, still within the fenced perimeter of the playground. A triangular, green, steel curb separated the parking lot from the softball diamond. So, again, we lined up behind this curb in deep left field waiting our turn to throw. Mr. Alt was standing at home plate, with the end of his tape measure and clip board chart ready to measure and record the distance of each boy's throw… kind of like measuring shot put throws. Some of the best throws were making it to home plate. When my turn came, I wound up and pegged a throw which went over Mr. Alt's head… another 15', and over the fence along the first baseline, and bouncing onto Wardman Ave.! This put a huge smile on Mr. Alt's face, and mine too. That throw instantly qualified me for the "BIG" Play Day competition at the Kenmore West High School athletic field on Delaware Rd. This was a Saturday morning competition between all of the elementary schools in the district – Washington, Roosevelt, Franklin, and Hoover. Each softball thrower (probably 20 of us) got three throws. I didn't have my best stuff, but still finished in the top 3.

Miss Gieger recognized my energy and my athleticism… so when it came time for a messenger to take or retrieve a message from the office, she would often call on me. Our classroom was on the 3rd floor, and next to the indoor fire stairs. The office was on the first floor, and on the opposite side of the building. The stairway had a landing halfway between floors, so it was a zig zag going down or coming back up. I became very fast at descending those (and any other) stairs. There was also a railing I learned to slide from landing to landing on. Anyway, it was fun being the messenger.

Another interesting note from elementary school… on one afternoon, each week for a couple of hours, the Catholic students would go to "Religious Instruction," and the Jewish students would go to "Hebrew School." This would leave maybe half the class behind for those couple of hours. So, we would have "free time"… maybe watch a movie or go to the auditorium for an assembly of some kind. Sometimes, the Jewish kids would bring in Matzo (a cracker like food) for show and tell. It was interesting, and I liked the stuff.

Chapter Six
1962

The most noteworthy of events for 1962 had to do with my brother. Jim was just 14, and he ran with a pretty fast crowd. Jim was very athletic and, sometimes, against my parent's wishes, he would leave home on the run headed toward Delaware Ave. Washington School playground was just five doors down, and surrounded by a 7' chain linked fence. The entrance to the teacher's parking lot was guarded by a gate (locked after school hours.) Jim and some of his buddies learned to scale and flip over that 7' gate in one swift and smooth move. Once you were clear of that gate, you were out of reach of any pursuers and on your way to any number of interesting destinations.

My recollection is Jim became ill (maybe German measles) around May and was supposed to stay home and rest. However, Jim was hard to keep down and escaped to run with his boys, even though he wasn't well. Anyway, Jim's illness escalated and he was taken to Children's Hospital in Buffalo. He was soon diagnosed with life threatening encephalitis, which made him paralyzed from the chest down. Dad was out of town when he learned the news and raced home in that hot 1959 Plymouth Fury I mentioned earlier. Of course, we were all devastated. Mom called Jim

"Jamesie," and it became quite a chore for her to visit and care for him daily AND to care for the rest of us, especially Wende, who was not quite 2-years-old. Again, Christian Science was called into play. My maternal Grandmother Smith and my uncle, Granger Smith, were devout CS, and they did all they could with the power of CS. The doctors warned us Jim may not walk again.

I can remember getting daily updates about Jim from my parents, and eventually he began to regain some feeling. That was such great news. After a period of time, Jim was moved to a rehabilitation facility on Delaware Ave., toward downtown Buffalo, where he would spend the next 9 months or so. Because of my age, I was not allowed to go up to his room, so I had to settle for a wave from his window. On a couple of occasions, I can remember Jim being wheeled out in a wheel chair for a visit.

My parents took our portable black and white TV to the rehab facility for Jim to have in his room. We're talking about the days before remote controls, so Dad fabricated a 7' long aluminum tube pole, notched at the end, to enable Jim to turn the channels from his bed.

Jim continued to make progress, and had to relearn to walk. It must have been early 1963 when Jim was finally allowed to come home… we were glad to have him. It was the beginning of a remarkable recovery! The power of Christian Science?

I have no doubt this is when Jim developed the patience and will power he has displayed ever since.

It was great having the Washington School playground just down the street. With all the time I spent there, I learned every square inch of that blacktop. It had two steel slides, adjustable teeter totters, a huge sand box, two sets of monkey bars, huge swings, and a basketball hoop. There was also a softball diamond and two "strike out" game set ups. "Strike out" was played with tennis balls and regular wooden bats with two man teams (pitcher and outfielder.) There was a rectangular strike zone painted on the side of a concrete wall behind the batter's box. You could strike out swinging, or looking, or you could walk. A ground ball caught by the pitcher was an out. A ground ball past the pitcher was a single. The base runners were invisible, but kept track of. A pop up caught by the pitcher or the outfielder was an out. A ball past the outfielder to the fence was a double. A ball that hit the fence on the fly was a triple and, of course, a ball hit over the fence (probably 150 feet) was a homer. The foul poles were clearly established, and games could last for hours. When I was 11ish, I would only get to watch the "older" teenage boys play. A couple of noteworthy "older" guys who were regular players were Norm Mineo and Chuck Vacario. Norm, a good friend of my brother's, would eventually become a self-made millionaire. He was also a member of the prestigious Royal Order of Knights, a high school fraternity my brother Jim and, later, I would be honored enough to become members of. There will be much more about the R.O.K in the pages to come. Chuck Vacario would become a successful front man (a la Mick Jagger) for the regionally popular rock and roll band, *Caeser and the Romans* and then later as *Big Wheelie and the Hub Caps.*

But every once in a while, I would get to sub into a game with these guys and wait for the time the younger guys could get their chance.

> SIDE NOTE: It was about this time that "Mike's Giant Submarine" opened on Delaware Ave. right across the street from Washington School. Submarine sandwiches were something new to us. When you went into Mike's, your eyes would start to water from the smell in the air of the freshly cut onions. You could buy a 16" fully loaded bologna sub on a fresh roll for 49 cents, ham 59

cents, and roast beef 69 cents – unbelievable. As far as I know, Mike's is still there... but I'm sure the prices have gone up10x.

When we couldn't play "strike out," we would resort to whiffle ball. There were many variations, but it could even be played one-on-one. John Johnston (another lifetime buddy) lived down the street at 160 Knowlton (an address which would become important to the Lakers) and we invented a game of one-on-one whiffle ball where the batter's box would be inside the garage, the pitcher would pitch in through the open garage door, and the batter would try to hit the ball back out of the open garage door. We made up our own interesting ground rules and they varied from 52 to 160 Knowlton. We would play home and away series, and games could go on for hours.

SIDE NOTE: I think this summer was the first season for the NY Mets.

That Fall, I was back to Washington School for 6th grade with Mrs. Churak. She was very professional and a disciplinarian. She especially enjoyed theatre, and we did two plays that year. The first was about the Solar System and Greek/Roman mythology. We did a skit about the planets in our Solar System, and some of us were planets while some of us were Greek or Roman Gods or Goddesses. I was the God of Saturn – Cronus, the Roman God of agriculture. The skit was pretty cheesy, but it helped us, and the other students who came to watch, learn more about the Solar System.

Then, there was "Oliver," our second production. This was a much more sophisticated production. Mrs. Churak took great pains to assure a very professional (for sixth grade) show. She had us listen to the Broadway version of the show over and over and dissect it. From the sets to the lighting to the costumes and make up, it was quite elaborate. I was cast as Mr. Bumble, who ran the orphanage. In my big scene, I came strutting on to the stage, swinging my cane and singing "Boy for Sale"....

"He's going cheap – only seven Guinee's…that's all there-abouts"…and so on.

We performed the play twice, including an evening show for our parents (who were instrumental in rehearsing us and helping us with costumes etc.) Anyway, it was a big hit, and we got rave reviews. It was definitely the highlight of my sixth grade experience.

Another thing I especially enjoyed was "after school" gym. As I mentioned earlier, there were three classrooms for each grade level at Washington School. We would compete against the other sixth grade classes in touch football, basketball, or softball depending on what season it happened to be. It was quite competitive, and bragging rights were at stake. Sometimes (if I had the money) after "after school" gym, I would go to Kays drug store and buy six (full size) nickel candy bars for a quarter ,or go to Henel's Dairy for 10 cent strawberry phosphate.

Sometime during the early 60s, my father and some other men from the Lafayette Presbyterian Church organized a "Sports Night" at the church. They were able to recruit a few of the Buffalo Bills, including Elbert Dubenion, Tom Sestak, and "Lookie, Lookie, Lookie, here comes Cookie" Gilchrist. It was a big thrill to meet those Bills who would go on to win the 1964 and 1965 AFL championships. The dinner was held in the upstairs gym of the church. It was catered, and each of those Bills addressed a crowd of about 80 Bills fans. This was about the time Dad had become a Bills season ticket holder at the old War Memorial Stadium AKA the "Rock Pile." The Rock Pile also became the home of the Buffalo Bison baseball team (International League) after Offerman Stadium was razed.

> SIDE NOTE: The "Rock Pile" was used in the filming of the 1984 movie, *The Natural*, with Robert Redford. In the famous scene where Redford's character, Roy Hobs (lefty batter), hits a dramatic homer over the right field wall… the catcher in the scene is none other than Bill Truman (another lifetime friend.) Bill was the point guard on our Kenmore West High School basketball team, and a tremendous athlete. This was his 15 minutes of fame.

Back to the Lafayette Presbyterian Church gym; the gym was multi-purpose. There was a full basketball court, a stage at one end, and a projection booth at the opposite end suspended high above the gym floor. After church on Sundays, my, previously mentioned, friend Bob Knight and I would go up to the gym and hope it was unlocked. If so, we would rare and tear (in our street shoes and Sunday clothes), and maybe shoot some hoops if we could find a ball. That wasn't enough excitement for Bob. He would climb up a steel ladder fixed to the brick wall which led to the projection booth about 25' up. From the top of the ladder, it required about a 3' stride across "mid-air" to the projection booth. As I said earlier, Bob was a dare devil with no fear. He made that step without a thought, and then shamed me into doing the same (against my better judgment and instincts.) I did it once, and that was enough for me… scared the hell out of me. It even makes me uneasy thinking about it now. It was one of those times when you were literally scared for your life. Much more about Bob to come.

Sometimes, during basketball season, our minister would invite basketball teams from other churches (mostly inner-city) to come to our gym at LPC Sunday afternoon for some games. There might be three or four teams, so we would do round robins. It was very loosely organized, but it gave all the participants the opportunity to compete. This was the first time I had played against black players, and I couldn't help but notice (in general) how quick they were and how high they could jump. This may sound politically incorrect, but as my basketball career ascended, the more blacks I competed against and had as teammates. I am not a racist... it's a reality. There is a reason why the NBA is made up of 85% black players.

Chapter Seven
1963

In 1963, my sister Amy was a senior at Kenmore West. She was an excellent student (National Honor Society) and a member of the prestigious sorority, Omega Theta Phi (better known as Theta.) So, she was scholarly and very social. The sororities and fraternities were a big deal at Kenmore West in the 60s. There were maybe three or four of each, and maybe 25 or so members of each. Keep in mind KW was grades 10 – 12 with over 800 students in each class. So, if you were a member of one of these sororities or frats, you were part of the social elite. However, Epsilon was the "sister" sorority to the Royal Order of Knights fraternity… so, there would be occasional "joint" meetings. Basically, these were parties for the guys and gals to get together. There may have been some beer consumed. Times were different then. You have to realize, 18 was the legal drinking age in NYS. Again, I will have much more to say about the sororities and fraternities as you turn these pages.

One of Amy's boyfriends was 6'5" Warren Plant. I especially remember Warren because he was the center on Coach Hubie Klein's KW Blue Devils basketball team, a position I would later fill. Warren was a great high school player. It was very impressive, to me, to watch him dunk a basketball with two hands. He would continue his basketball career as a division 1 player at Canisius College as a starter. My basketball buddies and I would go to Memorial Auditorium, "the Aud," (downtown Buffalo waterfront) to watch Canisius where they played their home games. We saw Warren and some other great basketball players there. More about "Little 3" basketball to come.

But, back to Amy. Because of our connection with the Lafayette Presbyterian Church, Amy met a young man named Bob Volk. Bob was a handsome and athletic guy who was two years Amy's senior. He lived with his family on Delaware Ave. at Gate Circle (NW Buffalo) upstairs from the family owned and operated VOLKS drug store. Bob's sports were crew (rowing) and cross country. If memory serves, Bob was an alumnus of Hutchinson Tech HS. He did his crew training and competitions at the Buffalo Rowing Club on the Buffalo River near the Peace Bridge. Amy and Bob became close, and eventually she went to work part time for the Volk's at the drug store. I remember Amy only having to walk five doors down from 52 Knowlton to Delaware Ave. where she could catch the NFT (Niagara Frontier Transit) bus straight south to Gate Circle – 10 cent fare. Sometimes, she would take the bus home, and sometimes Bob would bring her home. Anyway, Bob would come to our house regularly, and I liked him… he paid attention to me.

Amy graduated from KW in June of 1963. Bob, by this time, had 2 years at Alfred University under his belt, so it was no surprise Amy decided to go to Alfred State College in the Fall of 1963.

Meanwhile, I was finishing up the 6th grade at Washington School and about to turn 12 years old. I still loved baseball, and that summer I played for "Mike's Giant Submarines" in the grasshopper division. Along with grasshopper games, Johnny Johnston and I were still playing a lot of whiffle ball and a lot of "strike out" at Washington School playground.

My parents were quite socially active, and got together with other couples usually to play bridge. I can remember helping my mother prepare the house for "Couples Club" when it was their turn to host. I would help her set up the card tables & chairs, vacuum, and dust. She would be busy in the kitchen preparing hors d' oeuvres and goodies, music would be playing on the "Hi Fi" – maybe Ray Coniff Singers or Glenn Miller. Typically, there would be two tables to accommodate four couples. The couples would rotate. As the evenings wore, on the chatter and laughter from the group would get louder and more audible, making its way to my third floor suite. Over time, I learned to distinguish different laughs from different people... Mrs. Murphy, Marge Magner, and so on. They were having a genuinely good time, and it made me feel good too.

My baby sister, Wende, was turning 3, and I was doing my share of babysitting. We would play all sorts of games, and I would try to teach her some ball skills... rolling, bouncing, and catching. She caught on quickly, so it was a lot of fun for both of us. Even though I was 9 years older than Wende, I was the closest in age to her (compared to our older siblings) so I always thought we had a special bond.

That fall, I started 7th grade at Kenmore Junior High School. KJHS housed grades 7 through 9. It was a big change from Washington School for many reasons. First of all, it was different because you were changing classrooms each period for different subjects, unlike elementary school. Another big thing was you were meeting new students from two other elementary schools – Lindbergh, Roosevelt, and some Catholic kids coming from St.

Paul's parochial school. All of this made me feel more grown up and independent.

Oddly, I don't remember many of my classroom teachers' names, but I do remember my Physical Education teachers' names – Mr. Saliba, Mr. Whiles, and Mr. Kenney. Mr. Kenney was a character and near retirement, by now. He was a legend in Kenmore, and eventually Conway field (the one with the blue Navy jet) was renamed to Kenney field. Mr. Whiles, I think, recognized my potential as an athlete... especially for basketball. We had PE twice a week, one day for gym and one day for swimming. To this day, people tend not to believe me when I tell them the boys swam in the nude. Of course, the girls swam separately from the boys.

It was fun and interesting to meet new kids from other schools. It definitely broadened my horizons. That fall, I tried out for the Kenmore Bills football team and made it. This was the first time I played organized football (full pads.) The Kenmore Bills were part of a league run by the Town of Tonawanda Recreation Department, and every bit as competitive as the Town baseball leagues described earlier. I was used as a tight end on offense, and on defense, I was also an end. It was a lot of hard work and rough. I enjoyed it, but I knew I didn't really have a future in organized football. The team was made up of guys who came from Washington, Lindbergh, and St. Paul's schools. The very best players on that team went on to play for Coach Jules Yakapovich's Kenmore West Blue Devil nationally ranked football team.

Social life was becoming more important to me. The cool kids had to dress a certain way. For the guys, it was cool to wear really tapered slacks. It was cool to do your clothes shopping at *Roger Lewis Men's Store* on Delaware Ave. The coolest slacks were either "Blades" (tight fitting with horizontal slit pockets at the belt line) or "Casinos" (rounded slit cut at the cuff line.) Paisley shirts were also in style. Shirts had to be button down, absolutely no fly away collars. If the slacks were not tight enough, when they came from the store, Mom would turn them inside out and run a new and tighter inseam on her sewing machine.

Kenmore Bills 1963

I guess I was cool enough to be invited to join the SQUIRES. The SQUIRES was a KJHS fraternity which was a precursor to the High School fraternities at Kenmore West. There was an initiation period which involved pledging for several weeks and being paddled by your "superiors." Anyway, it was an elite fraternity for cool guys.

Being part of the SQUIRES led to being invited to some parties where there were girls. I have a vague recollection of some of these parties, which were no alcohol, but included music (Beach Boys, maybe,) dancing, and spin the bottle.

After my brother Jim's rough 1962, my parents thought it would be best for him to have a change of scenery. It was Jim's sophomore year in high school and they sent him to live with my Grandmother Laker (Nanny) and Great Grandmother Clements (MaMa) in Mitchell, Indiana, my Father's home town. It worked out great for Jim. He liked it and he did well. Jim was always well-accepted socially wherever he went. It was, and is, a wonderful trait he possesses. His classmates loved him and nicknamed him "Jim Shoes."

Meanwhile, as I mentioned earlier, my sister Amy was a Freshman at Alfred State College (they called it Alfred Tech, back then) and living in Brookside dormitory.

Things were about to change for the Laker Family, but before I go there, I want to interject another Bob Knight story. As another Buffalo winter was bearing down on us, and our first heavy snow, Bob introduced me to a new winter activity – "poggying." After a good snow fall, we would locate ourselves at a four-way stop intersection in a hiding position. When an unsuspecting motorist stopped, we would sneak out behind their car and hold on to the rear bumper in a squatting stance. We would then slide (ski) behind the car for as long as we dared, or until the driver got wise. This was back when automobiles had real bumpers which were easy to hold on to.

NOTE TO MY GRANDCHILDREN: DO NOT TRY THIS. IT IS VERY DANGEROUS!

This was yet another example of Bob Knight's bad influence on me. (But I loved him).

Now, back to the big change for the Laker family. Sometime late that Fall or early Winter, Dad was notified by ESSO he was being transferred to a new territory on the Southern Tier of

New York State (Steuben County.) His job of calling on and training ESSO gas station dealers and owners would remain basically the same, but in a new area of responsibility. This, of course, would require us to move to Steuben County, about 100 miles away from Kenmore.

Looking back, I think we all had a mix of emotions. On one hand, this would be a new adventure… moving to a new town, a new house, and meeting new friends. On the other hand, we would be leaving our beautiful home and friends in Kenmore.

We were now under the gun to find a new home in Steuben County. I can remember going on a couple of house hunting trips with my mother. My father pretty much left the house searching up to my mother (with the help of Winters Realty) as he was busy looking after his new territory. It didn't take my mother long to narrow the search down to Hornell and Bath. Outside of Corning, these were the two largest communities in the County. My mother was quite savvy as a house hunter, and she didn't mind telling the realtor just what she was looking for. Wende and I tagged along looking at a variety of homes. My mother's musts were four bedrooms and a big backyard. It was fun for me to do the walk throughs and try to imagine which bedroom would be mine. My mother coached me not to show too much enthusiasm, as it might impact later negotiations. Something in the area which struck me was the size of the hills. They were like mountains to me, and I envisioned myself one day hiking to the tops of them.

The more we looked, the more my mother was leaning toward living in Bath. ESSO put us up at the brand new Swiss Chalet Motel while we were house hunting. We had a luxurious suite, and Wende and I loved it. Finally, after much looking, my mother decided on a house at 213 East Steuben St. in the Village of Bath. My father gave his stamp of approval and it was a done deal.

213 East Steuben St. was a 4-5 bedroom, turn of the century Victorian with 1.5 bathrooms, a large living room, a formal dining room with a fireplace, and large kitchen. It also had a large back yard and a barn with a loft. One drawback was the traffic. This was before the Southern Tier Expressway (or later I-86), so East Steuben St. doubled as US Rte 15, and the truck traffic was kind of heavy. I didn't realize it at the time, but the loud rumbling sound we would often hear were the truckers engaging their Jake brakes as they approached a sharp curve in the road nearby.

As it went, we were able to make a deal and get moved into 213 East Steuben St. before the start of the school's second semester in January of 1964. I think ESSO took care of the sale of 52 Knowlton in Kenmore.

Since Amy was at ASC, and Jim was in Indiana, I had first dibs (after my parents) on which bedroom to choose. The one I chose was a big bedroom, and my parents allowed me to have the use of the "family heirloom," extra tall 4-poster double bed built by my Great Grandfather Bapa.

> SIDE NOTE: I never realized until years later, but before we knew we were moving, my Mother had arranged for me to get braces on my teeth at the University of Buffalo, School of Orthodontics. Of course, this got put on the back burner because of the move. Too bad!

Chapter Eight
1964

When school started in January, I was assigned to Mr. Cheplick, a guidance counselor. Haverling Central School was a relatively new building which housed grades 7 through 12. I remember being nervous as Mr. Cheplick escorted me into an arithmetic class being taught by Mrs. Mabel Watson, and introducing me to the class. Here was this new kid… a tall, skinny red head. I must have stuck out like a sore thumb. I could feel the eyes of the other students on me. You have to remember, Haverling was a very small school compared to Kenmore Junior High School and Kenmore West High School.

Anyway, I managed to make it through a couple of days of school pretty much as a loner. After interviewing me, and looking at my profile, Mr. Cheplick told me there was a 7th grade basketball team coached by Mr. Flanagan. The team had after school practices at the Vernon E. Wightman Elementary School gym just next door to Haverling. As I remember, Mr. Cheplick escorted me to my first practice and introduced me to Coach Flanagan and the team. The story of that first practice is best told by one of those teammates, and lifetime friend, Brian Friedland:

"It was the winter of 1963-64 Junior High Basketball 7ᵗʰ grade season as we gathered for a practice at the Vernon E. Whitman School gym. Sitting isolated from the group was this tall, skinny red-headed kid who just came to Bath with his family and I thought to myself, "I hope he isn't very good," since I was the 5ᵗʰ man, at the time, on our team. Well, his name was Greg Laker, as introduced by our coach Mike Flanagan. We started the layup drill and he looked pretty good. The basketball drifted away after one of our players attempted a layup. Greg went after the ball and, in one motion, picked the ball up and passed it behind his back to the next person in line, which happened to be me. Unfortunately for me, it was a perfect pass. Later in the practice, when we were about to scrimmage, Coach Flanagan started calling the first team's names, and the 5ᵗʰ name he called was Greg Laker. I said to myself, "damn, that skinny red head just took my 5ᵗʰ spot. So – as we all know, sadly for Greg, he developed Rheumatic Fever and had to stop playing... so I eventually got my spot back due to his illness. We ended up becoming good friends..."

After, that things opened up for me with my new friends at Haverling. Basketball had now opened the door for me like it would so many times in my life to come.

Brian became my friend, then. He had an older brother, David, who was also in 7ᵗʰ grade. David was a big guy, and excelled in wrestling and track & field. David had a great sense of humor and he would keep us all in stitches. He also cracked himself up, and could not hold back his own laugh, as much as he would try. Luckily for me, Brian and David liked me and took me under their wings. As a result, I got a direct pass into the inner circle of the 7th graders at Haverling. Now, in addition to my new basketball guys, like John Smalt, Ed Finnerty, Glenn Howe, etc. – I was accepted by many other 7th grade guys and girls simply because of my association with the Friedland brothers.

The basketball season went along, and we played against other schools such as Prattsburgh, Avoca, Hammondsport, etc. Things were going great for me, and I was having fun. Then, it HIT! Walking home from practice one of those winter nights, I felt ill – feverish.

That night, I could not sleep. I was in terrible pain. My legs ached and my parents sat up with me, massaging them and doing anything to try to make me comfortable. The next day, Dr. Kuhl came from Hammondsport to examine me. He had me admitted to Ira Davenport hospital, where I was diagnosed with Rheumatic Fever. The doctors detected a heart murmur. They kept me in the hospital a couple of nights, then brought me home with strict instructions, which included much bed rest and very limited physical activity. My parents set me up in the downstairs den as a makeshift bedroom. I was not allowed to climb stairs for weeks. Eventually, I was allowed to go upstairs once a day – even though I felt fine.

The school set me up with an "in-home" tutor. Mrs. Carlson was a young, pretty teacher (a la Miss Crump). She came in three or four days a week for two or three hours per visit to teach me lessons in social studies, science, math, and English. If memory serves, I think she tutored me from early March until the end of the school year. Thanks to her, it was a good school year and I passed the 7th grade.

Dr. Kuhl was telling my parents and me I would not be able to participate in physically demanding sports. This, of course, was terrible news to me. I felt fine and I didn't want to accept this assertion.

Occasionally, Brian and David would come to visit me and keep me in the loop. On one of these occasions, my mother was steaming up a batch of corn on the cob and offered some to the boys. David always had a big appetite, and quickly polished off a couple of ears. When my mother offered him some more, David replied, "Mrs. Laker, you keep on making it and I'll keep on eating it." I thought my mother would die laughing.

Then, to make matters worse, my mother became ill and, believe it or not, she was diagnosed with Rheumatic Fever. (No, it is not contagious). At that point Gramma Smith (her mother) came to stay and help out with things around the house. Somewhere around this time, I think, my Mother was beginning to feel homesick for Kenmore and her friends there. The move to Bath, so far for her, had been a rough experience. On the other hand, as far as I knew, Dad was doing just fine with his work. He knew his business and he was a good people person who got along well with his ESSO dealers.

With the end of the school year drawing near, we were looking forward to Jim's return from Indiana, and Amy coming home from Alfred for the summer. When Jim came home, he was full of Indiana colloquialisms, which were hilarious to me. To this day, many of these figures of speech are still in his repertoire and have, over the years, crept into mine. For example: "He's in like a porch climber," and "F___ you AND the mule you road in on." No doubt these were picked up in Grissom's pool room in Mitchell.

Amy had a good year at ASC and came home for the summer with her stenograph and portable typewriter. It was dazzling to me, to see the speed and accuracy she could make these machines work (and without even looking down). Of course, Amy was studying to become a secretary.

Bath is the Steuben County Seat, so the County courthouse and other county office buildings were located there.

The Steuben County Fairgrounds were also located in Bath, and for one week in August each year, Bath was overwhelmed with visiting fair goers of all ages. Somehow, Amy got a one week job working in the County Fair ticket office. At the end of each day, Amy would entertain us with stories (delivered sarcastically) about some of the characters who crossed her path at the fair.

But back to the subject of this book... me. I was getting healthier and allowed to do more physical activity. Still, I had to guard against a relapse by over doing it. Doctor Kuhl prescribed a daily dose of penicillin, which I took until I was 20 years old.

That summer, I would become a teenager, and Wende would turn 4. Her birthday was captured on the Laker 8mm films and attended by a handful of neighborhood kids... notably Amy and Ann, the Catherman twins from next door. I was the activities director and organized games of musical chairs and pin the tail on the donkey. Those were fun and happy times.

Being buddies with the Friedland brothers had its benefits, not the least of which was the location of their house on E. Washington St. Their house backed up to one of the 7 foot chain linked fences which surrounded the Steuben County fairgrounds. We would, stealthily, scale the fence and drop down right behind the tent which housed the exotic dancers. If we were lucky, we would go undetected and save ourselves the 75 cent entry fee.

It was that summer, during fair week, my buddy Bob Knight made his first trip to Bath (he hitch hiked the 100 mile trip.) By now, you are forming a clearer picture of Bob Knight and his lack of fear. The Friedlands and Bob Knight hit it off immediately. Bob had many quirks and figures of speech. For example: Instead of flipping his middle finger at you, he would simply say "the bird is yours." It cracked us all up.

By this time, I think Bob was pushing 15 and I had just turned 13. He was cool, tall (6' 3"), well built (sculpted), and handsome (blonde hair, blue eyes.) Oh, did I mention fearless?

As I said earlier, one of the features at 213 E. Steuben St. was a barn with a loft. The loft was a perfect place, in the summer, to camp out with old mattresses and sleeping bags. So, at least while Bob was there, we would sleep in the loft. Not much sleep, though… a lot of chit chat, stories, and X rated jokes.

Bob had a thing about signs. He was HELL bent on collecting signs of all sorts – NO PARKING, CURVE, STREET NAMES, manufacturing labels/placards – you name it. The loft became the home of an extensive collection of signs. But let me tell you about the "grand daddy" of all signs. That summer, the BEATLE'S movie "A Hard Day's Night" was released and was playing at the Babcock Theater on Liberty St. downtown Bath. Out in front of the theater, on the sidewalk, stood a two sided 4' wide by 5' tall "A" frame promotional poster (red, black, & white) for the BEATLES movie. It was a heavy duty structure being anchored down with cinder blocks. So, on a midnight outing from the loft, I accompanied Bob stealthily downtown to the Babcock Theater. Bob was able to get the structure loose from the cinder blocks and carry it (about 60 lbs.) 4 blocks back to the loft. Ahh! Did I mention the Babcock Theater was only a couple of doors down from the police station? Unbelievable!

Vicki Orvis, one of the girls in my class, had a serious crush on Bob, and was also a huge BEATLES fan, bought the poster from Bob. I think it was a hefty $20. Her parents, however, did not allow her to keep it, and so it was returned to the loft. The poster stayed with the Laker family for years. I only wish I had it now to put on E-Bay.

Another funny thing happened while Bob was in town during Fair week. On the midway, there was a guy set up in a booth hawking spaghetti. All you could eat for 75 cents. Between Bob, the Friedlands, Glenn Howe, and myself – the guy was forced to shut down when he ran out of spaghetti.

In order to protect our interests in the loft, Bob and I set up a booby trap system. The only indoor access to the loft was up a 10' wall mounted wooden ladder which led to a 24" x 24" hinged wooden door through the ceiling. We rigged it up so if anyone tried to enter while we were sleeping, they would get doused with a bucket of water. Of course, my brother Jim and my sister Amy were curious to know what Bob and I had going on up there in the loft. One night, late, we heard a loud crash, and a loud scream "OH SHIT!" The booby trap worked to perfection, and Amy was soaked. She could only laugh.

That Fall, I would start the 8th grade at Haverling. Looking back, it seemed, there was no lack of activity. On more than one occasion, a group of us 8th grade boys would hang out on Friedland's front porch with David's Daisy BB gun. Maybe it was David, Brian, Glenn Howe, and myself. Mostly we would shoot at inanimate targets but, occasionally, an unfortunate and unliked passerby would get a BB in the butt.

The Friday night home varsity football games were a big deal, and an opportunity for kids to hang out with their peers. The 8th grade guys and gals were checking each other out. Eventually, there was kind of a clique formed. The girls I can remember from that group were Mary Deegan, Sherry Foster, Jennifer Knapp, Marjean Lodge, Paula Walden, Liese Ness, Vicki Orvis, and Cathy Nielsen. Some of the guys were Brian and David Friedland, John Smalt, Ed Finnerty, Glenn Howe, Sam Balcom, John Roche, and Bob Murphy (class president.)

We would have parties at some of the homes of these kids (parents on premises.) There was music (a lot of Beatles and other

British invasion groups,) dancing, soft drinks, and snacks. There were dances, also, at the school and at some of the churches. I can especially remember there was going to be a Friday night dance in the basement of the Presbyterian church. It took me a while, but I finally worked up the nerve to phone Sherry Foster and invite her to go with me to the dance. She said yes; it was my/our first "date." She lived just a few blocks away, and when the time came, I walked to her house to pick her up. Of course, this would mean meeting her parents and siblings. I was sweating bullets, and I think her Father gave us a ride to the dance in their 1963 Oldsmobile station wagon. Those dances were great! It was all of our gang and then some. We were all into the music. All of the kibitzing would come when a ballad was played… who was going to ask who to dance? The hormones were kicking in. We had a lot of fun. The walk home was long, but worth it. I was on cloud nine when my new girlfriend kissed me goodnight. I vowed to myself I would never stay home on a Friday night ever again.

It was interesting, visiting the Friedland home. They had a large family – Brian and David had three older sisters. The oldest were twins, Barbara and Joan, next was Irene (about my sister Amy's age,) and then a younger sister Lisa. Mr. Friedland (Chester) was a high ranking administrator at the Bath VA (Veterans Administration.) The Bath VA resembles a beautiful college campus and employs hundreds. Brian bragged (rightfully) about his father – a Kansas University Jayhawk track & field star during the era of Phog Allen. There was also a family tie to the New York City entertainment world, particularly to Ed Sullivan, as pictures on the den walls would prove.

On some occasions, we would encounter Chet in his recliner, watching a ball game and enjoying a big stogie. He was a cool guy with a wry sense of humor. When Brian introduced me to him as Greg Laker, he, without hesitation, renamed me "Legs

Graker." To this day Brian still addresses me as "Legs."

What I remember about Mrs. Friedland was she was an avid golfer at the Bath Country Club. On any given Saturday, I would witness Brian or David hitting up Edna for some cash to go over to Hatfield's store to pick up something for lunch. The boys would return with a pack of Oscar Myer cold cuts and a loaf of bread – fix sandwiches and mauw!

At some point, there was a $5 bet made between me and Glenn "Funk" Howe. I needed to gain X number (maybe 5 or 10) of pounds within a certain period of time. David took it upon himself to fatten me up. David was a heavy weight wrestler, and a big guy for his age. He, himself, had no problem packing on weight when he wanted to. So, he would force feed me scoops of ice cream and spoon fulls of honey, etc. As hard as he tried, he got no results and I lost the bet to Glenn. It was no fault of David's. I eventually would grow to be 6'6" tall, but never weighed over 190 lbs. I like to describe my physique as slim.

Sometime later that Fall, around Halloween, Bob Knight made another trip down to Bath. During his first trip down, Bob met Liese Ness, a classmate and neighbor of mine. It was a mutual interest relationship. I think they had even exchanged letters. So, this time around, Bob and Liese were looking for some place to be alone. They ended up in Friedland's garage - in Chet's Buick. Somehow, Mr. Friedland became aware of this activity and approached the Buick.

"Is that you, Legs?" he inquired.

A ruffled Bob and Liese emerged and sought a quick exit.

Another Bob Knight story from that visit included Brian, David, and myself. Bob had observed there were some horses in a fenced in area right in the middle of the Village and adjacent to the Swiss Chalet Motel. Under the cover of darkness, the four of us entered the horse barn, mounted the horses "bare back," and took a little trot around the coral. None of the three of us would have had the balls to even consider this activity without the suggestion and urging of Bob Knight.

Because of my Rheumatic Fever, I did not play basketball during the 1964/65 season even though I was feeling fine and I had grown 5 or 6 inches in the past year.

While my sister Amy had returned to Alfred for her 2nd year, my brother Jim was now home and ready for his junior year at Haverling. In no time at all, Jim became buddies with the "in" crowd at Haverling. It was the era of hot cars and Jan & Dean music.

Jim helped organize a fraternity with his new Bath friends – "TappaKegga." Some of the guy's names which come to mind are Wayne Bubbs, Charlie Brown, John Chapman, Norm Smalt, Jeff Robbins, Bob McKee, and George Harkness. Jim could write a chapter about the Frat's summer cottage (Animal House) on Keuka Lake 1965.

Jim would meet Barb Beeke during his junior year. She would eventually become his first wife. Barb had two brothers, Bill and Brad, who we would also become close with. Bill, I think, was a year younger than Barb, and Brad was a couple of years younger than Bill. During the summer months, the Beekes operated "Wigwam Harbor," a camp ground high above Branchport with a beautiful southern view of Keuka Lake's west branch; a gorgeous piece of property.

That Christmas, the whole family was home for the holidays. Jim now, of course, living at home in Bath, and Amy home from Alfred State College. By now, my mother was recovering from her Rheumatic Fever and things were going pretty well for the Laker family.

Chapter Nine
1965

Although I was not allowed to play basketball in the 1964-65 season, I enjoyed going to watch the varsity boys play. They were very good, and there were a couple of TappaKegga guys – Norm Smalt (a bruising forward) and point guard Bobby McKee. Other key players on that team were swingman Bill Steele and low post man Gary Jacobs. The games were exciting and loud.

One of the classes I enjoyed that school year was Music. The teacher was Mr. Kendall. We spent one semester studying the musical "My Fair Lady." You know, "*The rain in Spain stays mainly in the Plain,*" and so on. He was an Ithaca College alumnus, and we had to learn the IC alma mater "*High above Cayuga's waters, beautiful to see...*" Anyway, I enjoyed that class.

Other memorable classes and teachers from 8th grade were Miss Sprague – French. "*Avezvous de bon bon 'o chocolat*"? Translation: "Do you have a piece of chocolate"? I also learned to count to ten in French... I can't begin to tell you how handy that knowledge has served me in my lifetime. Mr. Elmer Leach – English... he was a great story teller. At Halloween, he had us on the edge of our seats with the story of a headless horseman. He belted out the punchline, which scared the hell out of us.

Mr. Wesley Moore was our art teacher. He was very talented and taught us how to draw with one and two point perspective diminishing to the horizon line. This was very intriguing to me, and had a lot to do with preparing me for mechanical drawing courses I would later take in high school. Mrs. Mabel Watson (she must have been near retirement) taught Arithmetic. I did well in her class. We would try to solve such paragraph problems as: "If a train leaves Springfield at 10:00 AM and travels at 40 MPH, how long would it take…blah blah?" I can't remember our Science teacher's name, but I do remember learning about the 4-strokes of a gasoline engine: INTAKE, COMPRESSION, IGNITION, and EXHAUST. The more memorable thing I can remember about that class was being entertained by fellow student, Ed Peacock. Ed should have been a standup comedian. He was one of those few guys who could really make me "belly laugh." Oh, and I can't forget I made a 6"x8"x1" wooden cork covered hot plate holder in Wood Shop. That hot plate holder was used at the Laker dining room table for years.

Meanwhile, after school that spring, I would regularly walk Sherry Foster home from school. We would hang out, watch TV, or listen to music. She was a real Beatles freak, and so was I.

SIDE NOTE: By the way, this is about when the Beatles first came to the USA (actually, late 1964) and I can remember the family huddled around the "black & white" TV to watch them perform on the Ed Sullivan Show.

Sometime in winter, after a good snow fall, I introduced some of my Bath buddies to the sport of poggying. I can't remember who all was involved… but definitely Brian Friedland. There was a 4-way stop at the intersection of East William St. and Campbell Ave. It was a perfect place to poggy and we were having some good rides. Well, somebody must have called the cops because they, all of a sudden, showed up. Some of the guys ran, but at least Brian and I were stuck. The cop asked us our names and, for some unknown reason, I came up with Greg Quigley. The cop told us to knock it off. Our hearts were pumping and we were relieved when he let us off with a warning.

The Foster's house was on East Washington, at the bottom of a hill. Many of my friends and I made some of the first home-made skate boards (old roller skates nailed to the bottom of a random board) and spent many after school hours rolling downhill on this portion of East Washington St. You could get going pretty fast, and it was a little bit gnarly, but I can't remember any serious injuries to anyone.

It was sometime in Spring, I think it must have been during Easter vacation, Amy brought her new boyfriend home from Alfred. Jerry Labie was in his senior year at Alfred University, and had played football there for the legendary Coach Alex Univich. Jerry was a Jewish fellow from Long Island, and he had a brief "Meathead vs. Archie Bunker," relationship with my slightly narrow minded father. It was short lived, though, and Dad became very fond of Jerry, as we all did. Amy and Jerry would wed in July 1965 in Buffalo at the Lafayette Presbyterian Church.

For some unknown reason, that Spring, I was being bullied by an older boy, Elden Cutlip. It got to the point where he was threatening me, and I was afraid to see him on the street for fear he would beat me up. Finally, I brought this to my brother Jim's attention. It so happened one day, I had seen him (Elden) hanging out near the courthouse smoking with his buddies, and I came home and mentioned this to Jim. Without hesitation, Jim grabbed me and loaded me into the family 1959 Chevy station wagon and burned rubber out of the driveway and down East Steuben St. toward the Courthouse. I spotted Elden with his buddies and pointed him out to my brother. Jim whipped the car into the Courthouse parking lot, jumped out, and raced toward Elden. In one fluid motion, Jim grabbed Elden and gave him a knee in the "family jewels" while telling him, in no uncertain terms, "If you know what is good for you, you will be leaving Greg alone!"

Elden, doubled over, acknowledged he got the message. I never had a problem with Elden after that!

My mother was growing increasingly less happy in Bath. I think her illness, my illness, living on a truck route, along with her home sickness for Kenmore all factored in. She pleaded with my father to see if ESSO would transfer him back to the Buffalo area. I don't know all of the details, but somehow Dad was able to make it happen. So, at some point in the late spring of 1965, we knew we would be returning to Kenmore. Dad had to sacrifice his position of being an ESSO dealer sales manager, and take a position in the ESSO offices on River Road in the Town of Tonawanda. My feeling was he did it to please my mother and keep the peace. Jim and I had mixed emotions about the impending move. We had made good friends in Bath (we each had girlfriends) but on the other hand, we were going back to the familiarity of Kenmore, where we also had many friends.

Again, I don't want to get too far ahead of myself, because it was later in the summer before we moved back to Kenmore. That spring, there was an 8th grade formal dance in the high school gym. It was quite elaborate, with decorations, refreshments, and records spinning out our favorite tunes. Sherry Foster was my date, and I even got her a corsage. Of course, there was a secret ballet vote for the royalty of the dance. I was genuinely surprised when I learned I was voted King. Being the "new" kid in the class,

I was humbled. If memory serves, Mary Deegan (Sherry's best friend), was voted queen. We danced while the song *King of the Road* by Roger Miller was played.

Another memorable activity from that summer was being invited, on several occasions, to Sam Balcom's house to go swimming. Sam was the first friend I had whose family had an "in ground" swimming pool – diving board and everything. Sam was an only child, and I always thought of the Balcom's as "well-to-do." We would ride our bikes (towels draped around our necks) to his house out on Mitchellsville Road outside of the Village of Bath. After a raucous swim, we would go to the basement rec room for ping pong and snacks. Sometimes there were 6 or 7 of us. We had a blast. For some reason, I recall watching an NBA game there, in color, on CBS. It was the Celtics vs. the Lakers (Tom Heinson, John Havlicek, Bill Russell, Jerry West, and Elgin Baylor), so it could have been the finals; in June, sometime.

Since I was turning 14 that summer, I was getting anxious to drive. My brother, of course, had his license and I was jealous. Two things I remember about that were: number one, Dad helped me build a (motorless) go cart. Actually, I helped him. Actually, I watched him. It was a plywood chassis with lawn mower type wheels/tires, rope steering, and a hand brake. For power, you needed the benefit of gravity, which meant finding a hill (not too tough, around Bath). So, we folded down the seats in the 1959 Chevy station wagon and loaded the beast in there. Dad had a hill in mind. It was Mt. Washington, out by the Steuben County jail, and it was a county highway. I was oblivious, at the time, but looking back now, I realize how crazy it was. Nevertheless, Dad drove us halfway up the hill, a mile or so. He gave me a little push, and there I was – coasting down Mt. Washington – no helmet (never gave that a thought), going pretty damn fast, with a station wagon following. It was great though, and I had to do it a couple of more times. I think one of the wheels finally fell off and that was the end of it.

Number two, my mother would take me out on the Town of Bath dirt roads and let me drive. We were out near where the county landfill was, and there was very little traffic. She didn't think anything of it, and so, I learned to drive in the 1959 Chevy station wagon with 3-speed manual transmission on the column and "arm strong" steering. This will sound familiar to my daughters, Kaitlin and Joanna, as this is the way I taught them many years later.

I have a vague recollection of playing Babe Ruth baseball that summer. It may be vague because I think we moved back to Kenmore before the end of the season. However, I do remember feeling privileged to play on the beautiful baseball diamond (with dugouts) at the beautiful VA complex.

One more memory before we make the move back to Kenmore. There was a guy, a year older than me, who lived just down East Steuben St. from me. Frank "Nicki" Nicklaus was the son of Dr. Nicklaus, a dentist, and quite well to do. Dr. Nicklaus was uncle to Jack Nicklaus (famous pro golfer). Jack even made trips to Bath when he was younger, and lit up the Bath Country Club. Anyway, Nicki lived in this big Victorian home with all the comforts. His bedroom was state of the art, with all kinds of built-ins, electronics, and TV etc., really cool. In the basement was a rec room, complete with a 9' turn of the century (leather drop pockets) Brunswick pool table. To top it off, there was a carriage house out back. You would climb a wall-mounted ladder to the second floor, which was converted into a full (albeit short) basketball court. It was really cool, and Nicki was generous enough to let us play up there, even when he wasn't around.

In an ironic twist, our new home in Kenmore would be at 160 Knowlton Ave., just down the street a block from 52 Knowlton (our previous home in Kenmore). Not only that, but Mom and Dad bought 160 Knowlton from the Johnston's (Johnny's parents). Remember, Johnny was my whiffle ball buddy and lifetime friend.

> SIDE NOTE: Now that I'm reminiscing about Johnny, I recall he, too, made a couple of trips to Bath, and was in on some of Bob Knights antics. John had/has a special dry, sarcastic sense of humor, which always cracked me up.

160 Knowlton was a large, 1920s two-story, 4-bedroom house with a huge, unfinished walk up attic. It featured a double stairway, one from the kitchen to a landing, and one from the front entranceway to the landing. The house needed a little face lift and a kitchen update. While we were still living in Bath, finishing off the second semester of school and enjoying the early summer, Dad was busy in Kenmore. Not only was he busy with his new responsibilities at his new job at ESSO, but he was working his ass off doing the updates at 160 Knowlton. My brother and I would later reminisce Dad never really got the credit he deserved for all of the handywork he did – carpentry, electric, and plumbing. Jim says he got a lot of his training from his grandfather (Bapa.)

Looking back, I'm sure Dad was anxious to get the house ready, not only for us to move into, but in preparation for my sister Amy's wedding in July. Indeed, he did meet his self-imposed, deadline. Amy and Jerry's wedding (Saturday, July 17th) at the Lafayette Presbyterian Church was lovely, and Amy was a beautiful bride. Jerry started his career with IBM in Erie, PA, where they moved soon after the wedding.

That Fall, I would return to Kenmore Junior High School as a 14-year-old freshman. I was already very familiar with KJHS, having spent the first half of my 7th grade year there. Now, I was an upper classman, so to speak, SQUIRE (our junior high fraternity.) That was the core of my social life in Kenmore at the time.

As I mentioned earlier, Jim and I had mixed emotions about leaving our friends (and girlfriends) in Bath. Over the next several months, Jim and I would make many weekend excursions to Bath. Jim was 17-18, and I was 14. We would head out on the 100 mile trek to Bath with very little money and no concrete plans of where we would stay. As I remember, most of these trips were made in the family 1961 Ford Galaxy. Occasionally, friends would put us up (the Beeke's or the Friedland's), but other times, we rented cheap rooms or even slept in the Galaxy. The drives home on Sunday nights were painful, but we survived.

Sherry Foster & me at 160 Knowlton

Eventually, for me at least, it became impractical to keep up the Bath visits. The sabbatical was over and the Kenmore roots took over.

Being one of the SQUIRES guaranteed an elevated social status. I was part of a clique of guys and gals who hung out after school at Watson's café for Cherry Cokes, hot fudge sundaes, and Terryton or Lark cigarettes. Some of the guys and gals I remember from this clique were Tom Brown, Richie Ward, Rose Ann Mineo, Ann Gambino, Paul Zebrowski, Betty Skrobacz, and Bob Kelley... just to name a few. At night, the hang out was the new Dunk n Donuts (next door to Mike's Giant Submarines.) It didn't matter how cold it was, or how much snow – the guys would be wearing their penny loafers or wing tips with their blades or casino slacks. The gals were in short wool pleated skirts with knee socks. It was also cool for the guys to be wearing English Leather or Jade East cologne. So, on any given night, we were hanging around Dunk n Donuts, smoking Terrytons or Larks, and probably freezing. If we were lucky, we would go to somebody's house (basement) to hang out. It was natural one of the guys liked one of the gals or vice versa. It might go something like this:

Rose Ann says to me, "Greg, ya know, Annie really likes you." And that might be all it would take to spark a "going with" relationship. Anne McGuire lived on Wabash Ave., about 3 doors east of Elmwood, so it was a good one mile walk from there to 160 Knowlton. By now, I was about 6'3" and Anne was only 5'1". When I would walk her home, and be saying our good nights in her back hall, she would stand up one step just to get a good look at my chin. Anne and I would be an item, on and off, for a couple of years.

In October, basketball tryouts started. There were probably 25 boys trying out for 10 spots on the 9th grade team. The coach was a first year Physical Education teacher – Dick Harvey. Dick was a University of Buffalo graduate and a star basketball player there after a stellar high school career (All Western New York) at Dunkirk. Dick knew his stuff. I never had any doubt, I would make the team and be a starter… and I was right. The competition was fierce, and I was battling against 6'5" center Lynn (Arthur) Robb. This was about the time I became closer to Dave Casselman, Mike Vaccaro, and Bill Truman. There was no doubt these guys were going to be the key players on this team (and teams going forward.)

My social life and poor academics were on a collision course with basketball. When report cards came out late that Fall, I had 2 Fs, 2 Ds and an A. The A was in mechanical drawing (Mr. Kester) which, obviously, I loved and had a natural aptitude for. The other courses couldn't keep my interest, and I was negligent with my work. Oh, by the way, my attendance was atrocious.

Of course, Coach Harvey was privy to all of the player's report cards. I was soon beckoned to Coach Harvey's office where he closed the door and had me sit. He said, "Greg, I really wish I could keep you on the team, but because of your poor report card, you are ineligible for the next grading period."

He went on to tell me he would be working at the Washington School playground in the summer of 1966, and he would love to work with me on my basketball game (he could see my potential.) It was a wakeup call for me, to say the least. Again, I was unable to play organized basketball. I did get my grades up, and actually made the 9th grade baseball team that Spring (1966.) I did some pitching and played first base. Hitting was not my strong point, so I knew that was going to be the extent of my baseball career.

Backing up to January 24, 1966, Amy and Jerry had their first child. Caryn was born in Erie, PA. I rode with my mother on a wintry day, to Erie from Kenmore to be there (in the waiting room) to lend a hand to Jerry while Amy and Caryn were still in the hospital. Amy was just 20 years old, herself.

Chapter Ten
1966

We 9th graders were the Kenmore Junior High School class of 1966. That Spring, there were plans for a 9th grade talent show – "Talent 66." My fellow SQUIRES buddies, Bob Kelley, Pete Scanio, Richie Ward, and I had a plan to be the *Rolling Stones*. Of course, I was going to be Mick Jagger, and I was even allowed (against the dress code) to grow my hair long. Our performance was meant to be a lip sync version of *Spider to the Fly* (still one of my all time, favorite Stones tune.) There were many other fine acts, which did very well. The show was in the auditorium in front of the student body (grades 7-9) and lasted about an hour. I think it covered the last period of a Friday. We were the last ones to go on, and we were very nervous. As we strutted onto the stage with our instruments and everything, the music started but it was the wrong song – *West Coast Promo Man*. We faked as best we could, and got a strong ovation from the audience. All of the acts came out for a "curtain call." On stage, up front, there were 3' tall block letters which spelled out TALENT 66. We, faux *Rolling Stones*, thought it would be a cute idea if we turned the 66 into 69. The student body roared with approval, but not so much the assistant principal (Mr. Moskal.) The following Monday, we were summoned to Mr. Moskal's office where we were, not only verbally reprimanded, but all of us bent over his desk and were paddled with the so named, "board of education."

To get back at Mr. Moskal, I think we ordered a few pizzas and a couple of taxi cabs to his house. Don't know if he ever connected the dots on that.

That summer, I accepted Coach Harvey's invitation to the Washington School playground. With his encouragement, I began to work on my basketball game in earnest. The following basketball season (10th grade) at Kenmore West High School, our KJHS team nucleus merged with the same from Hoover JHS to form the Junior Varsity basketball team coached by Kenneth "Rocky" Welgoss. We had a great season and went 13-5. Coach Dick Harvey, meanwhile, was elevated to replace retiring Coach Hubie Klein as varsity basketball coach. Coach Harvey and his star front court player, Steve Waxman (All Western New York), led the varsity basketball team to a section VI class AAA championship, beating Niagara Falls in the final game in front of 7,000 fans at Memorial Auditorium. Again, I am getting ahead of myself.

Also, that summer, we took another memorable trip to Mitchell, Indiana (Dad's hometown.) I had just turned 15, and the four of us – my parents, Wende, and I made the trip. My grandmother Laker (Nanny) and great grandmother Clements (MaMa) lived in a small house on the outskirts of town where my brother Jim had lived with them while a Mitchell High School sophomore. We were there for maybe a week, and I remember getting a letter from my girlfriend, Anne McGuire, smeared with lipstick (she missed me.) The house overlooked the old elementary school, which was a few hundred yards away and had a basketball hoop in the playground there. I would dribble my way there in the heat of the day and shoot hoops. That soon became tiring, and I was looking for something better. The new high school could also be seen from Nanny's back yard – but no outdoor hoops (unusual, I thought, for a school in Indiana – home of the Hoosiers.) Come to find out, the outdoor court was in town (long walk) next to the "old" high school. It was a great court – nice, rectangular backboards and huge shade trees (lighted at night.) Once I discovered that court, I was golden, and spent a lot of my time there shooting hoops.

The other point of interest I found in downtown Mitchell was Grissom's Pool Hall. Grissom's was "old school" – even my father frequented the place in his youth. I think there may have been six or eight tables there, and at least two of them were Snooker tables. This was the first time, in my fledgling billiards career, I had encountered Snooker tables – 10' long, smaller curved pockets, smaller balls, and lighter weight cue sticks... much more challenging than regular 9' pool tables. Being a music lover, I was also impressed with their jukebox selections – a mix of country and rock. It was the first time I had heard one of my all-time favorite tunes, *For What It's Worth* by the Buffalo Springfield. All and all, it was a great experience I thoroughly enjoyed. By the way, the Grissom name was very important to Mitchell, as it was also the home of Virgil Grissom, the astronaut.

Interestingly, my next (and most recent) visit to Mitchell would be some 29 years later with my beautiful and wonderful daughters, Kaitlin and Joanna (14 and 12, at the time.)

A couple of other summer activities from around this time span come to mind. Johnny Johnston had a Courier Express newspaper route which had to be delivered by 6 AM. Many times, we would sleep out in tents in our backyards. The papers would get dropped off around 4 or 5 AM, and I would help Johnny deliver his route. We would then throw our golf bags over our shoulder, hop on our bikes, or get on the NFT bus, and go to Delaware Park City golf course. If you teed off before 7 AM, you could golf for free. On other hot summer nights, in the wee hours, we would go pool hopping. We knew where all the nice pools were, and we would stealthily slide in for a quick dip, undetected. On other occasions, we would wake someone and have to make a run for it. On one of our getaways, we were apprehended by the Town of Tonawanda Police and taken to the Brownschidle Station on Delaware near Sheridan Dr. They detained us long enough to have our parents come to the Station and retrieve us. We were lucky to get off with a warning. Our parents were not happy.

> SIDE NOTE: While I'm at it, I should report the first time I recall getting drunk was also around this time. It was at 160 Knowlton and my brother had some of his buddies over. (My parents were gone.) It involved a little too much Colt 45 malt liquor and puking off the front porch. Enough said!

Now, in the fall of 1966, I was 15 years old and entering my sophomore year at Kenmore West High School. It was a big step because now, the student body included students from KJHS and Hoover JHS, so, new friends were waiting to be made. I got an after school job as a stock boy at a store, next to Dunk n Donuts. I would describe it as a mini Dollar General. That was my first "real" job, and it was nice having a little income. The store was owned and operated by a couple of middle aged ladies. They were bitchly, and not easy to work for. I hung on until basketball season started in October.

The big deal, though, that Fall, were the rush bids coming out for the fraternities and sororities. If a fraternity or sorority wanted you – you would actually receive a hand delivered engraved invitation to a "rush tea." I received 2 such invitations. One from Phi Sigma Chi, and one from the Royal Order of Knights. My brother, Jim, had been in Knights and I was hoping they would rush me. It wasn't uncommon for brother tradition (Suttons, Santa Marias, Hartmans, Wingenbachs, Kelleys, Browns, etc. – and now Lakers.) The rush teas were formal affairs (coat and tie.) Soft drinks, tea, and hors d'oeuvres were served, and each prospective pledge was introduced to the member Knights. If you were accepted, you became a pledge. The pledging period lasted 6 weeks. I was with a group of maybe 8 pledges. As a pledge, you were expected (at school), to, at all times, wear a tie, carry chewing gum, and carry a note pad (for recording merits and demerits.) When encountering a member Knight (in the halls at school) you would greet and address him by name – hello Mr. so-and-so. He could, for example, ask you for a piece of gum. If you were not prepared, he would record a demerit in your note pad. Pledges were often requested to bake cookies or prepare Rice Crispy treats for a superior and deliver them to the cafeteria at lunch time. Pledges were also asked to make decorative paddles. Each pledge had a "big brother," who would help them and look after them. The Knights had weekly meetings. The meetings were typically in the basement of one of the member's homes. They would do their business meeting and collect dues. There were officers – President, VP, secretary, treasurer, and Sgt. at Arms. The pledges would be congregated upstairs in the kitchen, shining the shoes of the members. The pledges had to be prepared with all the shoe shining supplies. One-by-one, the pledges would be called to the basement where the members would be sitting in a circle. The pledge would address the first member in the circle, "Hello Mr. so-and-so, is there anything I can do for you Mr. so-and-so?"

Each member would make a request of the pledge, or let him pass to the next member in the circle. If a member had a problem with a particular pledge, he could ask the pledge to bend over and prepare to be paddled. The member would then have the option of paddling the pledge – sometimes just a tap, but other times a hard "whack" which could be heard from above in the kitchen. My hardest "whacks" came from Jim Hartman. It turns out, my brother Jim was hard on him the year before, and this was "pay back" (not an uncommon occurrence, considering the brotherly tradition.) This routine went on for six weeks, leading up to HELL NIGHT.

For the record, the guys I can remember from my pledge class were John Santore, Pete Scanio, Bob Kelley, Tom Brown, Mike Phillips, Buddy Boughton, and Pat Phillips. For HELL NIGHT, the pledges were instructed to wear old clothes. The members would load us into cars and take us to a remote field. The 20 some members would line up, gauntlet style, armed with paddles, eggs, lipstick, molasses, and saw dust. The pledges would have to navigate their way through the gauntlet while being mugged and covered with all of the above stuff. We were a complete mess, to say the least. Next, we were blind folded and loaded into trunks of members' cars. We were taken maybe 10 miles, but when we were dumped off, we had no idea where we were. Finally, we made our way to civilization and were able to borrow a phone to call our parents to come rescue us. By that time, though, we didn't care. We had survived HELL NIGHT… we were Knights.

Besides the comradery we enjoyed, there were organized activities. As I mentioned earlier, Knights' sister sorority was "Epsilon." We would have "joint" get-togethers, like parties or picnics (Ellicott Creek Park.) It was a great way for guys and gals to meet and get to know one another. We raised money via dues, and each year we had our own formal dance. We would rent out a banquet room at one of the nicer restaurants in town for dinner and dancing. Because our Knight's formals were so nice, I never did go to either the Junior or Senior proms at Kenmore West. Another activity we had were inter-fraternal "tackle" football games. I was used as a wide receiver. We had some very competitive (but friendly) games vs. Phi Sigma Chi, and I think Knights usually came away with bragging rights. Many of the guys in these two fraternities were "jocks," but I was the only varsity basketball player during my time at Kenmore West to be in Knights. By the way, Knights colors were red and white. We had red wool winter jackets, with two white leather shoulder stripes, our "coat of arms" patch, and our embroidered names. The summer jackets were white cotton with the "coat of arms" insignia and embroidered name. All of the jackets were done up at *Broadway Knitting* on the east side of Buffalo. I wish I still had my jackets and paddles.

My chronology here, I think, is a year off. So, I think it was back in 1965. Even though Bob Knight lived away from Kenmore (the west side of Buffalo – Parkdale Ave. off of Lafayette), and was a student at Lafayette HS, we were still buddies. Sometimes, when I would spend the night at his house, we would sneak out late and wander the streets of Buffalo (crazy.) The west side, at that time, was predominately Italian, and very nice. There were many (legal) immigrant families, and they kept the neighborhood nice. It was common place to see thriving vegetable gardens and to smell the smell of Italian meals being prepared.

The first pool hall recollection, with Bob, I have, was a joint (Italian) on West Ferry St. near Grant Ave. They had about 8 brand new Brunswick Gold Crown I nine foot tables. We were beginners, and I can only remember how awkward it was for me to force my left hand into forming a closed bridge grip. This was the beginnings of a lifetime love affair I have with the sport of pool/billiards.

About this time, now, maybe, we are back to 1966, the Knight family moved to the east side of Buffalo in a very nice area, not far from the intersection of Main St. and Hertel Ave. The house was a duplex which they shared with Bill's (Mr. Knight's) brother Ed. It had a lot of space with a huge back yard. This was closer to Bill's work at a Buick Dealership near Main St. and Delevan Ave. Bill worked in the service department there, and always drove a sharp looking, smooth running Buick.

Bob was now going to Bennett HS, predominantly black, and home of legendary basketball player, Bob Lanier. Bob now had a great part-time job in downtown Buffalo at the, now world famous, Anchor Bar (home of the original Buffalo chicken wings.) At that time, the Anchor Bar was more well-known for its late night live Blues music. Bob would work, cleaning up, from 4AM (close) until 7AM. I could not believe the amount of cash he would come home with he found on the floor and booths while cleaning up.

Bob soon saved enough money to buy his first motorcycle. It was a red Honda 90 dirt bike. Even though he did not quite yet have his license, he would walk (or ride) the bike across Hertel to some open fields adjacent to the railroad tracks. It didn't take him long to learn how to handle that bike, and soon, he was doing jumps and other dangerous maneuvers (no helmet.) I would mostly watch, but Bob would sometimes put me on the back of the bike. I didn't like that… too crazy. I did, however, get a few chances to drive the bike myself.

Being next to the railroad tracks meant we saw trains coming and going, and sometimes stopping. Of course, Bob couldn't resist the temptation of boarding some of these train cars even when they were moving. Under the strain of peer pressure, I joined Bob on a few of these train hoppings. Usually, the trains wouldn't go very far, or if they did, we were able to catch a return train and hope the train was going slow enough for us to jump off at the right time and place.

One time, however, we got on an east bound train in an empty coal car with sides up to our chests. It speeded up and, before it came to a stop, we were in a train yard looking at a sign which said Depew (about 10-12 miles east of Buffalo.) We waited, probably another hour, looking for a train going back west and near home. Finally, we rolled into an empty box car on a west bound train. The train picked up speed and was going too fast for us to jump off near our "home" area. The next thing we knew, we were on a bridge crossing over the Niagara River just north of the Peace Bridge. The train finally came to a stop in Fort Erie, Ontario, Canada. Believe it or not, even Bob was a little scared. We waited, what seemed forever, and finally we felt the clanking of the couplers as the train reversed its course, headed back east. As soon as the train got back to the USA and slowed down enough, we took our first opportunity to debark. What a relief.

My interest in pool was growing. Bob Knight liked it, too. The next pool room in Bob's new territory was much bigger... maybe 20 new 9' Brunswick Gold Crown Is. At the time, I didn't know a Brunswick from an AMF, but I did know they were high quality tables. Pool was very big in those days, and it wasn't uncommon to have to put your name on a waiting list and wait an hour for a table to open up. TIME!

As I mentioned earlier, in this chapter, the 1966/67 version of the Kenmore West junior varsity basketball team was now a mix of Kenmore Junior High School and Hoover Junior High School players. The heart of the team, however, was the nucleus of KJHS players – Dave Casselman, Bill Truman, Mike Vaccaro, and me – not to mention Carl Price and Lynn "Art" Robb. The Hoover stand out was Greg Witter (who became a lifetime friend of mine.) That team, under Coach Kenneth "Rocky" Welgoss, overachieved with a record of 13 wins – 5 losses, and showed signs of things to come. Another Hoover "groover" on that team was Harold "Buddy" Boughton. Buddy was a great athlete. He went on to be a standout on the KW Niagara Frontier League championship football teams. Buddy and I went through Royal Order of Knights, pledging together and became fraternity brothers.

This is also a good time to update you on my best friend from childhood, Gary Galbreath. Although Gary grew to be 6' 5", and had a similar physique to me, he wasn't quite able to make the team (tryouts were extremely competitive.) He did, however, volunteer to be a team manager and he diligently carried out those duties with dedication right through our senior years.

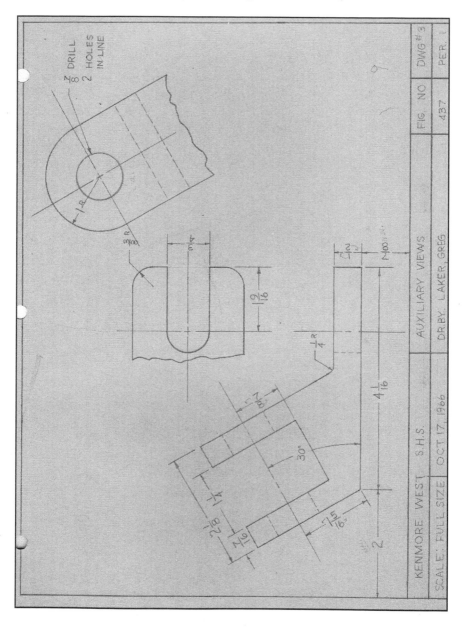

Chapter Eleven
1967 and 1968

Following that season, in early 1967, I became more and more obsessed with basketball. Basketball became a 24/7/365 interest of mine. My teammates and I realized that if we were going to become successful collectively, and individually, it was going to take dedicated, hard work. We were inspired by the KW varsity basketball team which had just won the Section VI AAA championship, led by (my idol) #24 star Steve Waxman. In the sectional quarter finals, semi-finals, and finals, Steve scored 30, 30, and 30 respectively. They beat Niagara Falls in the finals, 63 -60, at Memorial Auditorium to avenge an earlier season loss. We all had the same goal – win a Section VI AAA basketball championship in the AUD!

By the way, Steve Waxman went on to play college basketball, first at the University of Buffalo, and later at Canisius College. He was arguably the best player in Kenmore West basketball history, and the only one of two KW players to be inducted into the Ken-Ton Sports Hall of Fame, albeit posthumously. The other one, sadly, was our teammate Fran Moulin.

We would look for games of hoops everywhere. Our nucleus, soon to be known as the "neighborhood gang", would go to the

Belmont YMCA and play against the older, local men. We had nicknames for those guys, like Hal Greer, Truck Driver, and Banlon, etc. The games could be bruising, but it was good for us. Casselman, Vaccaro, and I each had hoops on our garages and, if need be, we would shovel the snow from the driveways in order to have a place to shoot around. By this time, the Laker family had moved a few blocks from 160 Knowlton to 51 McKinley Ave. When the weather warmed up that Spring, we would play at the (not so great) basketball court at the Kenmore West tennis courts behind the school. At one of these sessions, I came down awkwardly with a rebound and turned my ankle. I had never felt such pain, and it instantly swelled and became discolored. The x-rays were negative, but it was a severe sprain and I needed to be in a cast for 6 weeks. This was my first sports injury, and the 6 weeks seemed like forever. Since I couldn't play, I resorted to reading basketball magazines to get my "fix." This is when I became enthralled with following college and pro basketball. I was fascinated with team and player stats and bios.

Although basketball was probably the dominant activity in my life then, and for years to come, I still had other interests. After all, I had a girlfriend – Anne McGuire. We were part of the clique I mentioned earlier. One of the group's favorite warm weather hangouts was the Kenmore Pool at the corner of Mang and Elmwood. It was a beautiful, new Town of Tonawanda facility with an observation deck overlooking the diving board area. We would hang out there with the group – many of them smoking cigarettes. By now I had given up smoking cigarettes in favor of basketball conditioning.

Like most other kids my age, I was anxious to get my driver's license... maybe I was a little too anxious. Sometime late that spring (still 15 years old), I was home alone and one of the cars was in the driveway. The temptation was too much for me to resist. I got the keys and went for a little cruise downtown Buffalo. I wasn't nervous about my ability to drive, but I was nervous about getting pulled over or found out by my parents. Lucky for me, there were no problems and I returned the car safely. My parents were none the wiser.

When I did turn 16, I immediately got my learner's permit and scheduled my road test all at the same visit to the DMV. Just two weeks later, I took my road test and flunked (made a poor parallel park.) I quickly rescheduled, though, and the second time was the charm. Like when I got that 26" Raleigh bike back when I was 10, this was a game changer. Now, the streets were mine… at least until dusk.

When there was no car available for me to drive, my alternative means of transportation was hitchhiking. Hitchhiking was very common back then, and we didn't think anything of it. I can picture Johnny Johnston and me thumbing our way to the Boulevard Mall just for something to do. Bob Knight and I would hitchhike to Sherkston Beach in Ontario, Canada – spend the day, and hitchhike back. We would be standing right there at the Peace Bridge with our thumbs out – the authorities would say/do nothing.

By now, Dad had gotten me jobs pumping gas and doing L.O.F. (lube, oil change, and filter) at a couple of EXXON gas stations – namely Colvin & Sheridan and Niagara Falls Blvd. & Sheridan.

Many times, I had to hitchhike to and/or from work. Only one time can I remember being picked up by a guy who scared me. It was on Sheridan Dr. on my way home from Niagara Falls Blvd. The guy was obviously a homosexual, and tried to put the moves on me. Luckily, I was able to make a quick exit at a red light.

Amy and Jerry (and baby Caryn) were still living in Erie, PA, and I wanted to go visit them. It was afternoon on one of those hot summer days, and I just headed out on a 95 mile journey. When you are hitchhiking, you never know how long you will have to wait for a ride, or how far each ride will take you. It may take you multiple rides to reach your destination, and you may have to wait long periods of time between rides. In this case, I can remember standing, perilously, on the shoulder of I 90 (the NYS Thruway), at the east/west split near Cheektowaga. It was rush hour, and cars and trucks were whizzing by me. That was hairy, but I finally got to Erie and got dropped off somewhere on the east side of the city, with still a few miles to get to Amy's. I walked those last few miles backwards with my thumb out (in the dark and through some pretty dark neighborhoods).

> SIDE NOTE: If memory serves, two movies that were popular that summer were the *Beatles* HELP, and *The Graduate* with Dustin Hoffman's debut. The songs *HELP* and *Mrs. Robinson* (Simon & Garfunkle), got a lot of play by DJ Joey Reynolds on WKBW 1520 AM. Oh, "I have just one word for you-PLASTICS."

The greatest thing that happened that summer, for us hoopsters, was the creation and opening of the "CROSBY COURTS." The COURTS consisted of 3 short full courts on blacktop and with wooden, rectangular, overhanging backboards, allowing for a nice wide baseline… perfect for 4-on-4 games. Coach Harvey's summer job was now moved from Washington school playground to Crosby Athletic Field. It was a perfect set up for him, and for us. He would work there mornings and afternoons. Some of us would go there during the days for shoot arounds and games of PIG etc. Many milkshakes and popsicles were wagered. Usually, it was too hot during the day for 4-on-4 games ,and many of us had summer jobs – but in the evenings (after dinner), when the courts were more shade covered, the action heated up. Players came from not only Kenmore, but other parts of the surrounding area. High school, college, and older players came. Winners would stay on – losers would get in line behind the challengers. It was call your own foul, but it better not be ticky tack. The play was very physical and tempers could flare. The neighbors got an earful. At the end of the night, though, we were a tight knit group – friendships grew and we would have many laughs over a long neck Vernors or NE-HI at Romances on Nassau. There is absolutely no doubt, in my mind, that the " CROSBY COURTS had a significant contribution to the success of Kenmore West basketball during that era.

Also, that summer, Bob Knight added another motorcycle to his fleet – a 750 Norton. Bob already had a BMW road bike and, of course, the Honda 90 dirt bike, not to mention the use of the family Buick Special station wagon. According to my friend, Sam Balcom, Bob made a trip to Bath on the Norton… I wasn't around for that. Bob would make occasional trips to Kenmore, and more frequent trips when he was introduced to Anne's friend, Colleen Morin. We would hang out, listen to music, etc.

My interest in pool was also growing. I had now discovered the nearest local pool hall – Bobby Cue, run by the owner and proprietor, Bob Clark, and his wife, Billy. Bobby Cue was located on Sheridan Drive, just west of Military Rd. Too far to walk to from my house. Bobby Cue had eight, 9 foot "American" tables with blue cloth. Bob was probably pushing 40, at the time, and he had a way of making you feel at home. Before long, I was signed up for a straight pool league (handicapped.) Bob was a chain Camel smoker, and there was no nonsense in his pool room. I soon learned the do's-and-don'ts (billiard etiquette.) I had the hand/eye coordination, and I loved the game (still do), so I was hooked.

That fall, at 16, I would start my junior year at Kenmore West. I had plenty on my plate between Royal Order of Knights activities, schoolwork, Anne, pool, and, of course, basketball.

Many of my basketball buddies were recruited by coach Robert Lucia (great guy) to play fall volleyball. I opted against volleyball, in favor of practicing basketball. I would spend most of my fall after school hours at the Crosby Courts, shooting around – mostly by myself. Simultaneously, on the adjacent football field, I was observing the Kenmore West football team practice. These guys were some of the best athletes at Kenmore West (and that is saying something) being coached by legendary Coach, Jules Yakapovich, and his assistant, Dave Fleischman. Some of the notable, incoming sophomore football players were Rob Sutton, Bill Tepas, and Gary Streicher. They were all standout players, and they were all a part of the Royal Order of Knights Fall pledge class. All fraternity protocol, rightfully, was off when it came to sports practices and games. Those three, however, were well aware of me on the adjacent basketball court. All three of them were a hoot (roar), and I really liked them. They were all from Hoover JHS, and they would cautiously address me as Mr. Laker (their "superior") because they knew I had the power to paddle their asses at the next Knights meeting.

After those guys made it through pledging and their HELL NIGHT, and became my "brothers," they christened me with a nickname. There was a 6' 6" 210lb. linebacker from Miami (FLA) University named Ted Hendricks. Because of his tenacious play and slim build (for a linebacker) they called him "Mad Stork." So, from that time forward, I was branded "Mad Stork," hopefully for the same reasons. Anyway, it's a moniker, which I am proud of and it has stuck with me to this day. More "Stork" stories to follow.

By the way, Bill Tepas was/is a music lover. We shared the same passion for the Beatles, the Rolling Stones, and other British invasion groups. As a matter of fact, Bill recently stopped at my home (while on business) in Canisteo to say hello, and give me a CD of the Dave Clark's Five greatest hits. Too cool!

Although it took me three tries to pass the Algebra regents with a 65, I knew I had a great math mind. Even though I could come up with all of the correct answers (isn't that the bottom line?) I couldn't show all the xyz formulas correctly. So, in my junior year, I took business math from Mr. Patterson… 99% grade – 'nuff said.

Sports and school spirit were huge at Kenmore West, especially when it came to competition vs. Kenmore East. That Fall, on a Friday afternoon before a Saturday afternoon football game vs. Kenmore East, there was a last period pep rally in the school auditorium. It was bedlam – the most exciting event I had been a part of to date… loud enthusiasm… goose bumps! Players were introduced and spoke – cheerleaders, at their best – pep band, it was awesome. Kenmore West 47 – Kenmore East 20!

SIDE NOTE: At the time, Kenmore East and Kenmore West football shared Crosby Field as a home field. So, if you were a home team fan, you sat on the stadium side while visiting fans were seated in the (cross field) green wooden bleachers. When it came to an East vs. West football game, it was hard to find a place to park, and the game noise could be heard for blocks. As youngsters, we knew the best place to crawl under the fence on Crosby Ave. behind the green wooden bleachers in order to save the 50 cent admission price.

Basketball tryouts began in October. Some of the guys were still involved with Fall sports, but with a few exceptions, it was a foregone conclusion of who would make the team. When you stop and think about it – it was quite an accomplishment and honor to be one of the 14 guys out of some 850 + junior and senior guys in the school to make the varsity team. No sophomores played varsity, at that time. Junior varsity was for sophomores only. In other words, we were an elite group. There was no doubt our 14th man would have been a starter at a lot of other schools.

Coach Harvey was a stickler for details and statistics. His tryouts and practices were well organized. Tryouts lasted about a week, and there were two cuts – each list of survivors was posted on the locker room bulletin board.

The tough Niagara Frontier League action opened up December 1st and we were at Lewiston – Porter. Kenmore West was the Section VI class AAA defending champions, albeit, now, without the services of star Steve Waxman. We lost a close game 63-60 in overtime. In my varsity debut, I scored 11 points and pulled down 13 rebounds.

Except for a few highlights, I will not go into detail about that season. However, for those interested in more detail, they are well documented in my Ken-West Basketball 67-68 scrapbook.

> SIDE NOTE: Academically, besides business math, I was most interested in Art (George Kontos) and Mechanical Drawing (Dave Fleischman.) Because of my artistic abilities, I was allowed to do many of the game program cover art. It was a tricky mimeograph procedure. I enjoyed that task, and many of those programs can be found in the above mentioned scrapbook.

The NFL was made up of 10 teams (schools) – Niagara Falls, LaSalle, Trott Vocational, Tonawanda, North Tonawanda, Kenmore East, Lockport, Lewiston Porter, Niagara Wheatfield, and, of course, Kenmore West. Senior guards Sandy Vogel and Gary Fries were the leading scorers, respectively, and I was the leading rebounder and only junior who started regularly. We got through the first round of the season with 5 wins and 4 losses.

We played our home games at the Kenmore Junior High School (formerly Kenmore High School) gym – appropriately nicknamed, THE PIT. It was old – probably from the 1920s. The seating was stadium style seats wrapped around three sides of the court, with the front row some ten feet above the floor. It could get very loud, but it was a great place to play... unique. We all knew right where our parents sat each game. My father was my biggest fan, and he wasn't above giving the officials a little help when he thought they needed it.

As I mentioned earlier, the NFL had 10 teams, so we played 9 opponents home and away. In the first round, we beat Kenmore East 50-46 at their "modern" gym. When they came to THE PIT February 2, 1968, it was the loudest I've ever heard. Whenever Kenmore East came to THE PIT it was necessary to bring in auxiliary bleachers. That night, more than 4,000 fans (according to the Tonawanda News,) somehow, packed into THE PIT... it was wall-to-wall – standing room only. You sometimes could not hear yourself think, let alone hear the official's whistle.

As with every game, a group of my Royal Order of Knights fraternity brothers would plant themselves in the front row (10' above floor level) directly behind the basket on the south end of the court (where we warmed up.) They would chant "Mad Stork – Mad Stork" as we did our layup line with our special blue and white ball, and to the sound of the Harlem Globetrotter's version of *Sweet Georgia Brown*, talk about an adrenalin high - WOW!!

Unfortunately, that night, Kenmore East got the best of us 56-53... that would not happen again during my high school career. By the way, Dave Casselman came off the bench to score 14 points that night.

Saturday, February 10th, in practice, I rolled an ankle for the second time. It was a severe sprain and I would miss the last 4 games of the regular season. I was also unable to play in the first round of the Section VI AAA playoffs at Erie Community College vs. Lackawanna. Lackawanna, led by All-Star Dave May, and future National Football League All-Star quarterback Ron "Jaws" Jaworski, beat us soundly.

Sandy Vogel, Gary Fries, and I were named to the Courier Express Niagara Frontier League All-Stars as honorable mentions.

During the basketball season, we typically had Saturday morning practices. On many of those Saturday afternoons, a few of us would get together to play poker (nickel/dime). The usual group included Casselman, Vaccaro, Greg Witter, and me – we would rotate homes. It makes me chuckle to myself to recollect our first of many poker games at Witter's house. Greg Witter had a younger 9th grade brother, Gary, who wanted to hang with us "older" guys. At the time, Gary was a skinny little guy with thick, black framed glasses. Much to his mother, Vonnie's, dismay, Gary would bring his piggy bank to the poker game. I can hear Vonnie now (from upstairs) say, "Geeeery, your gonna lose all of your newspaper route money!"

Gary was defiant though, and learned to play poker the hard way. Similarly, Mike Vaccaro's younger brother, Steve, was in the same boat. Some of the games we played were GUTTS, KINGS, AND, FOLLOW the QUEEN, ACEY-DUECY and, of course, CONJAHOOTY. If you had a really bad night, you might drop $20, and vice versa for a good night. When we played at Witter's, though, it was customary to hold aside at least 60 cents so you could buy a "John & Mary's" sub on the way home.

We all had nicknames, and there was constant ragging. Greg Witter was "Big Witter" – eventually just "Big." Gary was "LW" for "Little Witter." Mike Vaccaro was "Bird," and Steve Vaccaro was "Niffer." Casselman was "Cass" and, of course, you had the "Stork," AKA "Stretch."

> SIDE NOTE: Speaking of nicknames, if you read far enough into this book, I will tell you about a trip Cass and I took to Geneseo in 1975 to visit LW… one of the biggest roars I ever had.

A lot of times, after a Friday night basketball game, we would be so wound up, we would have a poker game to wind down. We would have an ear and one eye on the TV if there was a basketball game on. Little Three (St. Bonaventure, Canisius, and Niagara) basketball was at its peak. Bona's mascot, back then, was the Brown Indian, and we would beat the drums to cheer them on. It has always bothered me the so-called "do-gooders" and PC crowd have to go overboard to eliminate a mascot name which was, after all, chosen in the first place to be something to be proud of. They chose the "Brown Indian" to honor him. I digress… anyway, Bona had All-American big Bob Lanier (6'10" lefty post player with a soft touch), a local product from Bennett High School in Buffalo. Niagara had Calvin Murphy (another All-American) who was a 5' 8" scoring machine, equaled only by Pistol Pete Maravich at LSU. Canisius' star player was Tony Masiello, another scrappy Buffalo product who would eventually become the Mayor of the Queen City.

During my high school years, we would make many trips to the AUD to watch college basketball double headers. It was amazing to watch Calvin Murphy put up 50+ points in a game. You have to keep in mind, Murphy and Maravich were putting the numbers up before the benefit of the 3-point arc, where they made many shots from. Some of their 50+ point games could easily have been 60+ point games. By the way, Calvin Murphy was an expert baton twirler and performed at half time of many Buffalo Bills football games (then at the old "Rock Pile.")

That spring, I attended my first Royal Order of Knights formal dance with Anne. If memory serves, it was held in the basement lounge of the upscale Four Seasons restaurant on Niagara Falls Blvd. There were about 30 of us for dinner and dancing. Somehow, I remember I was drinking 7 & 7s… most of the rest was a little fuzzy (50 years ago),but I do recollect it was the last time I was in possession of my Royal Order of Knights fraternity pin.

> SIDE NOTE: About this time, the BEATLES put out the "Sergeant Pepper" album. I had never seen or heard anything like this album before – I was in awe. Funny how time can be marked by the music of the day. That album got extensive play on our HI-FI.

By now, I'd had my driver's license for almost a year, but I signed up for summer school Driver's Education. It was a multi-benefit decision. I would get my "blue card," which would not only allow me to drive at night when I turned 17, but it gave me school credit and gave my parents a discount on auto insurance. It worked out great. I was the only Driver's Education student that summer who actually already had my license. There were four of us in the brand new, "Lou Awald" provided Chevrolet Biscayne with our instructor Mr. Rambus (Ramblin' Rose.) The four of us were Jeff Armon (Sugar Bear – no driving experience,) Lynne Sutherland (Sweetie,) my buddy Dave Casselman, and me. I would swing by and pick up Cass in the morning and head up to Kenmore West. The class was half in the car and half in the classroom. We even had to learn to change a tire. That was a fun class, with lots of laughs. Bottom line was, when I turned 17 in July, I was able to drive at night... that was another game changer.

Crosby courts was going full bore that summer. There were always new faces. Notably, there was a trio from Riverside: Charlie "Chuckie Wow" Forness, Joe Erman, and Bo Bazinski. They were a little older – Charlie was a football player - 5'10" 250 lbs. (heart of gold) and a fierce competitor. Joe Erman, also a football player, was about 6'5" 290 lbs. and solid as a rock (he played at Syracuse, and later for the Baltimore Colts.) Bo was a "crazy" scrappy 2-guard who pushed the boundaries of "clean" play. They definitely added a new dimension to "THE COURTS."

As for us Kenmore West guys, we were developing our games on a day-by-day basis. Casselman, Vaccaro, Fran Moulin, and I were pretty much every-nighters. Guys were vying for one of the 13 spots on the 1968/69 edition of the Kenmore West varsity cagers. The Witters, LW and Big, were also regulars at THE COURTS. LW would be on the JV that Fall, and Big would become our valuable 6th man.

There were a few other notable activities that summer. The Lakers took a family trip for a week at Keuka Lake. We were familiar with Keuka Lake from our days in Bath... just 8 miles from the beautiful Village of Hammondsport, which was located at the very south end of Keuka Lake. Keuka is the Finger Lake which is shaped like a "Y." On the east side, it is about 21 miles north from Hammondsport to Penn Yan, and on the west side, 18 miles from Hammondsport to Branchport. In between the "Y" is the lofty "bluff." We stayed in the motel units at "Gibson's Landing," about halfway up the west side of the lake, adjacent to the end of the bluff. It was a rustic lake setting... beautiful. Amy and Jerry were there with Caryn, and I think Jerry rented a boat for cruising and water skiing.

This was the first of several vacations we had at Gibson's Landing over several years, so the chronology may be slightly skewed.

The Casselman family vacationed there at least a couple of times during those years, also. There was a family there from Ohio, and Dave's younger sister, Sue, made friends with one of the daughters, Colleen; they became lifetime friends.

Not too far down the road was a vintage roadhouse named the "Wheel Inn." That place would get rockin' with its "red hot" juke box. I seem to remember getting drunk there on 7 & 7s. Pretty sure I was with my brother Jim.

That may have been my first water skiing experience, maybe for all of us. People, unfortunately, didn't give too much thought to sunscreen in those days, so there were a lot of burnt bodies. From what I remember, there was shuffle board, horse shoes, and a swim area which included a high diving board, slide, and swim out anchored float. Also up and over, across the road (Rte 54A), there was a general store.

Earlier, I mentioned I read a lot of basketball magazines. One of the advertisements which kept catching my eye was one for Kutsher's National All Sports Camp near Monticello, NY in the Catskill Mountains. The camp was run by legendary L.I.U. Hall of Fame coach Clair Bee and featured such names as Dave Bing, Wilt Chamberlain, and coach Bobby Knight (then at Army.) Campers came from all over the USA and Canada. It was wall-to-wall basketball drills and coaching for a solid week. Of course, for me, meeting Wilt Chamberlain was the highlight of the experience. Wilt gave each camper a basketball and a team photo op. Later that summer, Wilt would be traded from the Philadelphia 76ers to the L.A. Lakers for Darryl Imhoff and others. I think Wilt got the first NBA $100,000 contract.

Coach Bee and Bobby Knight were all business. I was among 10 players (out of hundreds) chosen to take part in a late night filming session. It was a professionally produced basketball training film directed by Clair Bee depicting various drills. The drills had to be executed to perfection, so sometimes it took multiple takes. I had kind of forgotten about that film, but I sure wish I could get my hands (eyes) on it now. YouTube?

One of my roommates there at Kutsher's was a black dude from Kansas City named Curtis Washington. He was my age and size, and was very talented. Coincidentally, later, Curtis would go on to play at Neosho C.C. (Kansas) in the Eastern Division of the Kansas Jayhawk Junior College Conference, at the same time I played for Seward County C.C. in the Western Division of that conference. We never competed against each other, but we were both named to the NJCAA Region VI (all of Kansas) All-Star team. Another example of "small world." By the way, during those years, Curtis' older brother Russell was playing, as a huge lineman, for the Kansas City Chiefs. For the record, that camp cost $125 which I split with my parents.

Gibson's Landing - Keuka Lake with Wende and Mom

KENMORE WEST SENIOR HIGH SCHOOL
KENMORE, NEW YORK

Laker, Greg _____ HR *306*

Honor _____ X

has done Above Average _____ work

Average _____

in *Driver Education* _____

EVALUATION OF PUPIL'S TRAITS
ONLY unsatisfactory traits are checked

SOCIAL ATTITUDES	WORK HABITS
1. Co-operation	6. Daily Preparation ....
2. Dependability	7. Accuracy ....
3. Courtesy	8. Promptness ....
	9. Initiative ....
	10. Neatness ....
4. Reporting for Individual Help	11. Use of Class Time ....
5. Class Attendance	12. Working to Apparent Ability ....

Comments : _____

_____

_____

_____

_____ Unit State Credit - Final Exam *91* _____

_____ Unit Local Credit - Passed on Average

Report Period Ending: _____

Teacher _____

Ken West senior picture

Another rebound

Also, that summer, we (Casselman, Vaccaro, Fran Moulin, Greg Witter, myself, and a few others) represented Kenmore West in an outdoor high school basketball league at Erie C.C. I recall the court seeming extra-long, especially after playing at THE COURTS. What I remember most are the trips out to

ECC. Five of us would cram into the Laker family red '63 Mercury Comet. We were always running late, so we were racing. The Comet had a 6 cylinder engine with three on the tree manual transmission, and we were overloaded. So, we would be speeding down the Youngman (I 290), no seat belts… crazy. I think we did pretty well, and gained some valuable experience. It was before the days of AAU.

Looking back, it was a very busy summer.

Again, that Fall, while many of my teammates were playing fall sports, I was spending many of my after school hours at THE COURTS shooting around – mostly by myself.

With Wilt Chamberlain

When it came to sporting goods in Kenmore, the place to go was Erv Dells on Delaware. Erv was an older, white-haired gentleman who, I think, was a retired "big leaguer." He had a wide variety of sporting goods for all sports. We bought our white high top Converse "Chuck Taylor" basketball sneakers there for $9.95/pair. Converse pretty much had the sneaker market cornered, in those days. Erv also sold uniforms (all sports) and New Era ball caps… Spalding, Rawlings, and Wilson baseball gloves, golf clubs, etc.

One day that fall, I came home to 51 McKinley to find my father in a "bad way." He was hurting, so I loaded him into his company car and rushed him to Kenmore Mercy Hospital. We soon realized he was suffering a heart attack. Knowing his heavy smoking habit, and overall lack of a healthy lifestyle, it should have come as no surprise. Luckily, it was a relatively mild heart attack and Dad was back to work within a couple of weeks. That may have been when he made the big effort to switch from Camels to a filtered Viceroy cigarettes… OMG!

At the same time, I mustn't forget about my interest in pool. This is about the time Bob Clark moved the Bobby Cue business from Sheridan and Military to Delaware and Princeton Blvd. This move not only gave him more space (now 9 tables,) but put him right down the street from Kenmore West High School. This made it a lot easier for me to frequent Bob's place. Also, on quiet Sunday evenings, my brother Jim and I would often drive into Buffalo to the new Golden Cue pool hall in a plaza at Hertel and Military across from Casey's biker bar. That was a big place… probably 20 Brunswick 9' Gold Crown I tables with gold cloth – beautiful.

Kenmore Business District

For a while, around then, the family car was a 1962 Pontiac Catalina. It was black and it was fast. I can mark this period of time cruisin' with the Doors, *Light my Fire*. Fall was in the air, the excitement of Ken West football on a Saturday afternoon at Crosby Field was awesome.

SIDE NOTE: *"Mischief"* – A couple of stories from the Fall of 1968. The first was a prank Bob Knight and I had pulled before while, still living in Bath. This time, it was Casselman, Vaccaro, and me. We first had to find a house that had a front door with a door knocker, with no storm door to encumber the door knocker. We found the perfect target at a house on the north side of McKinley Ave. near Myron. We could see a man, through the front window, sitting in his chair, reading his newspaper. When it was dark enough, we stealthily went to the front door and tied thread to the door knocker. We then unspooled the thread all the way across the street where we were out of sight in some bushes. Then, we would give a few yanks on the thread to activate the door knocker (knock, knock, knock.) We could hardly contain ourselves as we watched the man put down his newspaper and go to answer the door. He opened the door, looked around, and saw no one, so he closed the door and returned to his chair and newspaper. We were roaring with laughter. We gave him enough time to get comfortable, then tugged on the thread a few more times. The man got up, this time visibly annoyed, and again saw no one when he opened the door, hands on hips. Again, he went back to the comfort of his chair and newspaper. We were hysterical. The third time, he hopped up quickly, but this time when he opened the door, he discovered the thread and could see where it was coming from. We popped up and ran like hell. He was in pursuit and we made our way (top speed) down the McKinley/Crosby alley. This may have been the fastest I have ever run. We finally sought refuge at Joe Henafelt's house, which backs up to the alley on McKinley. After waiting a half hour or so, we figured the coast was clear and we made our ways home, still laughing. It was all pretty harmless.

The other mischievous escapade which happened sometime in the same era, involved pea shooters. It might have been after a ball game, when we were pumped up and looking to blow off some steam. Casselman, Vaccaro, Moulin, and I were in the red '63 Comet (I was the wheel man) on our way to Witter's. We all happened to be armed with pea shooters and ammo. As we turned down Winterwood, we noticed the silhouette of a "couple" in a steamed glass car parked at the curb. They were obviously making out. If memory serves, it was not just any car, but a late 60's black Olds 442 muscle car. We thought we could add a little excitement by pelting them with peas. We pulled up next to them, rolled down our windows, and opened fire. We then sped off, laughing all the way. As I gazed into my rear view mirror, I could see his tail lights come on and realized he was making a U-turn. It was soon apparent he was in hot pursuit, and now there was a chase. I got us out onto Sheridan Drive, but the old Comet was no match for the Olds 442. He quickly caught up to us and forced us to the side of the road. He pounced out of his car and came directly to the driver's door, pulling it open. The other three (Casselman, Vaccaro, and Moulin) were cowering (rightfully) to the other side of the car. He was pissed (rightfully) and we were apologizing profusely. After a few anxious moments, he let us go with a clear warning. We were sweating bullets. It was, however, not the end of our pea shooter days – read further on!

Speaking of pranks and mischief, my father used to delight in telling us about some of his high jinxes. I will not elaborate now, but it occurred to me that if any of you readers are interested in the details of my father's antics, you can ask me. This way, I will know if anyone has had the interest and patience to read this far in my book.

Once again, in October, it was time for basketball tryouts and, once again, there were no surprises as to who would make the team. This time, though, we were on a mission. Our tight knit group – Truman, Vaccaro, Casselman, and I were soon dubbed, in a newspaper account, "The Neighborhood Gang." We all lived within a couple of blocks from one another. On school days, Bill Truman would pick up Vaccaro, then Casselman, and finally, me. Bill drove a 60s something red Chevrolet Corvair convertible, which was our primary mode of transportation to school and home after practice. We sometimes practiced in THE PIT, and sometimes in the drab Kenmore West High School gym. By the way, Fran Moulin was the only junior starter – he was our 4 and enforcer. Truman was the point guard, Casselman the 2, Vaccaro the three, and I was the center. We had a deep bench – juniors Mark Shafer, Jerry Dziura, and senior Vic DeGeorge were all capable backup guards, and juniors Bob Bartholomew, Bob Miller, and Rich Ashcraft were our strong backup forwards. Greg Witter, however, was our valuable 6th man and utility type – defensive stopper. As I mentioned while describing our 1967/68 team, many of our bench players could have started for many other high school teams. A good example was junior guard Mike McArdle. Mike was a good player, but we were loaded, and as a result, he didn't get much playing time. At some point, late in the season, Mike calculated he had sat on the bench for 500 consecutive minutes. When that 500th minute ticked off on the game clock (in the Pit) Mike stood in front of the bench and turned to the crowd to display a premeditated sign, which illustrated his frustration. Coach Harvey was not amused.

Greg Witter, Bob Miller, Fran Moulin, Rich Ashcraft, Mike Vaccaro, Bob Bartholomew, Greg Laker, Gary Galbreath, Coach Harvey, Charles Hemstreet

Mark Shafer, Jerry Dziura, Mike McArdle, Bill Truman, Vic DeGeorge, Dave Casselman, Ron Katz, Jim Rider, Dave Nies

We opened our season December 6, 1968 in front of a raucous full house in Lockport. It got physical, and punches were thrown. Some over-zealous fans came on the floor and order had to be restored by the officials. When the dust settled, both Fran Moulin (our enforcer) and Tony Williams of Lockport were ejected, and we went on to win easily 75 -50. The box score read: Vaccaro 19 points, Casselman 17 points, Truman 17 points, and Laker 17 rebounds.

Again, other than a few important highlights, I won't get into all of the details of each game that season. The details are, however, well-documented in my KEN-WEST B-BALL 1968-69 scrapbook.

Coach Harvey (for $50) signed me up to a college basketball placement bureau. I completed an application which included all of my personal data – height and weight, along with my stats, and a testimonial from Coach Harvey. From that point on, hardly a day went by when I wouldn't come home to letters from colleges from all four corners of the country. Granted, many of the letters were "form type," but there were also many which showed genuine interest. It was fun to read the letters and browse through the literature, looking on the map and imagining myself going to play basketball for some of these colleges.

We went into our Christmas break undefeated at 5W – 0L, and our confidence was building. Over the break, I can remember purchasing the Beatles' *Double White* album. Dave Casselman and I would take that album to his attic bedroom, which he shared with his older brother, Dick, and played it repeatedly. Dick was 2 years Dave's senior, and an aspiring actor who was pursuing his dream in New York City, at the time. He was probably home for Christmas vacation, and I'm sure Dave, myself, and the Beatles were a little much for him. Back then, the cut *Rocky Raccoon* was my favorite song on the *Double White* album and I learned it by heart. Stay tuned!

Chapter Twelve
1969

Going into the New Year, we were on a roll – 5 and 0. We continued through the first round of the tough Niagara Frontier League season undefeated at 9W - 0L. The press was now, regularly, referring to the team's nucleus as the "Neighborhood Gang" because the four of us – Truman, Casselman, Vaccaro, and I lived within a couple of blocks from one another. In win number 8 vs. North Tonawanda, I achieved 2 individual school records: 25 total rebounds broke a school record previously held by, my idol, Steve Waxman's 23. Of those 25 rebounds, 16 were offensive rebounds. I'm proud to say, as of this writing, 16 offensive rebounds in one game remains a school record at Kenmore West. What makes the record even sweeter is it came against North Tonawanda's star center, Varick Cutler, who went on to play for Coach Lefty Driesell's University of Maryland Terrapins.

We had many happy bus rides on our way home from victories. It was traditional for the team to sing the school's alma mater: *"We sing to you, oh Alma Mater, we spread your praises far and near.*

We're proud to be your sons and daughters. Your honor we uphold as dear… etc. fight, fight, fight!"

On one of those raucous bus rides home, after we sang the Alma Mater, I decided to sing (solo) *Rocky Raccoon*. I must say it got a favorable response, and from then on, it became requested by popular demand.

The second round of games, for us, began Friday, January 24 at home vs. Lockport – a team we had beaten soundly the first game of the season. This time, we were without the services of our point guard, Bill Truman, who had missed school all week due to illness. Lockport was a much improved team, but we missed Bill. Lockport 51 – Kenmore West 45; our first loss. Next, we faced a tough Lewiston-Porter team at their gym, and we were stone cold, again. Lewiston Porter 67 – Kenmore West 58. (I fouled out of that game with 3 minutes remaining.)

We got back on track vs. our next opponent, Kenmore East, and ran the table from there, winning the last 7 games of the regular season.

SIDE NOTE: In game 16 at LaSalle, we clinched the NFL title in a close and **ROUGH** battle, 46 -42. In the last few seconds, tempers flared between the players. Both benches emptied and some LaSalle fans came on the court and threw punches at us. We finally made it to our locker room, but as we boarded our bus, we were surrounded by a mob of angry LaSalle fans banging on the sides of the bus and throwing rocks. Finally, order was restored when six Niagara Falls City Police cars arrived at the scene. That NFL Championship was Kenmore West's first since 1960.

Going baseline in the pit

So, we finished the regular season with a 16W – 2L record, and we were now facing West Seneca (led by Junior star, Tom Basher) in the quarter finals of the Section VI AAA playoffs at Erie Community College. We had no problem beating West Seneca 82-66, our highest scoring total of the season.

Now, we were faced with a tough Jamestown team led by 6' 7 ½" Donn Johnston. At Erie Community College, again, the game was very close and came down to a 12' jumper from the corner made by Jamestown's Denny Turner, with just two seconds on the clock – Jamestown 56, Kenmore West 54. We were devastated… our dream of a Section VI AAA championship in the AUD was not to be. Jamestown would go on to beat Niagara Falls in the finals in the AUD, and Donn Johnston would go on to play at the University of North Carolina.

The pain of that loss to Jamestown stayed with us for a long time. Even now, as I write about it, I can still feel the pain. But, trying to look at it all objectively, we knew we had a tremendous season, and we had nothing to hang our heads about.

When the Niagara Frontier League All-Star team was announced, it was no surprise Mike Vaccaro was named to the first team. Mike finished 2nd in the league's scoring race, only because Tom Wrobel from Niagara Falls was force fed the ball by his teammates to score 38 points in their final game, and took the title away from Mike. Dave Casselman, rightfully, was named to the second team, and I was an honorable mention.

Our parents, along with Coach and Mrs. Harvey, arranged for a nice banquet for us in late March at the Apple Grove Inn in Medina. It was a buffet affair, and all of the mothers received gifts. Coach Harvey got a little emotional as he expressed his pride in our team.

It was now time to look forward. As I mentioned earlier, my name and vitals were registered with an athletic placement bureau, and I was receiving letters and inquiries almost daily. I was honored to receive letters form such schools as Syracuse, Cornell, Northern Arizona, and the University of Buffalo. UB seemed the most interested, and assistant Coach Norbert Baschnagel recruited me aggressively. Because my grades were marginal for acceptance to

UB, it would necessitate my successfully completing some summer school courses on campus. I wasn't crazy about the idea of summer school, but I was willing to do whatever it took.

Meanwhile, when the weather broke, we were all back to playing hoops at Crosby Courts. But there was more going on than just basketball. I was working, pumping gas, and preparing for my final exams, which were of great importance to my collegiate aspirations. The class of 1969 was one of the largest at Kenmore West to date. There were 850+ of us, and it would necessitate splitting the class in half for two sessions in order to accommodate seating enough for parents and families in the auditorium for graduation.

> SIDE NOTE: It was traditional at Kenmore West to have a "Senior Day." Normally, in the past, this meant breaking the dress code, skipping classes, and maybe a few harmless pranks. At the time, the Kenmore West dress code forbid blue jeans, sneakers, or shirts without collars (for the guys), and skirts and dresses had to be a certain length (for the gals.) Anyway, things got out of hand that day, and there was chaos! The worst thing I remember doing myself was wearing blue jeans, sneakers, and a T-shirt. Some of the stunts, however, went over the line.

Bags of marbles spilled out on the hard hallway floors and made people slip and fall. Black shoe polish was applied to black toilet seats. Grease on stairway bannisters, a goat's head in a drinking fountain, and some broken windows. There were several injuries, and the school was a mess. It took a weekend to clean up the mess. I can't remember the consequences for some of the more serious offenses, but there were arrests made. I witnessed some of it early on, but some of my Royal Order of Knights brothers and I had planned on skipping out and meeting at Ellicott Creek Park for a picnic with the Epsilon gals. I was actually ashamed at what happened.

In late May, or early June, I received my first phone call from Coach Virgil Akins at Seward County Community Junior College in Liberal, KS. Coach Akins wanted me to come to SCCJC (southwest Kansas) and be a part of the very first class. SCCJC would pay for my books and tuition. They also promised me a part-time job, which would pay for my room and board. There were no dorms or cafeteria, and the campus was comprised of a repurposed hospital (Epworth Hall,) a repurposed Hardware store (Reno Building,) and some designated classrooms at Liberal High School. Coach Akins was very persuasive, and convinced me I would love to play in the very tough Kansas Jayhawk Junior College Conference. After many phone conversations with Coach Akins, and discussions with my parents (who were slightly leery,) I signed a letter of intent on June 21, 1969. It was probably one of the best decisions I have ever made.

The summer went on, and I continued my part-time job pumping gas at the Exxon station at Colvin and Sheridan. Most evenings, we were still all playing hoops at Crosby Courts. The basketball action there was as intense as ever. By now, both Dave Casselman and Mike Vaccaro had committed to go to Buffalo State, Bill Truman was going to Genesee Community College, and Greg Witter was headed to SUNY Geneseo.

There was a lot going on during the summer of 1969, the Viet Nam war, race riots, and college campus demonstrations, not to mention the USA put a man on the moon. At the time, I was not as keenly aware of all the ramifications of these events, as I would later become. My priorities were, by far, basketball and preparing for my adventure to Liberal, Kansas.

Earlier that year, my buddy Bob Knight had enlisted in the United States Marine Corp, and was doing his basic training at Paris Island. We would write to each other, off and on, even when I went off to school. Bob was a perfect fit for the Marines.

Sport: __Basketball__

This copy is to be retained by student

19<u>69</u>

KANSAS JAYHAWK JUNIOR COLLEGE CONFERENCE

19<u>70</u>

LETTER OF INTENT

1. FINANCIAL AID AGREEMENT

This is to certify that _____Gregory Laker_____ will be awarded financial aid at

Name of student

<u>Seward County Community Junior College</u> to the extent of _____

Institution

Books and Tuition

The above will be paid if he meets the admission and financial aid requirements set forth by the above-named institution and the KJJCC. Jobs may also be provided by the school or assistance may be given to help procure a job. Assistance may also be given in finding room and board facilities; however, no part of these expenses may be borne by the school or any supporting agency.

The above award becomes effective <u>September 1, 1969</u> and may be renewed each semester of the students athletic

Month   Year

eligibility. This agreement will not be canceled except for failure of the student to comply with the rules and regulations of this institution and to cooperate fully with its officials and teachers.

6/18/69   _James M. Miller_   June 18, 1969   _Virgil Akins_

Date   Dean or President   Date   Athletic Director

2. PRE-ENROLLMENT APPLICATION

This is to certify my intention to enroll at __<u>Seward County Community Junior College</u>__ in

Institution

the fall or spring term of the 19<u>69</u>-<u>70</u> academic year. My decision is subject to acceptance by this institution and fulfillment of its admission requirements.

I understand that other members of the KJJCC are obligated to respect my decision. I also understand that if the application is approved and filed with the KJJCC Commissioner, my eligibility at any other conference institution will be limited in accordance with the regulations printed below.

I accept the conditions as listed in the above Pre-Enrollment Application and Financial Aid Agreement and certify that I have not received financial aid or promises of financial aid in excess of that allowed under KJJCC rules. Both my parents (or guardian) and I understand that my failure to meet the admission and financial aid requirements of the above-named institution by the fall will render this agreement null and void.

Gregory G. Laker   6/21/69   _James L. Laker_   6/21/69

Student   Date   Parent or Guardian   Date

51 McKinley Avenue   Kenmore   New York

Street Address   City   State

(Please Type or Print Address)

Regulations and Procedures for Letters of Intent

1. By the signing of the Letter of Intent, the student-athlete and his parents certify they have not signed another such letter with an institution which is a member of the Kansas Jayhawk Junior College Conference and that no financial assistance may be given athletes that does not go through the school administrations and it is limited to a maximum of tuition, remission of fees and furnishing of books.

2. After signing a Letter of Intent with a KJJCC institution, should a student-athlete elect to enroll at another KJJCC institution, he would not be eligible for athletic competition at the institution in which he enrolls until he shall have been in residence one year, and in no case for more than one year in any one sport.

3. This form must be completed in triplicate, one copy to be retained by or returned to the prospective student-athlete, one copy to be forwarded within one week to the Commissioner's office, and one copy to be retained by the institution.

4. THIS FORM IS NOT TO BE SIGNED BY THE STUDENT-ATHLETE AND HIS PARENT PRIOR TO:

A. 8:00 A.M. (LOCAL TIME), FEBRUARY 1, 19____, FOR A STUDENT SIGNING A FOOTBALL APPLICATION.

B. 8:00 A.M. (LOCAL TIME), MARCH 22, 19____, FOR A STUDENT SIGNING A BASKETBALL APPLICATION.

C. 8:00 A.M. (LOCAL TIME), MAY 21, 19____, FOR A STUDENT SIGNING A GOLF, TENNIS, OR TRACK AND FIELD APPLICATION.

There was one monumental event which happened that summer I and millions of others were very aware of. A little music festival down at Yasgar's Farm turned huge; WOODSTOCK!

"The New York State Thruway is closed man! Can you dig it?"

The music and activity which came from the event had a tremendous impact on our culture. The music lives on today, and my generation lived it in real time.

Coach Akins was anxious for me to get to Liberal, and so was I. He thought it would be a good idea if I arrived a week or so before classes started so I could get settled and comfortable with my new prospective teammates. Classes were scheduled to begin September 3rd, so I planned to arrive in Liberal sometime during the last week of August. I was excited! It would be my first time on an airplane when I boarded a United flight out of Buffalo to Chicago – O'Hare. O'Hare was recently overhauled, and state of the art. I couldn't believe it only took an hour and change to get to Chicago from Buffalo. I had a couple of hours to kill before making my connection to Kansas City, MO., so I wandered around, gawking at the sights and the people. Since I checked my suitcase, I was traveling with just a gym bag. The bulk of my stuff was being shipped in a huge trunk (about the size of a Volkswagon) to Liberal. It ultimately arrived about two weeks after me. So, my next stop was KC, MO. The KC airport was old and more like a "Greyhound" bus terminal; complete opposite of O'Hare. My layover in KC would be a long 6 hour wait. I was bored to death and anxious to get to Liberal. At one point, I inquired where the nearest pool hall was, but it would have meant a lengthy cab ride into unknown parts of downtown KC. So, to kill the time, I walked the full length of the terminal numerus times, checking out the people. Finally, I boarded my

Frontier Airlines flight. It was a prop job, but back in those days, they would actually serve you something to eat. The plane made one stop in Wichita to drop off and pick up passengers before heading on to Liberal. By the time I got to Liberal, it was late and dark – probably about 10:00PM. Coach Akins was there, at the small airport, waiting to pick me up in his 1960 something maroon Chevy Corvair. He, and most of the local people I met, had southern drawls and, of course, they all thought I spoke with a funny accent. Coach drove me to a nearby "Ma & Pa" motel where we had a brief visit, and he told me he would be back in the morning to pick me up. I was a little apprehensive; after all, I was just 18 years old, 1,400 miles from home, and totally on my own.

When I woke up the next morning, I looked out the window to see a barren landscape and tumbleweeds rolling down the highway. As promised, Coach Akins arrived to pick me up and take me to the campus for a tour. Of course, the tour did not take long since, as I mentioned, it was pretty much "make shift." Don't get me wrong, everything was very nice, and the people I met could not have been more welcoming. I felt comfortable. Coach explained there would be more recruits arriving later that day, and some of them would be living in the same house with me. At that point, Coach Akins handed me off to fellow recruit Mike Howell, who was from nearby Tyrone, OK and familiar with Liberal. Mike was also 6'5" with a rugged build, and dressed like he was ready for a rodeo (big belt buckle for his Wranglers and cowboy boots.) He was soft spoken and easy going; easy to like. Tyrone was about 8 miles down the road in the Oklahoma panhandle. Coach Akins directed Mike to show me around Liberal, and later we would meet up with the other guys who would be living in our house. Mike loaded me into his green 1964 Chevy Chevelle SS – 4 on the floor, and a V-8 with plenty of pep. Liberal, at the time, was a small city of about 12,000 – 13,000 population. I soon learned the largest industry there was a new meat packing plant. Mike cruised me around town and showed me the sights. Liberal was big enough to support such things as an A&W drive in, Sonic drive in, a daily newspaper (The Southwest Daily Times,) a hospital, a semi-pro baseball team, a drive in theater, a K-Mart, and now a fledgling Community College. My initial impression of Liberal was not a bad one, but flat, dry, hot, and dusty. Although Mike's home was nearby in Tyrone, he planned to live in the house in Liberal with the rest of us. Since we had some time to kill before we would meet up with the other guys later that afternoon, Mike decided to take me to Tyrone to show me the family farm/ranch. This was the first time I had been in a car traveling in excess of 100 mph. Needless to say, it didn't take very long to cover the 8 mile trip to Tyrone. Mike's family farmed/ranched it. They had both crops and livestock on their substantial piece of property. I was introduced to his father (who looked like the Marlboro Man) and mother, along with his younger sister. They could not have been more welcoming. Mike also showed me his man cave; a small barn was set up with a vintage leather drop pocket 9' Brunswick pool table, pinball machine, and other games – very cool.

> SIDE NOTE: Sometime that day, I think it was about when we were traveling at 100 mph, Mike disclosed to me he could only see from one eye. It was not physically noticeable, and Mike never made a big deal about it, but from that point on, I always marveled at how well Mike was able to play basketball, play pool, drive, or perform some other challenging tasks. It was inspiring.

It was now time to return to Liberal to meet some more of the guys and see the house we would be living in. When we got to the house (203 W. Walnut St.), we were greeted by Coach Akins and our new landlord, Tom Kitch. 203 W. Walnut St. was a 2-story Victorian home which had been divided into 3 apartments – two up and one down. The house was a little on the rough side, but I think it was the best Coach Akins could come up with at the time. We didn't love it, but we were more interested in basketball and having our new found independence. Here is a brief introduction to my new housemates: Downstairs apartment - Mike Howell – Tyrone, OK, Danny Love 6'5" (6'10" wing span) Montezuma, KS, and Jim Ziegler 6'4" Springfield, IL. Upstairs apartment A – Art Tippit 6'2" Topeka, KS and Dominic Accarpio 5'8" Berlin, CT. Upstairs apartment B – Danny Shaffer (track man) Holyrood, KS, Fred Besthorn 6'2" Holyrood, KS, Dale Reed 6'3" Little River, KS, and me. Our landlord (slumlord), Tom Kitch, was a local undertaker and did rental property on the side. I think we only paid about $50 each/month but multiplied by 9 tenants = $450. That was pretty good income for that property back in 1969. How we determined who would get which apartments, and who would room with whom, I think, came down to who spoke up the most. Dale Reed and the boys from Holyrood were already acquainted, since they had competed against one another in high school sports. Dale was outspoken (to say the least) and somehow, I got shepherded in with those guys. We had one big bedroom with 4 beds – barracks style. There was a large living room (no TV), small kitchen, and one bathroom. Danny Shaffer lasted only a short period of time. He was home sick for his girlfriend back in Holyrood. With Danny gone, it made it quite a bit more comfortable for Dale, Fred, and me. Looking back, it was pretty amazing how quickly we became close. Dale had a way (still does) of telling you about people and places, from his life, as though you should already know about these people and places. He would, for example, tell me a story about "Dale Doll" or "John Nelson" (Little River guys I never heard of) as though I should already know who these people were. It worked for Dale, though, and pretty soon, I knew about all 557 people in Little River. Dale grew up on a farm and was the baby of the family. His siblings were considerably older, and thus his parents were older, as well. Dale was very sure of himself and wasn't afraid to tell you his opinions. My first impression of Dale was a 6'3" slim guy, maybe 165 lbs., short brown hair (Brillo pad), braces on his teeth, T-shirt, slim fit wrangler jeans (ankle length), low cut white "Chuck Taylor" Converse sneakers, and white tube socks. He was acutely aware of his hair (slept with a knit hat on) and for any developing facial blemish, he carried a tube of Clearasil. Dale walked with a cocky strut and he never met a mirror he didn't like. All kidding aside, he and I became very close and have stayed in touch through the years. Much more about Dale ahead.

My other roommate, Fred Besthorn, was a rugged built, 6'2" 200 lb. guy with a shock of light blonde hair. He liked to wear his short sleeved shirts rolled up to show off his guns. Fred was soft spoken, compared to Dale, and would have been well-suited to be an evangelist minister.

Both Dale and Fred had cars and I, of course, was carless. Dale drove a sharp looking, bronze colored 1961 Chevy Impala with a 283 V-8 and automatic transmission. It featured the full vista rear window and was tricked out with a custom steering wheel and an 8 track stereo tape player. Fred drove the family 1956 Chevy Bel Air station wagon. It was Robin's Egg blue with a white top. They both took pride in keeping those vehicles looking and running good. Both of these cars would be classics in today's market.

A little more background on my other housemates: Dominic Accarpio and Art Tippit shared the apartment across the hall from us. Dominic was very homesick for his family back in Connecticut, and sought comfort in hanging with us. He was a little insecure and we playfully nicknamed him Wap. Tippit, from Topeka, was the closest thing we had to a hippie. Art had his own car, and he made himself pretty scarce, hanging out with a crowd away from the house and the team. Downstairs, again, were Mike Howell (who you already know about,) Danny Love, a really bright guy from nearby Montezuma, and Jim Ziegler, (painfully shy) from Springfield, IL. Those guys had the only TV (black & white) in the house, so naturally their apartment was the place to hang if there was a good ball game or something on. The only phone in the house was a pay phone on the second floor. Back in the day, we would pretty much be limited to calling our parents once a week, collect, for about 5 -10 minutes. It was expensive.

We did have a record player in our apartment. I had recently bought The Beatles' *Abbey Road* album, which I played enough to make my roommates crazy.

"Come together right now over me...."

By the way, we had 3 black players on the initial roster – Lionel Hoover, Roger Logan, and Ron Clark. They were all from the Wichita area, and they lived in a house (the Palace,) literally on the other side of the tracks. We occasionally visited their house, and the accommodations were similar to ours. As a point of interest – Jimi Hendrix was what I can remember hearing played while visiting there.

So, 203 W. Walnut St. was about a ten minute drive to campus – too far to walk, so we had to depend on carpooling. Fred,

Mike, and especially Dale were very generous about giving rides or even loaning us, carless guys their cars. Somehow it all worked out, since I don't ever recall not getting to class or being stranded on campus. Once you were on campus, all of the classrooms were within walking distance. I had declared my major to be Physical Education, but most of my classes were generally required courses... probably a 16 credit hour load with a couple of electives.

As promised, Coach Akins found part time jobs for the guys who needed them. My first job was at the school working as a custodian in Epworth Hall (the old hospital.) The third floor was being renovated, and I was basically a broom and dust pan man. That job was short lived, then Dale and I got the opportunity to work at Brown's furniture store out on Highway 54. We had a variety of responsibilities, including moving furniture around the store, building and painting display dividers, and making deliveries in the one ton flatbed truck. Courtney Brown (the owner) was in his 40's at the time. He was a suave, handsome, and smooth talking guy; a natural salesman. Courtney was firm but fair with us and kept us busy. We were supervised by Courtney's right hand man, Joe – an older gentleman maybe in his late 50's. Joe, I think, was a recovering alcoholic but a very hard worker and taught Dale and me the ropes. He was a no nonsense, but kind guy. I think our favorite thing to do was to deliver furniture. Usually, deliveries were near or around town, but sometimes they could be as far as 50 miles away. Those long deliveries could take up the better part of a work day for us. It intrigued me to observe how friendly the people in Kansas were. When you passed someone on the road, while driving, they would invariably wave. It may seem like a little thing, but it really made an impression on me. One of the fringe benefits of working at Browns was the 24" console color TV in Courtney's office. Sometimes we could catch a little TV if we were on break or not too busy. One Saturday afternoon that Fall, we got to watch Lew Alcindor's NBA debut with the Milwaukee Bucks and teammate Oscar Robertson. That was a thrill for us. All-in-all, it was a pretty good part time job for us. I think we worked about 12 – 15 hours a week. For what it's worth, Joe drove a new Plymouth Barracuda with a hatch back, and I think Courtney drove a Lincoln Continental.

Before we started official basketball practice on October 15th, we did a lot of conditioning and pick up scrimmages at various Liberal middle schools and the high school. Since we were sharing the high school gym (Rindom Hall) with the boys' varsity and JV – scheduling for these facilities was sometimes challenging. One of the facilities, which we frequently used was an old dungeon gym deep in the bowels of the Liberal High School. It was a short, full court with steel fan backboards located adjacent to our "Saints Green" locker room. This is where we used our "Exergenies" and worked with free weights. An Exergenie was a piece of apparatus which included a gas cylinder (similar to that used with a storm door) and ropes, which would create resistance in a number of different exercises performed by the user. We each had one.

SIDE NOTE: Dave Baker was our assistant Coach. Dave was a black man in his mid-twenties, 5'10", stout, and very athletic. He was the head track coach and, as I mentioned earlier, some of his track recruits came out for basketball. Dave was an alumnus of Emporia State College (Kansas.) He had a younger brother, Wendall, built just like him whom, when in town visiting Dave, would always like to challenge me one-on-one. It got very spirited, but I think I got the best of that series.

For the record, even though the colors – green, gold, and white, were established, it was not until mid-October the school's Board of Trustees chose the name "SAINTS" from a list of 4 names presented by the student body. The other 3 were "The Cobras," "The Fighting Irish," and, heaven forbid, "The Jolly Green Giants." It always made me wonder how our jerseys were ready for our opening game at Panhandle State College November 20th. That was some fast turnaround.

Between school, work, basketball, and our part-time jobs, there was little time for socializing. One of the popular activities was cruising the "Main Drag." We would load 4, 5, or 6 of us in a car and cruise from one end of town to the other. The girls would be doing the same thing, so there was a lot of hootin' and hollerin' from car to car. The A&W Drive-In was a good spot to turn around and check out all of the hot cars parked there. We might make 2 or 3 laps in an evening – just checking things out.

There was a "real deal" pool hall on the Main Drag (Kansas Ave.) They had the only full size tables in town, including a couple of 10' snooker tables – the first ones I had seen since Mitchell, IN when I was 15. At this pool room, there was a "rack boy" who would come and rack the balls when the game was done. It was a quarter a rack.

The Kansas and Oklahoma guys had been telling Dominic (Connecticut) and me they wanted to take us on a "Snipe" hunt. They explained it would be a night hunt, since "Snipe" were nocturnal, and that it would be great eating. Anyway, a bunch of us went down to Mike Howell's farm/ranch in Tyrone for a "Snipe" hunt. We played pool and other games in his man cave until dark. We got a nice bonfire going, and then it was time for the hunt. We were each equipped with gunny sacks (burlap bags) and flashlights. Turns out the Kansas and Oklahoma boys had quite a laugh watching the "city boys", Dominic and me, diligently hunting for the non-existing "Snipe." Major ball busting.

The team started official practice October 15ᵗʰ at Rindom Hall. There were 14 of us, but only 12 would survive the cut. Two guys – Roger Logan (Wichita) and Billy Williams (Adams, Ok) did not make the cut. When the 12 man roster was established, we had a team meeting to discuss our goals and to set some team rules. At the meeting, Dale Reed and I were named co-captains. Among our training rules were no smoking and no drinking alcohol during the season. Soon after, it came to the team's attention that Art Tippit had been drinking wine at a party. Coach Akins left Art's destiny up to a team vote. The team voted Art off the team for the first semester. Lionel Hoover made the team, but was academically ineligible for the first semester. That left us with a ten man roster. Lionel was allowed to practice.

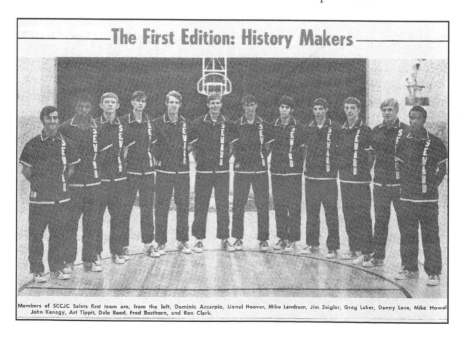

The First Edition: History Makers

Members of SCCJC Saints first team are, from the left, Dominic Accarpio, Lionel Hoover, Mike Landrum, Jim Zeigler, Greg Laker, Danny Love, Mike Howell, John Kenagy, Art Tippit, Dale Reed, Fred Besthorn, and Ron Clark.

Bob Williams was the Sports Editor for the "Southwest Daily Times." Starting before the season, Bob did a weekly feature called "Meet the Saints." Each of us was interviewed by Bob, and a brief bio with our picture appeared in the Sports Section. At the same time, we each did a videotaped interview which appeared on the local cable TV station. We were quite the celebrities in Liberal.

While we were busy practicing and preparing for our upcoming season, it was hard not to notice the SAINTS cheerleaders doing the same. It was natural for us to become acquainted with them, and soon we became friendly. There were six original SAINTS cheerleaders (all girls.)

SIDE NOTE: Although Seward County Community College started organizing in 1967, we were the first students when the doors opened for classes in early September 1969. The plan was to build a new campus with money secured from a bond issue. Students (including some of us basketball players) actually went door-to-door promoting the bond issue, but on October 23rd 1969, the $2,820,000 bond issue went down in a 1,361 to 1,437 vote. It was, of course, a big disappointment to the Board, the administration, faculty, and students – but there was still hope ahead.

MEET THE SAINTS

In more ways than one, 6'5", 185-pound Kenmore, New York native Greg Laker is a big man for the first edition of the Seward Saints.

As one of the bigger Saints, Laker is going to be called upon to do double duty at both forward and center.

"I don't know how much relief I can give Greg," head coach Virgil Akins frets. "It just depends on how fast some of the other big kids come along.

It's a big adjustment from high school ball to junior college. Some of our young men are ready now. It will take others longer," Laker has apparently nailed down a starting berth for Thursday's season opener at Goodwell, Okla., against the Panhandle State junior varsity.

"Greg is the young man we are counting on quite heavily in the rebounding department," explains Akins. "He has got to clear the boards on defense to limit the opposition to just one shot while triggering our fast break offense, and he has to be underneath our boards to haul in our missed shots."

But being called on as the No. 1 board clearer isn't new to Laker. He had the same job at Kenmore West High School and responded with a team high of 15 caroms per game, 4 assists and a 10 point scoring senior season earned him all-league honors after his ball club posted a 17-3 overall record.

Laker lists several reasons for coming to SeCo Juco: "new school, to go to school someplace besides in the east, basketball and academic opportunities."

ties."

Besides attending classes, practicing, studying, the Saint also holds down a part-time job at Brown's Furniture.

Perhaps it's because of this busy schedule that Laker has already developed a strong fondness for SeCo Juco and Liberal.

Greg likes to dabble in art in his spare time, but his professional pursuit lies in obtaining a degree in physical education in order to be a teacher and coach.

One of Lakers most important assets is his leadership ability. This quality has already rubbed off on his teammates as he has been elected one of the Saints first set of co-captains.

The New Yorker says that he is looking forward to a learning, exciting and winning season in the Saints first basketball season. Laker sums his feelings up this way:

"I fell very proud to be a member of the first Seward County Community Junior College basketball team."

NEXT: Wichita's John Kenagy.

GREG LAKER
Saints Big Man

> **ONE OF A SERIES** of articles on the players who will makeup the first SeCo Juco basketball team. The Saints open their season Thursday night at Goodwell, Okla., against the Panhandle State junior varsity.

Another social event which comes to mind from early that Fall was at Ormiston's farm. The whole basketball team and cheerleading squad were invited for a BBQ picnic. Debbie Ormiston was a cheerleader, and her father Frances was on the board of trustees for the college. Their farm was in Kismet, Kansas, less than 10 miles from Liberal. We were treated royally and served steaks bigger than any I had ever seen. To top off the BBQ picnic, they brought out this crazy crank bucket. They all laughed when this naïve city boy did not know it was a homemade ice cream maker. It made the best strawberry ice cream I have ever tasted. The Ormiston's could not have been more hospitable.

A mutual interest was developing between me and another one of the cheerleaders – Susan Smith. She was an attractive brunette and she was always dressed to the hilt. (By the way- jeans and a sports shirt were pretty much how I rolled back in those days.) Although her family now lived in Liberal, she had roots both in Texas and Louisiana (Shreveport), and had a thick southern Belle accent. I think we were each struck by our very different backgrounds. She drove the family 1969 emerald green Oldsmobile Delta 88. Since I was carless, she would occasionally pick me up for school or other social activity.

Coach Akins was much like a father figure to me and the other guys, and he would sometimes show up at the house unannounced. He frowned on girls being at the house, so that was kind of limiting to any of the guys who had girlfriends. One of the more popular meeting spots, believe it or not, was the school library – to do homework.

That brings to mind a humorous dating story. As I mentioned earlier, my roommates were Dale Reed and Fred Besthorn. Fred was a little less self-assured than Dale, but he had mustered up the nerve to ask one of the gals from school on a date. In preparation for his date, he was very nervous. Fred was perspiring so badly, when he would put on a clean shirt, it would instantly get stained at the arm pits. This routine spoiled a couple of shirts, so Dale and I laid Fred down on his bed and covered his torso with baby powder. He was finally ready, however nervous, to go pick up his date (in the family 1956 Chevy Biscayne – robin's egg blue station wagon.) Dale and I were cracking up.

Back to basketball. We were now ready for our first game of the season; actually, the first basketball game in Seward County Community College history, and my first college game. Our first game would be, not too far down the road, in Goodwell, OK. vs. the Panhandle State College Junior Varsity on Thursday, November 20th. We traveled in two, brand new 1969 white Ford LTD station wagons with 3rd row seating facing rear. By the time we loaded our gear, team manager, 2 coaches, and 9 or 10 players, it was pretty cramped.

We played hard, but there were some first game jitters. Panhandle State College Junior Varsity 59 Seward County Community College 53. In my first college game, I had 22 points and 14 rebounds – both game highs. The key to the game was free throws – they shot 35 and we shot 15, quite a discrepancy.

As I have done describing the past basketball seasons, I will not detail every game, but will try to hit some of the highlights. For those interested in more details, they can refer to my "A Basketball Season to Remember" 1969-70 scrapbook.

Most of the players' hometowns were close enough for them to go home for Thanksgiving. I accepted an invitation to go home with Mike Howell in Tyrone, OK. The Howells, of course, were very gracious, and it was a beautiful feast. Sometime after Thanksgiving, a group of us went back down to Tyrone to watch a girls' basketball game Mike's sister was playing in. It was a strange game for me to watch. They played 6 on 6, with 3 girls playing defense and 3 girls playing offense. None of them were allowed to cross half court (very different.)

First 2 college career points on a sky hook

After our season opening loss to PSC-JV, we reeled off 3 straight wins and were prepared to play our first Jayhawk Junior College Conference Western Division game against Cowley County Community College. The game was to be played at the beautiful new Southwestern Heights gym in Kismet, Kansas, and it would count as a home game. The Jayhawk Junior College Conference was arguably the toughest Division I JUCO Conference in the country. We were not up to the task – CCCC 99 SCCC 74. Next would be a conference game vs Pratt Community College at home just before Christmas break. Pratt had an All-American player, Paul Stovall. Stovall was a powerful 6'5", about 240 lbs. and could jump out of the gym. He would later play at Arizona State, and then for the Phoenix Suns. Pratt CC 115 – SCCC 94.

So, we headed into the Christmas break 3W – 4L and 0-2 in the Conference.

> SIDE NOTE: Not really a side note, but my parents and Wende had made the trip (in the red 1963 Mercury Comet) in time to see the last 4 games before the break. They were graciously hosted by the Ormistons in Kismet for nearly 2 weeks. The master plan was for me to return to Kenmore with them for the holidays. Through his connections with (legendary) Coach Ted Owens, Coach Akins was able to arrange for us to stop in Lawrence on our way home and see a Kansas Jayhawk basketball game in the famous Phog Allen Field House. When they turned out the lights and the "packed house" slowly and quietly began the "Rock Chalk Jayhawk" chant, it grew faster and louder, and finally to a fever pitch; it was spine tingling!

It took us a full day of driving to reach Erie, PA, where we stopped to visit the Labies (my sister Amy, Jerry, and Caryn). Finally, we made it back to Kenmore and 51 McKinley. The break went fast. I did a lot of sleeping in and, in the afternoons, I would go to the Belmont YMCA for hoops with Vaccaro and Casselman, who were on break from Buffalo State. There were a couple of poker games, as well, and several trips to Bobby Cue.

Chapter Thirteen
1970

Happy New Year! It was now time to get back to Liberal and get ready for our next game, January 8th at Dodge City. Coach Akins had taken Dale and me to Dodge City early in the season to watch their Thanksgiving tournament. Not only did we get to see some great basketball, but we got to see some of the sights of the city, including Boot Hill. There is actually an "Old Town" section of the city depicting what you might imagine seeing on "Gunsmoke." Anyway, Dodge City smoked us 92-65 and I had a terrible game… 3 points. We had to try to remember we were all freshmen and lacked the experience the other conference teams had.

Our next conference game was notable because it was at Hutchinson at their beautiful "Sports Arena." The Sports Arena was significant because it was the yearly site of the NJCAA Division I basketball tournament, and the home of the perennial powerhouse, Hutchinson Blue Dragons. We played pretty well, but again fell short – 75-55 in front of 7,000+ "Sea of Red" Hutch fans (largest crowd I had played in front of to date)… very exciting. By the way, the Hutchinson Coach, at that time, was Gene

Keady, who would later gain fame as the Coach of the Purdue Boilermakers.

We finally had our first conference win against Barton County CC (another first year school) 71-66 at home. So, through the first round of Jayhawk Junior College Western Division play, we were 1-6 and 5-9, overall.

It was now time to hit the road east in the two 1969 Ford LTD station wagons to Butler CCC in El Dorado (Wichita) and Cowley CCC in Arkansas City in back-to-back nights. In both cases, we played well early, but were unable to hold our leads. At Cowley CCC, six of us fouled out. They shot 49 free throws, we shot 29. My 31 points (most in my career to-date) was bittersweet. Later in the season (February 13th) vs Dodge City at home in Liberal, I scored my career high 34 points, albeit in a 97-93 loss.

The season was winding down, and our last game was home vs power house Hutchinson. It was "parent's night" and admission was free for those wearing green. Although my parents had already been to Liberal earlier in the season, the next best thing was to have my brother Jim there. He and his future wife, Barb Beeke, made the trip (in the red 1963 Mercury Comet) as part of a trip which would take them on down to New Mexico to visit friends. It was great having them there… unfortunately, after being tied at 61, we lost 95-79. So, we finished the season 1-13 in the conference and 6-16 overall. Considering we were a first-year team with all freshmen, we competed fairly well – but we were not satisfied.

Finger roll

With the season over, we had more time on our hands. Still, we were drawn to the gym for shoot arounds and pickup games. Spring break was approaching, and Dale invited me to go home with him to Little River. As I mentioned earlier, Dale grew up on a farm there and was, by far, the youngest sibling. It was almost like being an only child to his parents, Francis and Helen. I happily accepted Dale's invitation... now, I was finally going to get to see these people and places Dale had been describing to me. Little River was in Rice county, not too far from Hutchinson, and maybe 2-3 hours from Liberal. Most of western Kansas was very flat, and the roads are mostly straight. Dale would tell me there were roads at every square mile (mile markers.) Some of the mile markers were no more than a tractor path, but they were there, none the less. When the team was on a road trip, in the twin white 1969 Ford LTD station wagons, traveling throughout western Kansas late at night, you could see lights 10-12 miles in the distance. You would see towering lights in the distance, as though you were approaching a metropolitan sky line. But as you got closer, you realized what you were seeing were the lights on a, small town, CO-OP grain tower. It was no different on our trip to Little River. With the windows of Dale's 1961 Chevy Impala rolled down, and the Crosby, Stills, and Nash "couch album" blasting on the 8 track car stereo, we had it made. The unfamiliar, fresh new smells of the plains were rolling through my nostrils – they were wonderful; life was good.

It didn't take Dale long to show me "downtown" Little River before we headed to the farm. Main Street may have had a 4-way stop sign, or a flashing 4-way red light. He took me past the LR High School, and I also remember Dale pointing out Max (a beloved local with Downs Syndrome) who had been a part of some of his Little River stories.

Finally, we made it to the farm and, finally, I got to meet Dale's (somewhat elderly) parents, Francis and Helen. Dale's father was a hard-working, no nonsense farmer who had a hard time understanding the value Dale and I placed on a silly game like basketball. Francis was 60+ and worked "hands-on" from dawn to dusk. He had a rugged, but slightly bent over, build and when he removed his hat, there was a sharp line separating the red of his face from the white of his forehead and slightly balding scalp. He had strong hands that could crush you like a vice when you shook his hand.

Dale's mother, Helen, was a sweet, matronly lady with a warm smile. In a way, she reminded me of Dennis the Menace's next door neighbor, Mrs. Wilson (and that is meant to be a compliment.) She was also a "no nonsense" person, and she kept an immaculate farmhouse. Dale didn't hesitate to load her up with his dirty laundry and ironing, which she happily took care of. Dale had also been bragging to me about his mother's cooking. She did not disappoint. Much to his parent's dismay, there were a couple of mornings Dale and I slept in (typical for teenage spring breakers.) However, when we did rise and shine, Helen would have a breakfast fit for a king ready for us. It was my first encounter with "sour dough" waffles, with real maple syrup, and accompanied by bacon or ham and 'taters." What a treat!

We did, however, have to earn our keep. Following Francis' instructions, I can remember loading hay bales on a tractor drawn wagon in the fields. There were other assorted chores to be done, as well. I'm pretty sure I got to drive a farm tractor and a farm truck. Dale's parents were exactly the essence of "salt of the earth" people.

During the day, Dale and I would head to Hutchinson. The timing was perfect, because the NJCAA Division I basketball tournament was (as it is every year) being held at the Hutchinson Sports Arena. The week long tournament featured 32 teams from around the country. At the time, there were consolation games, so each team was guaranteed at least two games. There was action from morning until night, and we were enthralled with the fast-paced style of play and great players. Many of the star players would go on to NCAA Division I schools, and some even to the pros (NBA/ABA). The Sports Arena was crawling with scouts. Dale and I spent a couple of days watching wall-to-wall hoops. Ultimately, Vincennes, Indiana Junior College led by Bob McAdoo (as a freshman) would win the tournament. McAdoo would go from Vincennes to Chapel Hill, NC and play for Coach Dean Smith's Tar Heels. From there, McAdoo was drafted by the Buffalo Braves and became an NBA All-Star. Fortunately for me, I was able to see McAdoo play many times in Buffalo at the Aud.

Meanwhile, back in Little River, Dale had a girlfriend – Kelly Schmidt, who was now still a high school senior. Kelly had an older sister, Kristen, who Dale was dying for me to meet. As I recall, their father was the local doctor, and they were rather well-to-do. Kristen was a freshman at Kansas University, and also home for spring break. Anyway, Dale and I visited their home one evening and hung out with the sisters in their basement rec room. Kristen and I hit it off, and I would see her a few times over the next year and a half. We would also write to each other.

SIDE NOTE: For those reading this book who are one or two generations behind me – people would actually write letters to family and friends. Some of the letters (written or received) would, for me anyway, become treasures or keepsakes – not to mention a means of tracing history. Try to imagine yourself with NO cell phone, NO texting, NO Facebook, NO Facetime!

Back on the farm and Helen's cooking, you already know the breakfast routine. (By the way, Dale Reed is the only person I've ever met who insists on eating his cereal with half & half.) A typical dinner at the Reed house might be a (melt in your mouth) beef roast with mashed potatoes, green beans, and homemade bread. She always had some kind of dessert – maybe homemade apple pie or chocolate chip cookies. It was awesome.

Soon after returning to Liberal from Little River, I learned of two personal honors. First, during our last home game vs Hutchinson, the SCCC Saints fans voted me "Most Valuable Player" for the 1969/70 basketball season. That was a great honor, and I was humbled. Secondly, I was named to the Jayhawk Junior College Conference Western Division All-Star Team. That was an honor I did not expect. What made it more satisfying to me was the All-Stars were voted on by the opposing coaches

> SIDE NOTE: Speaking of honors – W.A. Shufelberger ("Shuf," an older gentleman and local business owner) received a well- deserved "Community Service" award from the Chamber of Commerce that Spring. It was significant to us because Shuf was an avid supporter of the Saints basketball team, and was always looking out for us. He could often be found in the company of Coach Akins… almost like another assistant.

As the school year was coming to an end, many of the guys were becoming increasingly homesick, especially the out of staters, Dominic Accarpio (Kensington, CT) and Jim Zeigler (Springfield, IL). They and I were a long way from home. To pass the time, silly bets were being made. I collected $25 from the guys for winning a bet I would shave my head. There were other bets made which are better off left untold.

Laker Named To West Juco All-Star Team

TOPEKA. — Seward County has its first All-Star basketball player. He's Greg Laker, the office of the Kansas Jayhawk Junior College Conference announced today.

The 1969-70 KJJCC All-Star team was selected by divisions. Players were nominated by their own coaches and were then voted upon by opposing coaches in their division.

A 12-man Western Division team was selected after Laker, Brent Baum of Dodge City and Mark Nelson of Garden City finished in a three-way tie. A two-way tie in the East created an 11-man All-Star team.

Five players were unamious choices. They were Charles Pipkin, Dodge City; Paul Stovall, Pratt; Alex Scott, Coffeyville; Lee Roy Bowie, Highland and Curtis Washington, Neosho County.

Those repeating on the select teams for the second consecutive year are: Pipkin, Stovall, Clint Davis an Sdcott of Coffeyville, and Fort Scott's Lawrence Allen.

Western Division champion Pratt placed two on the All-Star team, Eastern Division winer Coffeyville landed three berths and Independence, the Region 6 champion, placed two players on the elite group.

ALL-WESTERN DIVISION

Barton County — Tom Cline, 6'9", freshman.

Butler County — Eldon Lawyer, 6'1", sophomore.

Cowley County — Danny Jones, 6'7", sophomore; John Woodworth, 6'3", sophomore.

Dodge City — Brent Baum, 6'6", freshman; LeRoy Martin, 6', sophomore; Charles Pipkin, 6'2", sophomore,

Garden City — Mark Nelson, 6'4", freshman.

Hutchinson — Bob Moser, 6'3", sophomore.

Pratt — Paul Stovall, 6'5", sophomore; Chris Boyle, 6', freshman.

SEWARD COUNTY — GREG LAKER, 6'5", FRESHMAN.

GREG LAKER
1st All-Star

New York Product High Among Leaders In Final Statistics

Greg Laker, Seward County freshman from Kenmore, N.Y., was the only Saint to make the final top 10 in the KJJCC Western Division statistics, it was announced today by League Commissioner Nelson Hartman.

Laker's scoring average of 19.2 was the sixth best in the West, Paul Stovall of Pratt topped the entire league in scoring with an average of 37.6 per conference game.

Laker's rebounding average of 9.3 caroms per conference game was the fifth best. Stovall also topped this department with an average of 25.6 rebounds per game. A distant second was Danny Jones of Cowley County with 12.5.

The Saint was second in free throw shooting with 84 per cent at the line. Laker made 63 out of 75 attempts in league games. Best in the West was Chris Boyle of Pratt with 88 per cent. Boyle made 47 out of 58 in league games.

Stovall finished with the best field goal percentage in the West with 66. Brent Baum of Dodge City was runner-up with 60 per cent. No Saint placed in this category.

Laker Spreads the Word
For Kenmore in Kansas

You would hardly expect many people, if any, in Liberal, Kan., to have heard of Kenmore, N.Y.

Greg Laker, a 1969 Kenmore West High graduate, has been spreading the word, though, and he's been doing it with his prowess on the basketball court.

This year, the 6-5 red-headed forward made the starting lineup at Seward County Junior College in Liberal and earned a first team berth on the Kansas Junior College Conference all-star team.

Laker, who set a Kenmore West rebound record last year with 25 in one game, led Seward in practically all of the school's offensive departments, and was also the team's leading rebounder.

Nicknamed the "Blonde Bomber" by the color blind Liberal Times sports editor, Laker led the club in scoring with an average of 17.7 points-per-game, and was the top rebounder with 199 (nine per game).

Laker set a single game school point record of 31 against Cowley College and later reset it with 34 points against Dodge City College.

His high rebounding effort was 17 against North Platte College. He connected on 82.4 per cent of his free throw attempts and 42 per cent of his tries from the field.

Seward County College is only in its first year of existence and Laker placed his name in school annals as its first player to make the all-star team.

As I mentioned earlier, there was not a cafeteria at SCCC, so we had to fend for ourselves. It was not uncommon for a group of us to pool our money and go to the local deli and buy a pack of Oscar Mayer bologna with a loaf of bread. We'd wash those sandwiches down with a quart of chocolate milk each. For dinner, if we were really splurging, our favorite place to go was the LaFonda restaurant. There we could get a chicken fried steak, mashed potatoes, a vegetable, and ice tea all for $1.25 – what a deal!

For several weeks, I had my eye on a used car at the CONOCO gas station where we often bought our gas. Although my house-mates were very generous about loaning their cars or giving me rides, I still felt like I was imposing, and I was anxious to have my own wheels. The car I was looking at was an emerald green 1947 Ford convertible with a flat head V8 and 4 on the floor. It was a sharp car, and it came with a $500 price tag. I was lucky if I had $100 in my checking account. To make a long story short, Dale offered to loan me $500 from his savings account. Looking back, at the time, that was a lot of money for Dale to trust me for. We made an agreement I would pay him back incrementally over the summer.

203 W. Walnut St.
May 1970

When the school year ended, I loaded up the emerald green 1947 Ford convertible and headed east. The trip from Liberal to Kenmore was about 1400 miles. The first leg got me into Missouri via Wichita and Kansas City. That night was spent sleeping in my car at an I-70 rest area, guarding all of my worldly possessions. The next day, I made it all the way to Springfield, IL, where my housemate Jim Zeigler had invited me to spend the night. Of course, I had been bragging about Kenmore's "Crosby Courts," and Jim was anxious to show me Springfield's version. Their courts were great; right in the Town Square and even under the lights! It was great to get a hot shower and a clean bed. The next day (3), I set my destination sights on Erie, PA, where my sister Amy lived with her family – husband Jerry and daughter Caryn. This route took me by Indianapolis, Columbus, and Akron. (You have to remember, there was NO GPS. I navigated with the use of state maps I had picked up at gas stations along the way). Looking back now, I think I did pretty well for an 18-year-old in a 23-year-old car. It was quite late when I arrived in Erie, but I was welcomed with open arms. Thankfully, the next morning, Amy took a cherished picture of me proudly standing next to my '47 Ford. After spending some time visiting with the Labies, I headed out on the last leg of my journey (90 miles) to Kenmore.

My 1947 Ford Convertible

It was good to be back in Kenmore – home. Amazingly, the '47 Ford performed well, and gave me no problems on the road. I was happy to see my parents and little sister, Wende. I even had my own bedroom. 115 Warren was a fairly typical 1920's vintage, Village of Kenmore house. Among other things, it featured a nice front porch with a swing and an above the ground swimming pool in the back yard.

I couldn't wait to drive my '47 Ford to the "courts." There was no denying it was a cool car. Crosby Courts were going as strong as ever, and now we all had another year's experience under our belts. Now, more than ever, there were college level players, and it forced the younger players to step up their games. The play was fiercely competitive, but at the end of the night, we were all buddies.

Most of the guys had summer jobs. Somehow I was able to get a job as a janitor's assistant at Hoover JHS. I think Mr. Robert Lucia (PE teacher) paved the way for me. The job mostly involved moving desks and chairs out of class rooms and preparing floors to be sealed.

Sometime after hoops on a Friday evening, guys would make plans to go out for a few beers. One of the bars I can remember going to that summer was Provo's in Riverside (I think.) It was a neighborhood Polish bar, owned and operated by Mr. Provesnic. It became over run by a younger crowd with still a few "old timers" sprinkled in. Although the drinking age, at the time, was 18, and I was about to turn 19, there were still many minors in the bar. Draft beers were 25 cents, and it was there I developed a taste for beer nuts with my beer. The other thing to keep in mind is the bars in Erie County could stay open until 4:00 AM. It was a fun place for guys and gals to hang out.

Of course, I couldn't come back to Kenmore without making several trips to Bobby-Cue. It was a different group there. Not my basketball buddies. When I first entered the pool room that summer, Bob Clark greeted me by "Mad Stork!" One of the guys I played a lot of 9 ball with during that era was John Lannon. We were classmates and in the same homeroom. Our games were very competitive, so little money changed hands over the long run. John cracked me up with his dry sense of humor and sarcasm. Typical Kenmore.

Another night spot I remember driving to with some buddies was the "Edgewater" on Grand Island. It was more of a roadhouse, and located on the East (Niagara) River Road. It was a cool place with live music and a great atmosphere. Cruising there and back with the top down on the '47 Ford on a warm summer night was awesome.

One morning, in July, as I was getting ready to go to work at Hoover JHS, I heard a partial blurb on the radio about a Buffalo Marine losing his life. I didn't think too much about it, and went on to work. Sometime later that morning, in the hallways of Hoover JHS, my father appeared and approached me. He didn't have to say anything, I knew – it was Bob Knight. We hugged and cried. As the story goes, on their off time, Bob and some of his Marine buddies were exploring an abandoned gold mine in Yuma, AZ (typical Bob Knight activity – right up his alley). While exploring, some of the guys were overcome with gas fumes, but were able to make it out – including Bob. Bob then realized one of his buddies did not make it out, so Bob went back in to try and save him. Bob died trying to rescue his fellow Marine buddy.

This is the worst thing I can remember ever happening to me. Of course, his parents, Bill and Mary, were crushed. Bob had a full military funeral with a 21 gun salute. I remember seeing the pain on Mary's face as the shots rang out. Bob, I think, was close to 21-years-old, and I am certain we would still be buddies if he were alive today. It was hard – still is, as I write this.

Coach Akins kept in close contact with me over the summer. He wanted to make sure I was playing ball and running. He also wanted to make sure I was planning to return to Liberal in August for my second year at SCCC. He kept me abreast of his recruiting efforts, and at one point, he thought he was going to sign Spencer Haywood's 6'8" younger brother. Unfortunately, that didn't materialize. Meanwhile, Dale and I were writing each other and I was punctual about sending him checks to repay the $500 car loan.

The summer went fast, and it was time to prepare for my return to Liberal. My father was encouraging me to sell the '47 Ford and find another car when I returned to Kansas. (The warmer, milder climate in southwest Kansas was more forgiving to automobiles – so, maybe I could get more for my money). Reluctantly, I took my father's advice and put the '47 Ford on the market. Through an ad in the Buffalo Evening News, I found a Canadian buyer at $650. So, the '47 Ford served its purpose, and I made a profit, to boot. (Wish I still had that car, today.) With the proceeds from the sale of the car, and money I had earned over the summer, I was able to pay Dale off and still have some money to buy another car when I returned to Kansas. (By the way – my parents had to contribute very little money throughout my college career.) That is not a complaint – they helped where they could. I was proud of the fact I earned my way through college, working and playing basketball. Unless you have been a college student/athlete, you may not realize how much work it takes and how hard it is.

Late that August, when I returned to Kansas, I was immediately in the car shopping mode. My budget took me toward the used car lots which were decorated with colorful strands of triangular pennants. At one such used car lot, I fell in love with a white 1963 Buick Wildcat. It had a 425 CID V8, red interior, automatic transmission, and Armstrong steering. The fuel economy was figured by gallons per mile. I had to have it.

Coach Akins had lined up some new places for the players to live this school year. Dale and I would once again be roommates. This year, the accommodations would be much nicer. 1142 North Jordan was a family residence in a very nice neighborhood of Liberal. The home owner was Mrs. McLean. She was a single mother of 2 teenagers – a boy and a girl. Her son, Mike, was a standout football player and track star at Liberal High School. Dale and I shared a very nice (above the garage) apartment with **our own** bathroom. The apartment was luxurious compared to where we lived last year, so we were very happy about that.

Only 5 of us players returned for a second year at Seward County Community College... Lionel Hoover, Mike Howell, Art Tippit, Dale, and I. Mike Howell was still recovering from a bad ankle injury, and would not be on the roster until second semester. It was going to be really interesting to meet and check out the new freshmen Coach Akins had brought in. There were nine new freshmen. By the way, the enrollment at SCCC that Fall had grown to 515 compared to 339 the year before.

Here is a brief introduction of the nine incoming freshmen: Chuck Minster 6'4" (Pittsburgh, PA), Stan Fisher 6'0" (Meade, KS), John Greenwood 6'3" (Chicago, IL), Greg White 6'1" (Little River, KS), Jay Myers 6'4" (Wichita, KS), Raymond Nealy 6'4" (Detroit, MI), Jim Zito 6'7" (Chicago, IL), Val Hammerschmidt 6'4" (Victoria, KS), Brian Novinger 6'0" (Kismet, KS), and Tom Schulte 6'7" (Victoria, KS).

Also new this year was, Coach Akins' assistant, Fred Cotrell from Victoria, KS. Our first year assistant coach, Dave Baker, moved onward and upward to Creighton University to become an assistant coach for both basketball and baseball.

Again, we would open up vs the Panhandle State College (Oklahoma) JV, this time on our home court. Our home court was still Rindom Hall (shared with the high school). Rindom's seating capacity was maybe 1600 or so. Coach Akins promoted several ticket packages, most notably, there were a group of 57 designated prime seats which could be had for $10 for all 12 home games, if you wore green. For this game vs Panhandle State College JV, however, admission was free for those fans who wore green and donated a bar of soap. (All bars of soap went directly to the Saints locker room).

Rindom Hall may not have been huge, but we got great supportive crowds. Our cheerleaders were very enthusiastic, and we had a great pep band. Overall, it was a terrific atmosphere.

Not only did we beat the Panhandle State JVs in our first game, but we won our next three in a row – Colby CC of Kansas – then Frank Phillips and Clarendon, both from the Texas panhandle. So, we were now 4W-0L and getting great support from our freshmen – especially John Greenwood, Chuck Minster, Raymond Nealy, and Greg White.

Coach Akins scheduled 27 games this season compared to 22 the year before. The idea was to make us more prepared for the tough Kansas Jayhawk Junior College Conference schedule. Our next opponent was Amarillo CC, another Texas panhandle team. Led by 6'9" freshman Larry Kenon (Dr. K), they would be a real test for us. We hung tough, but in the end, Kenon's 30 points and 21 rebounds were too much. Amarillo CC 93 – SCCC 78. Larry Kenon was a great player, and would go on to Memphis State where his team was beat in the NCAA finals by UCLA and Bill Walton. Later, he would be drafted by the San Antonio Spurs (then of the ABA.)

Off the court, Dale and I were hanging out with some of the freshman – especially Chuck Minster, Jay Myers, and Greg White. We would introduce them to some of the eating establishments and, of course, the pool hall. None of these guys had anywhere near the pool experience I had, so I got into their wallets a little bit. Again, we socialized with the cheerleaders – it was a natural fit, and we became good friends.

For me, having a car this year gave me a new found sense of independence. I also had a new job this year doing the team's practice gear laundry. This involved laundering practice jerseys, gym shorts, tube socks, and jock straps – sometimes sweat suits. The laundromat served as both my work place and my study hall.

School was going OK – my gpa hovered around 2.8. My mind had a tendency to wander throughout my school years. Reading speed and comprehension was never my strong point. Basketball was on my mind most of the time, followed by visions of pool balls caroming around a pool table, and I have to admit, I was distracted by girls (proving I was a red blooded American boy.) The bottom line, for me, was school went hand and hand with basketball. My goal was to play basketball at the highest level possible, and prepare myself to coach basketball and teach.

Back to the basketball season at hand – we were now into December. After our loss to Amarillo CC, we bounced back with a second win vs Panhandle State College JV. We then lost two road games to the Texas teams we had already beaten earlier – Borger (Frank Phillips College) and Clarendon CC.

Our first conference game was December 12th at Pratt CC. We were a little cold that night, and lost 71-63. Our next game was a conference game, and the last game before Christmas break, vs Dodge City CC. We were "red hot." I had 29 points (season high to date) that game, and we won 96-86.

So, we went into the break 1-1 in the conference and 6-4, overall. I was averaging 19 points per game. Back in Kenmore for the Christmas Holidays, it was great to see family and friends. Frankly, looking back some 48 years, it's hard to distinguish between the Christmas breaks of 1969 and 1970, except now in 1970 my parents and Wende had moved a few blocks to 115 Warren Ave.

Come to think of it, I'm sure the Labies (Amy, Jerry, and Caryn) were in Kenmore for Christmas, and my brother Jim was visiting with Barb Beeke (his future wife). Jim had graduated from Alfred State College in June of 1970 (marketing), and was immediately hired by A.L. Blades & Sons, Inc. to manage their International Truck dealership in Hornell, NY. Jim was proud to show up in a brand new 1970 International Travel-All (one of the first "full-sized" SUV's). That was his company car.

For sure I was playing basketball daily at the Belmont YMCA with Casselman, Vaccaro, and others. No doubt I was sleeping in, spending some time at Bobby Cue, and organizing some poker games with the guys.

Coach Akins stayed in touch with me over the break to make sure I was working out, behaving myself, and planning to return for the second semester. Although, at times, I had to overcome temptation, I kept the training rules (during the season) throughout my years at Seward County.

> SIDE NOTE: Because many early years' scorebooks were lost in a fire at Rindom Hall, some early records did not make their way to the official record book. One such scoring feat that should be noted is Greg White's 36 points vs Pratt in February 1972.

Chapter Fourteen
1971

All of us players were due to return to Liberal by January 3rd (Sunday) in time for classes on Monday and prepare for our three game road trip to Eastern Kansas. When Friday rolled around, we loaded into the twin white 1969 Ford LTD station wagons, and headed to Allen CC in Iola, KS for a game that night. Next was down the road to Coffeyville CC Saturday night, and finally Monday night at Marymount College in Salina, KS. We went 1-2 on that road trip and would play two more road games (five in a row) before our next home game vs. nationally ranked Hutchinson.

During this stretch, before the Hutch game, our roster underwent some changes. John Greenwood returned to Chicago (homesick.) Mike Howell returned to fill that "out of state" roster spot. Kansas Jayhawk Junior College Conference rules allowed for only 5 "out of state" spots on each roster. 6'7" Jim Zito (Chicago) was diagnosed with diabetes, Scott Valarius (6'6") transferred from Coffeyville, and 6'1" Phil Barrett from Wichita joined the team.

We were on a roll going into the Hutch game. We had won two conference games in a row and were in second place behind Hutchinson in the Western Division – 3-1 in conference and 9-

6 overall. Our good play continued, and we led the Blue Dragons by 5 at the half. Hutch, nationally ranked in the top 20, was big and quick, and we had a hard time with their press. With about 7 minutes left in the game, I got a hard finger in the right eye which forced me to the bench for the remainder of the game. My vision was blurry and Hutch was too tough – 87-65. Later that night, Coach Akins took me to an ophthalmologist in Liberal for a checkup. The Doctor put me through some tests, but there was not much he could do other than give me some drops. I had a scratched right eye, which created some spots and floaters I still have today. The injury has not been debilitating, but it has been a nuisance.

At this point, there was a bottle neck at second place in the Western Division of the KJJCC with a lot of games still to be played. We were in the thick of it, but stumbled down the stretch and fell out of the race.

One interesting, nonconference, game late in the season had us matched up against the University of New Mexico freshmen on a neutral court (Southwestern Heights – Kismet.) The UNM freshmen had a 7'3" center, Paul Kruse. It was a close game, but we prevailed 77-61. Kruse was the tallest player I ever played against.

The highlight of our season came February 19th at Hutchinson. We were 4-7 in the Western Division, and 11-13 overall. Hutchinson was 11-0 in the Western Division, and 21-3 overall. They were ranked 12th in the country for NJCAA Division I basketball. Remember, they had beaten us earlier in the season at Liberal. We had been working on a new offense (4 corner) that week. It was a packed house at the Hutchinson Sports Arena with 7,000+ fans, all in red, cheering on the Dragons. Hutch held a 5-4 lead early, but after, that it was all Saints. We ran the 4 corner offense to perfection and shocked the Dragons and their fans 74-

55. We were an unbelievable 22 of 30 from the field with layups and short jumpers on great picks, movement, and passing. It was, by far, our best game of the year, and for SCCC to date. That game was the most memorable and satisfying win of my entire college basketball career. We were on cloud 9 after the game and on the trip home. When we arrived back in Liberal, after 1:00 AM, there were Saints fans (who had listened to the game on the radio) waiting for us in the parking lot and honking their horns – welcoming us home.

> SIDE NOTE: This is about the time 4 year college Coaches and their assistants were scouting and recruiting in earnest.

Below is a summary of some of the 4-year schools/coaches which were recruiting me. Not in any particular order.

- **TCU (Texas Christian University)** Division I – Southwest Conference. After a phone interview with me, Coach Johnny Swaim sent me airline tickets to Dallas that spring. I was met there at the Dallas airport by a sharp, well-dressed TCU undergraduate basketball player who was assigned to "wine and dine" me during my stay. He picked me up in a brand new Cadillac Fleetwood and chauffeured me to the TCU campus in Ft. Worth. Although I can't remember his name, I gleaned his father was a commercial airline pilot for American Airlines and his family was "well-to-do." He was a friendly guy and happy to give me a tour of the campus. Everything was purple – from the huge football stadium to the 10,000+ seat basketball arena. He finally brought me to the athletic dormitory where I was assigned to a single room. When he dropped me off, he told me he would be back at 6 o'clock to pick me up for dinner. At 6 o'clock sharp, he picked me up and we went directly to a palatial women's dormitory where he and his date introduced me to my date for the evening. From there, we went to an upscale restaurant where we enjoyed a lovely dinner, which included cocktails (7&7s for me) and a Texas-sized steak. After dinner, we went to a night club where we had more cocktails, danced, and visited. My memory is a little fuzzy from there, but eventually I was returned to my room with instructions to be ready for breakfast at 9:00 am. That next morning I was definitely hungover, but made it to breakfast. What I didn't know or anticipate was there were 3 or 4 other recruits visiting campus that weekend and there was going to be some scrimmaging with some of the TCU players (observed by the coaches.) Needless to say I was not at my best. It was a memorable trip, but I realized on the flight back to Liberal, TCU was probably not the best fit for me.

- **ETSU (East Texas State University)** NAIA - ETSU is in Commerce, Texas, also not far from Dallas. Coach Jim Gudger had written me a couple of letters on stationary from a hotel room in Kansas City where he was attending the NAIA national tournament. Come to find out, Coach Gudger had previously coached at Western Carolina. He also coached the USA men's PanAm basketball team, and he was on the Olympic basketball committee to the great "Hall of Fame" USA Olympic Coach – Henry Iba. So, he definitely had the pedigree. My memory is a little unclear here, but I think he was trying to get both Dale Reed and me to come as a package. I never visited the campus, but Dale did go on to ETSU, where he had a great couple of years playing for a tough, great coach. By the way, there would be ironic twists which would connect ETSU with other people I would meet later in life. Small world stuff.

- **Marymount College** – Salina, Kansas. Coach Ken Cochran recruited me very aggressively. Marymount had a relatively new basketball program and we (SCCC) actually played them earlier in the season at their small, but nice, gym. Up until about 1966, Marymount had been an "all-girls" school, and they still had a predominantly female enrollment. Coach Cochran didn't hesitate to play the 3:1 ratio card in his pitch to me. He scouted me a couple of times, including our big win at Hutchinson. He even offered to set me up as roommate with Doug Campbell, a 6'7" forward who was graduating from Hutchinson. Doug was from Lyons, KS, not far from Little River, so I had become friends with him through Dale Reed. Coach Cochran was confident he was going to build a powerful NAIA championship contending basketball program. Marymount was one of four campuses I went to visit, and I was seriously considering. Actually, it finally came down to Marymount and UB. Coach Cochran was very persuasive – a great salesman. He stressed I may be just a bench sitter at the Division I level vs being a standout at Marymount. Cochran's teams went on to win 5 NAIA District 10 championships in 11 years and posted an unbelievable 401-118 win/loss record. Ironically, in 1972, Marymount would lose a very close NAIA District 10 championship game to Pittsburg State College (Kansas) coached by Bob Johnson. In 1973, I would go to Pittsburg State College to complete my BS degree and serve as an undergraduate assistant basketball coach for Coach Bob Johnson (great guy and coach.) I have often wondered how my life would be different had I made a different college decision back in the spring of 1971. By the way – Coach Cochran (various H.O.F.) retired early from coaching because of health concerns, but in 1982 he invented the "Pop-A-Shot" electronic basketball game where you actually shoot basketballs into actual basketball hoops. If you've ever been to an arcade, you've probably seen a Pop-A-Shot game.

- **Northwestern State College** – (Alva, Oklahoma) NAIA. Coach Keith Covey was also recruiting me aggressively. Coach Covey was more of a mild mannered gentleman. On one of our (SCCC) road trips, Coach Akins arranged for the team to have a light practice at the NWSC gym. Coach Covey was there to observe. It just so happened I had one of those practices where I could do no wrong. It was like a Greg Laker "highlight" reel. From then on, Coach Covey pursued me aggressively. He was also recruiting Dale Reed, but made it clear our recruitments were separate. He did not want either of us to feel pressured that it was a package deal. I did return to campus later for a visit, but for no particularly ill reason, decided against NWSC.

- **Northern Arizona University** – (Flagstaff) – Division I – Big Sky Conference. Coach Herb Gregg, another H.O.F. coach, wrote me several letters and offered me a "full ride" sight unseen – but by my reputation and Coach Akins recommendation. Again, for whatever reason, I declined. I was narrowing down my decision.

As a point of interest, at the time, an NCAA Division I Scholarship (full-ride) consisted of room, board, books, fees, tuition and $15/month. The NAIA schools could do something similar based on need and smoke & mirrors.

- **University of Buffalo (NY)** – Division I NCAA, Independent. Coach Ed Muto and his assistant, NorbBaschnagel, had been scouting and recruiting me since my days at Kenmore West. As I mentioned back in chapter 12, had it not been for my grades (not up to UB standards) and Coach Akins persuasiveness, I would have enrolled at UB as a freshman. Muto and Baschnagel were both UB alumni and had both played there for iconic Coach Dr. Len Serfustini (Serf). By the way, my high school coach, Dick Harvey, also played for Serf in the early 60s. Basically, there were two things which appealed to me about UB. Number one – they were an NCAA Division I program with a great schedule which would allow me to play against some top notch competition. I could find out how I measured up. Number two – I would be close to home, living on or near campus, with access to family and friends. It was important my father (my number one fan) and family could easily come to home games. Although I didn't really need to visit the UB campus, they flew me up from Liberal. I toured the campus and had a nice lunch with Coach Ed Muto at the Lord Amherst. While in Buffalo, I spent a couple of nights at home at 115 Warren.

• • •

Meanwhile, in the middle of all of this recruiting activity, I would receive maybe my greatest basketball accolades. On Tuesday March 9th the Kansas Jayhawk Junior College Conference named its All-Star team. For the second year in a row, I was named to this prestigious team. This time around, though, I was a unanimous choice by the opposing coaches. No doubt this had an impact on my recruiting stock. I was very humbled.

Laker Is Unanimous All-Star Pick

Seward County's Greg Laker was one of five players who were unanimous choices for positions on the 1970-71 Kansas Jayhawk Junior College Conference All-Star basketball team which was announced this morning by KJJCC Commissioner Nelson Hartman.

Besides Laker, other unanimous selections include Mark Nelson, Garden City; Martinez Denmon, Coffeyville; Chester Fuller, Independence; and Darryl Minniefield, Independence.

The All-Star players were nominated by their own coaches and then were voted on by opposing coaches in their division.

Laker is also one of eight players to repeat as an All-Star selection. Others include (in the West) Brent Baum, Dodge City; Nelson, and Chris Boyle of Pratt. In the East, Denmon, Fuller, Minniefield and Ronald Russell of Kansas City.

Region VI Western Division three players on the dream team and Eastern Division champion Independence also place three. Laker was the only Saint honored.

The 1970-71 Kansas Jayhawk Junior College Conference All-Star teams:

Western Division
GREG LAKER, Seward County, 6'6" soph.
Fred Johnson, Butler County, 6'0", soph.
Ray Johnson, Butler County, 6'1", soph
Brent Baum, Dodge City, 6'7", soph
Mark Nelson, Garden City, 6'4", soph
Steve Ostmeyer, Garden City, 6'3", soph
Stan Blackmon, Hutchinson, 6'7", frosh
Richard Morsden, Hutchinson, 6'5", frosh
Martin Terry, Hutchinson, 6'4", soph
Chris Boyle, Pratt, 6'2", soph

Martinez Demon, Coffeyville, 6'2", soph
Charles Henderson, Coffeyville, 6'1", frosh
Bob Babb, Highland, 6'1", frosh
Eric Johnson, Highland, 6'0", soph
Chester Fuller, Independence, 6'4", soph
Darryl Minniefield, Independence, 6'8", soph
Ronnie Tillis, Independence, 6'2", frosh
Deon Kayhill, Johnson, 6'3", frosh
Terry Smith, Johnson, 6'1", frosh
Mark Augustus, Kansas City, 6'8", soph
Ronald Russell, Kansas City, 6'4", soph.

GREG LAKER
All-Star Repeat

At the same time, the NJCAA Division I basketball tournament was taking place in Hutchinson. The Hutchinson Blue Dragons (whom we, SCCC, had had that huge upset over) made it to the tournament semi-finals, where they lost 67-66 to the number one seed Ellsworth, Iowa team.

As the school year wound down, we were all preparing for final exams. No more games or practices – but we still went to the gym for "shoot arounds" and pickup games. Sometimes it might be just Dale and me playing one-on-one like we did so many times after practice during the season. Our one-on-one games were very intense and looking back, those games were as instrumental in our basketball development as any other drills or exercises.

More should be said about the freshmen teammates I had become good friends with. Greg White (Little River) had become a standout player on our team. He was a straight arrow from a solid family, and his parents were at most of our games. Greg had a brand new 1970 jade green Pontiac LeMans (bought with money he had earned "putting up hay" in the summers.) Being a nice, new car, everything worked on it – especially the heater. Sometimes on cold winter nights, after practice, I would be lucky enough to catch a ride in the LeMans with Greg.

Chuck Minster (Pittsburgh, PA) was also a key player as a freshman. Chuck was a quiet guy, but a hardnosed competitor. I think he and Greg White were roommates.

And then there was Jay Myers (Wichita, KS). Jay was the most outgoing of the trio. He and I got along well, I think, because our, sometimes sick, senses of humor overlapped. One of the black players nicknamed Jay's car as the "Blue Ass Falcon" – that stuck. The car was a sky blue, early 60's Ford Falcon in fine looking shape. Jay always had a laugh in his voice and was quite amused at some of my Buffalo style humor and antics. He and I would exchange letters throughout the remainder of our college years. As a matter of fact, I still have a handful of Jay's letters which, when read today, still crack me up. Jay's strong sport was track. Coach Akins used to love to watch Jay run on the track. English and writing were his academia. He would correct spelling and grammar in my letters until I threatened to stop writing him. I'm now tempted to send him a rough draft of this book for him to edit.

Anyway, those three, along with Dale and me, would socialize together – pool, snooker, cruising the main drag, eating out or just hanging out. It was all good fun.

Before I forget, it should be noted that (on the second time around, on February 2nd) the bond issue for the new SCCC campus passed - this time by 300+ votes. In an open letter, the school President, Dr. James Miller, praised the student body for their efforts in promoting the bond issue to the public. The passage of the bond issue paved the way for plans for the new campus to proceed.

Another event I almost forgot about was Pancake Day. Liberal, Kansas is known as the "Pancake Hub of the Universe." Festivities included a parade and a pancake race where contestants carry a frying pan with a pancake and, at given intervals, flip the pancake in the pan – quite challenging. This year's speaker was none other than Bill Russell – Hall of Famer from the Boston Celtics. He spoke on social issues.

Every guy, at 18, must register with the Selective Services. At the time, you were also assigned a lottery number based on your birthday date. Guys with the lowest numbers, and otherwise eligible, were the first ones drafted to serve. Although I cannot remember my number, I know it was somewhere in the middle (maybe 149.) Anyway, that Spring, I got a notice to report to Amarillo, Texas for a physical. I remember taking the bus there – about a 100 mile trip south of Liberal. I was not feeling well that day, and it was kind of like a blur; surreal. There were dozens of us lined up to see various doctors for various tests. It was weeks until I got the results, but the bottom line was I was rejected due to my history of a heart murmur and Rheumatic Fever. Here I was, a high level college athlete, but not fit for military duty. Go figure.

As far as my dating life, I was on and off with Susan Smith (the head cheerleader) – mostly off. When she broke it off with me, I was heartsick for some time. Years later, while exchanging emails, she blamed breaking up with me on her mother. Her mother, supposedly, was afraid I would take her daughter away to New York. Later that Spring, I also dated Debbie Ormiston (another cheerleader). As I wrote earlier, the Ormistons were big farmers in Kismet, Kansas, and a "salt of the earth" family. Remember, they hosted my parents and Wende when they visited Liberal. Anyway, things just kind of faded away for Debbie and me, although we wrote to each other occasionally over the next several years.

On May 5th I signed my letter of intent to enroll at the University of Buffalo. A press release followed May 14 with articles in both the Buffalo Evening News and the Courier Express. This was a very exciting time for me and my family, especially my father. I know he was proud to put his signature on the letter of intent.

But school was not quite over, yet. We still had to get through final exams. It was hard to concentrate. Spring like weather comes early in southwest Kansas, so the mild conditions were a distraction. Finally though, the exams were over, the grades were posted, and I had made it. I had earned my Associates of Arts degree. Fifty-one of us made up the first graduating class for SCCC. There was a cap and gown ceremony in the high school auditorium.

It was bitter sweet saying our goodbyes to fellow teammates and other friends whom we would likely never see again. I distinctly remember Dale and I going to say goodbye to Coach Akins' wife Denise (also an SCCC teacher.) She told Dale and me we should stay in touch with each other. For some reason, I (we) really took that to heart, and Dale and I have remained close through the years, and to this very day.

It was now time to load up the '63 Buick Wildcat and head east. Over the last couple of months, I had noticed the Wildcat heater was not warming up. So, I changed the thermostat and hoped for the best on my trip home. My plan was to make it as far as Lawrence to stop and see Kristen Schmidt, who was finishing up her year at KU. The Wildcat radiator was heating up, and I had to make several stops to add water. Ultimately, I made it to Lawrence and had a nice visit with Kristen. I now knew I could not gamble on trying to nurse the old Wildcat all the way back to New York, so when I left Lawrence, I was on the lookout for used car lots to see if I could find a buyer for my car. Eventually, I found a dealer who would buy the Wildcat, so I cut my losses and put the proceeds toward a flight from KC to Buffalo. The 1963 Buick Wildcat is another car I wish I had today. What a boat!

Greg Laker
... *junior all-star*

Junior Star Enters UB

Greg Laker, a 6-6, 190-pound transfer from Seward County Community College in Liberal, Kan., Thursday became the third junior college transfer student to accept a basketball grant-in-aid at the University of Buffalo.

Laker is a Kenmore native who averaged 19.1 points and 9.1 rebounds during his two seasons at Seward. He also was impressive at the free throw stripe, converting 83.2 per cent. Laker established 10 Seward records during his stay there and was a two-time Kansas Jayhawk Junior College All-Star.

Laker will join 6-2 Bob Varnaian from Leicester, Mass., Junior College and 6-6 Jim Tribble from Missouri Baptist College, previous UB grant recipients, for the Bulls' 24-game 1971-72 schedule. "We are particularly looking to strengthen our forecourt next year," said UB Coach Ed Muto. "Laker gives us good scoring and rebounding potential."

SCCC graduation

174 | Gregory Granger Laker

STATE UNIVERSITY OF NEW YORK AT BUFFALO

Pre-Enrollment LETTER OF INTENT ___Basketball___ Date _4/28/71_

* * * * * * *

GENERAL STATEMENT OF FINANCIAL AID
(see details on reverse side)

This is to certify that ___Gregory Laker___ will be recommended by the Department of Inter-collegiate Athletics to the Committee on Financial Aid to Students, for financial aid to the extent of:

___X___ Full Grant, to cover costs to the University of: Tuition, Fees, University Housing and Board on campus only, unless married, and Books and Supplies up to $75 per semester. NCAA Rules permit member institutions to award an educational grant of no more than the actual costs (normal charges) to the University. Therefore, if you receive any additional scholarship awards (including Regents, Scholar Incentive, Educational Opportunity Grant, etc.), then this recommended award will be adjusted downward accordingly. X

_____ Partial Grant, to cover Tuition and all University Fees.

_____ Partial Grant, to cover University Housing and Board, on campus only unless married.

The recommended Award will be for the _1971-1972 ,1972-1973_ academic year, but it may be renewed during the period of the student's athletic eligibility. Application for aid must be filed annually with the University Office of Financial Aid.

This award is subject to enrollment at the University on a full-time basis (12 semester hours minimum per semester), and you will be required to maintain normal progress toward a degree.

If you should incur an injury which would preclude your participation in actual competition, your award will not be affected, but you will be expected to contribute otherwise to the sport of your primary interest or another intercollegiate sport to the best of your ability.

The commitment of the University to the Student-Athlete and the Student-Athlete's commitment to the University is described in greater detail on the reverse side of this letter.

The University requires a written statement, as indicated below, of your intention to accept this commitment by _5/5/71_

_____ _____
Athletic Director   Head Coach

* * * * * * *

I accept the recommended offer of financial aid as described above, and I state that it is my intention and desire to enroll at the State University of New York at Buffalo and to participate in its athletic program.

My decision is subject to acceptance by the Director of Admissions of the University, and by the Committee on Financial Aid to Students. I understand that before any award becomes final, I must present scores made on one of the following nationally recognized college entrance examinations, the S.A.T. of the College Entrance Examination Board, or the tests of the American College Testing program.

I also understand that any award made to me must conform to the provisions of the constitution of the NCAA, pertaining to the principles of amateurism, sound academic standards and financial aid to students (see enclosed sheet). By my acceptance I mean to state that I agree with these principles, and I acknowledge that both the University and I are bound by them.

I further state that I am unmarried, that neither the University or any other person has offered or given me any consideration other than the recommended grant-in-aid described above, and that I have read and fully understand this Letter of Intent.

Signed: _____ Date _____
(Student-Athlete)

Signed _____ Date _4/28/71_
(Parent/Guardian)

(This form should be executed in triplicate, with the white copy sent to the Committee on Financial Aid to Students, the canary copy to the Director of Athletics and the pink copy to be retained by the prospective Student Athlete.)

One of the perks I had at UB was a summer job working on campus with the painting crew. There were a handful of student athletes mixed in with the full timers. I painted everything from fire hydrants to dormitory rooms. My supervisor was an Archie Bunker clone. He liked his cigars and his racing forms and he didn't want any basketball player messing up his routine. We did our work – not too fast, not too slow. I actually learned a lot about painting from that experience.

So now, with no '63 Buick Wildcat, I was carless except for the use of the good old '63 Mercury Comet family car. Near the campus, on Bailey Ave., I found another one of those used car lots with the bright, multi-colored pennants. Soon, I had my eye on a maroon 1964 Chevy Impala SS with a 283 V8, with bucket seats and an automatic stick shift on the floor. This car was something like you would see in SoCal, tricked out with air hydraulics. I'm thinking I paid maybe $750 for that car – and I loved it.

Of course things were still hot and heavy at the Crosby Courts. The competition was tougher than ever, and it was great to see all my buddies again. So, I was painting by day, hoops at the courts in the evenings, and sometimes the bar scene at night with a group of guys checking out the breance' (colloquial for nice young ladies.)

When I had some spare time on my hands, I would go to Bobby Cue Billiards. Usually, in the evenings, you would have to be on a wait list for a table to become available. John Lannen and Fran Kenney were a couple of guys about my speed who I played a lot of 9 ball with – 25 cents a rack. Nobody got hurt too bad. One Saturday afternoon, there at Bobby Cue, a big guy walked in and asked Bob Clark (owner/proprietor), "Who is the best 9 ball player in here?"

It wasn't me – but Bob set him up with one of the better players who happened to be there.

As it turned out, John Leypoldt (place kicker for the Buffalo Bills) was the big guy who walked in looking for a game. John was a pretty fair pool player, and he was working summers selling cars for Kenmore Ford right across the street on Delaware Ave. As it turned out, later that summer, Bob Clark set up an exhibition featuring World Champion Steve Mizerak. Among many other championships, Mizerak was the 1970, '71, '72 and '73 World Champion for straight pool (14 and 1.) In front of a packed house at Bobby Cue, the "Miz" was incredible, making some impossible shots. Part of the exhibition was a 9 ball match with John Leypoldt. Even though Leypoldt was a very good player, he was no match for Mizerak. You may remember seeing the "Miz" in a series of commercials for Miller Lite beer in the early '70s. In one of the commercials, while making a complicated trick shot, he would proclaim, "You can really work up a thirst, even when you are just showing off."

It was the greatest pool exhibition I had ever seen!

That Summer (actually late Spring), my brother Jim would marry Barb Beeke on June 19th at St. Mary's church in Bath. I was honored to be Jim's best man. It was a Catholic ceremony, in the church chapel, followed by a reception in the adjoining banquet room. Barb's brothers Bill and Brad were ushers, and her father William gave the bride away. If memory serves, Wende was a flower girl. The maid of honor was, Barb's best friend at Alfred State College, Sue Ensminger. Sue was a cute, petite gal from Niagara Falls, NY. With the prodding of Barb and Jim, Sue and I spent time together at the reception dancing and visiting. By the end of the night Sue gave me her phone number and encouraged me to call.

It was a busy Summer, between work (full time), social life, and, most importantly, basketball. My focus was on preparing to play basketball at UB. Besides hoops at Crosby Courts, I now had access to Clark Gym on campus. Sometimes there were random pickup games, but mostly just shoot arounds. There was also a weight room in the basement of Clark and I worked on the "Universal" there. I was working hard on my conditioning, and trying to gain a few lbs. I ate everything I could get my hands on. Usually I would take four or five sandwiches to work and drink a lot of "Nutriment." My weight may have spiked at 200 lbs., but I leveled off at 190ish. My cardio conditioning was at its peak. I was doing a lot of distance and intermediate running. If I was going to compete for a spot on the UB basketball roster (let alone compete against some of the tough players on the tough teams on our tough schedule), I would have to be at my best.

So I finally worked up the nerve to call Sue Ensminger. By nature, I was a pretty shy guy – especially when it came to women. She was a soft spoken gal, and quite shy herself, so it was a little awkward. We made a date and she gave me directions to her house in a residential part of Niagara Falls where she lived with her mother. Driving to Niagara Falls from Kenmore was a good half hour each way, and it involved crossing Grand Island and it's bridges over the Niagara River. The '64 Chevy Impala was serving me well, and I was proud of it. On my first date with Sue, I had to do the "sit down" with her mother to see if I was fit enough to escort her daughter. My parents had raised me to be a gentleman, and I had no trouble making a fine impression on Mrs. Ensminger (I think her father was deceased.) After having a cocktail with her mother, Sue suggested she and I go to a local cocktail lounge for a couple of drinks. In those days, wrongfully, I did not pay much attention to the dangers of drinking and driving. Not to make excuses, but at that time, the legal level for DUI was .10 – which gave me a lot of leeway. Over the course of the summer, I think I made that trip to Niagara Falls about 5 or 6 times.

As the Summer came to an end, it was time to move to the campus and get registered for Fall semester classes. Even though I had grown up in greater Buffalo and spent the summer working on the UB campus, it was culture shock once the 25,000+ students inundated the campus that Fall. It was quite different than little old Seward County Community College. UB was predominantly made up of students from down state – Long Island and the greater NYC area. For the most part, they exhibited an air of sophistication and it was a little intimidating. It was also a time (early 70s) of student unrest. It seemed like there was always some kind of protest going on at the student union or on the quad.

Assistant Coach NorbBaschnagel, was charged with assigning housing for the basketball players. Five of us were designated to live in a 3-bedroom townhouse in the Allenhurst (23A Yale) neighborhood just off campus. The townhouse featured 3 bedrooms with one bath on the second floor. On the first floor there was a living room, dining room, and a full kitchen. The basement was a drive under garage. The 5 of us were all newcomers to UB – two freshmen and three of us Junior College transfers. Bob Vartanian was from Worcester, MA via Leicester Community College. Jim Tribble was a Cleveland native by way of Missouri Baptist College. Those two shared one of the bedrooms. My roommate was Bob Dickinson from Kennedy HS in Plainview, LI (NY). The other freshman was Chuck Axe from Sharon, PA – not sure how he ended up solo in the third bedroom.

There were shuttle buses which made regular runs from Allenhurst to various stops on campus, including the cafeteria. Our meal plan, of course, was a part of our scholarships and it was especially enjoyable to me after having no such thing at SCCC. We all (my roommates and me) took full advantage of our meal plan, even though it sometimes meant getting up early to get to the cafeteria for breakfast before classes.

My school schedule was quite demanding. As a physical education major, I was required to take a number of "activity" courses. Activity courses ranged with instruction for such subjects as archery, golf, swimming, and wrestling to gymnastics and so on. Gymnastics, in particular, came very hard to me. Our instructor expected us all to reach a certain level of competency on all of the apparatuses, including the parallel bars and the rings (iron cross? I don't think so.) I just was not built for it, but when it came to basketball as an activity class (different instructor) we were not expected to perform at any particular level. I never thought that was fair.

On the other hand, I had to choose some electives. There was a rumor going around a good class to sign up for was "Jazz Appreciation." A couple of my teammates and I bit on that course, which convened in a large auditorium of the Music Department. There were probably 100 or so students in the class. The professor was a young, black hipster. He explained we could show up for class when we wanted and we would grade ourselves. He played various Jazz records from John Coletrane to Louis Armstrong, and then opened the floor up for discussion. I quite enjoyed that class, and my grade.

Preseason basketball was mostly conditioning. Coach Muto, class of 1950, was "old school," carrying on the traditions of his iconic predecessor, Dr. Leonard Serfustini. Even though I was not the fastest player out there, I had as much endurance as anyone. Generally, I was out front in any of the distance runs. When tryouts started in earnest, there were about 25 guys trying out for 12 spots. By the way, there was a freshman team coached by Jim Horne (legendary player at UB in the 50s – looked like Earl "the Pearl" Monroe), so there were no freshmen on the Varsity.

Here is a quick look at the 12 man roster at the start of the season, using todays terms to describe their positions: 1=point guard, 2=shooting guard, 3=small forward, 4=power forward and 5=center. Of course, some of the players could play more than one position.

- Curtis Blackmore - 6'6' 260 lbs. Junior – Selkirk, NY (5) was our star. He was a stud and averaged 20 points and 16 rebounds as a sophomore.
- Bob Vartainian – 6'3" 180 lbs. Junior – Worcester, MA (2), very talented, could do it all.
- Jim Tribble – 6'6" 210 lbs. Junior – Cleveland (4), quietly solid and tough.
- Greg Bruce – 6'1" 170 lbs. Junior - NYC (1), clever.
- Neil Langelier – 6'4" 205 lbs. Senior Captain (3-4), solid fundamentals.
- John Forys – 6'1" 180 lbs. Junior – Buffalo (1-2), solid backup guard.
- OrvCott – 6'2" Senior – Buffalo (2-3), experienced lefty.
- Joe Evans – 6'4" sophomore – Sharon, PA (2-3), led the Frosh in scoring last season.
- Eric Rasmussen – 6'5" Senior – (2-3), long backup
- Don Van Dueson – 6'6" 230 Senior (5), tight end for the football team. Curt's backup
- Rick Matanle – 6'4" 190 Senior – Elmira, NY (3), backup
- Abe Gruenwald – NYC – our very capable team manager.

SIDE NOTE: Once the roster was set, Coach Muto took us all to the, well-known, Riverside Men's Shop, where we were all tailor fitted for red polyester blazers and gray knit slacks along with a short sleeved, white, mock turtleneck shirt. This was our travel attire for when we were on road trips.

1971-72 Varsity Basketball Bulls

(l-r) John Forys, Orv Cott, Joe Evans, Eric Rasmussen, Greg Laker, Curt Blackmore, Don Van Deuson, Jim Tribble, Rick Matanle, Bob Vartanian, Greg Bruce and Manager Abe Gruenwald. Front - Assistant Coach Norb Baschnagel, Captain Neil Langelier and Head Coach Ed Muto.

tastes better

A few of us came into the season nursing injuries, including me (ankle). That didn't help. In late November, Coach Muto lined up two scrimmages for us to prepare for our opener at Syracuse. The first was at SUNY Geneseo, led by my old nemesis, Tom Basher (West Seneca), and the second was at St. Bonaventure, led by Matt Gantt (Bob Lanier heir apparent). We did not play well in either scrimmage, and Coach Muto let us know it.

NOTE: See 1971-72 University of Buffalo basketball schedule, attached.

December 1, 1971 – It was now time to get on the bus and head down the NYS Thruway to Syracuse. This was before the existence of the Carrier Dome, or the Big East Conference – Syracuse was an independent. Jim Boeheim was an assistant to Head Coach Roy Danforth, and the Manley Fieldhouse was where the Orange played their home games. Manley was a mini-dome, which also served as an inside venue for the football team to practice. The basketball court was elevated, and the stands held about 7,000 fans. Syracuse rarely lost there. As a matter of fact, when Boeheim became head coach, he did not want to leave Manley when it came time to move to the Carrier Dome.

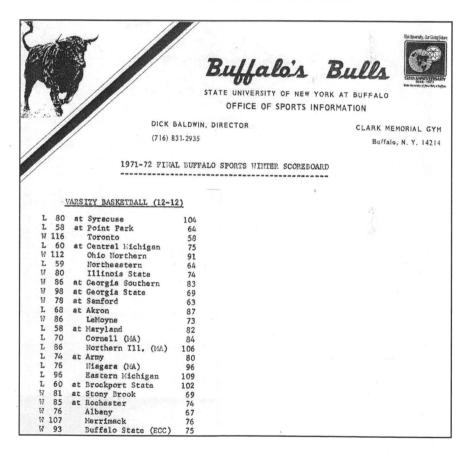

Buffalo's Bulls

STATE UNIVERSITY OF NEW YORK AT BUFFALO
OFFICE OF SPORTS INFORMATION

DICK BALDWIN, DIRECTOR
(716) 831-2935

CLARK MEMORIAL GYM
Buffalo, N. Y. 14214

1971-72 FINAL BUFFALO SPORTS WINTER SCOREBOARD

VARSITY BASKETBALL (12-12)

L	80	at Syracuse	104
L	58	at Point Park	64
W	116	Toronto	58
L	60	at Central Michigan	75
W	112	Ohio Northern	91
L	59	Northeastern	64
W	80	Illinois State	74
W	86	at Georgia Southern	83
W	98	at Georgia State	69
W	78	at Samford	63
L	68	at Akron	87
W	86	LeMoyne	73
L	58	at Maryland	82
L	70	Cornell (MA)	84
L	86	Northern Ill. (MA)	106
L	74	at Army	80
L	76	Niagara (MA)	96
L	96	Eastern Michigan	109
L	60	at Brockport State	102
W	81	at Stony Brook	69
W	85	at Rochester	74
W	76	Albany	67
W	107	Merrimack	76
W	93	Buffalo State (ECC)	75

When we made our entry onto the court, we were funneled through a gauntlet of Syracuse fans. As we passed through this gauntlet of fans, I could hear a familiar chant... "MAD STORK! MAD STORK! MAD STORK!" I turned my head, and there was Rob Sutton (my high school fraternity brother/SU quarterback) and his Syracuse football teammate, Joe Ehrmann (another Crosby Courts player.) Rob had coined that nickname for me, and I was pleasantly surprised to hear it in that venue and context.

Syracuse smothered us with their full court trap, 104-80. They were very quick and long. Their star player was a quick and talented black guard – Dennis DuVal. Dennis would eventually become Chief of Police for the City of Syracuse.

As I've done while describing previous basketball seasons, I will try to touch on the highlights. For those interested in more details regarding the 1971-72 Buffalo Bulls basketball season, they may refer to my "BUFFALO" scrapbook. By looking at our 1971-72 schedule (attached) you will see four of our opponents (Central Michigan, Akron, Northern Illinois, and Eastern Michigan) all became members of the MAC (Mid- American Conference) along with UB.

Fast forward – we were 2-4 going into a home game at Clark gym vs. Illinois State. This game was highlighted on our schedule because the team featured All-American 6'6" guard Doug Collins. Like Syracuse at Manley, we were tough to beat at Clark Gym. Collins scored 26 points, but we prevailed 80-74. My contribution in that game was clutch free throws down the stretch at "crunch time." We would then have a few days off for Christmas before departing on a southern swing.

> SIDE NOTE: Over the break, I stayed at home in Kenmore (115 Warren Ave) with the family. One night, I got an invitation from my Kenmore buddy, Dave Casselman, to

go out for a couple of cold ones. He wanted to take me down to the River Boat on the Niagara River. He said, "You've got to see this guy!"

John Valby ("Dr. Dirty") was a concert pianist by trade, but with the encouragement of his raucous beer drinking audience, played his original "smut" music. His lyrics were vulgar, but hilarious (at least to a 20 year old in 1971.) It was kind of like not being able to look away at the sight of an automobile accident. If you have the nerve – and you are not a minor – and never heard John Valby before, check him out on YouTube. Anyway, Cazz and I were hysterical watching and listening to John Valby.

The day after Christmas, the team flew out of Buffalo to warmer weather. We would play three games in four nights – Georgia Southern, Georgia State, and Samford (AL). We won all three games, which made for an enjoyable trip home, especially going into the New Year's break. It would be 20 days until our next game at Akron 1/19/72.

> SIDE NOTE: Just to back up a little, earlier that Fall, October 4th, my sister Amy gave birth to twins – my nephew Chris and niece Susan. What a joyful addition to the Labie family.

Chapter Fifteen
1972

It was nice to have some extended time off, although I went to the Belmont YMCA several times just to keep my legs under me. If memory serves, I think there were a few poker games with the Kenmore guys, and some time spent at Bobby Cue. By the way, I wasn't seeing too much of Sue Ensminger, although we did exchange letters. She was busy at Alfred State College (nursing program) and I was busy with school and basketball. It was expensive to make long distance phone calls in those days.

The break went fast, and we were back to practice at Clark Gym well before the rest of the student body returned to campus. At this point of the season, I had been the starting 3 forward and getting my share of playing time. When we went to Akron, I was able to secure a block of tickets for my family (the Christy's.) For some reason, I remember the shoot around warmups before that game. I got in a rhythm from the left wing about 18' out and banked in about 10 in a row. I was hoping my cousins were watching. It was all for naught, though – Akron 87 – UB 68.

The next highlight on the schedule was at the University of Maryland, coached by the flamboyant Lefty Driesel. Lefty had come in and turned the Maryland basketball program around. He was high energy and knew how to recruit. Maryland had two All-Americans – 6'11" Tom McMillen (Mansfield, PA) and 6'9" Len Elmore. Both would eventually play in the NBA. McMillen was a Rhodes Scholar, and later became a U.S. Congressman.

It was a Sunday game, and still there were 13,500 fans, all dressed in red, packed into Cole Field House. Maryland had plenty of other great players besides McMillen and Elmore. They were too big and too deep – UM 82-UB 58. Even though we were over matched, it was still a great experience to play in that venue and atmosphere.

> SIDE NOTE: While in our locker room before the game, Varick Cutler (North Tonawanda HS star) walked in to say hello to me. We had been fierce competitors back in the Niagara Frontier League. Varick was a freshman player for Maryland, then.

Finally, I got my chance to play in the Aud (Memorial Auditorium) against a tough Ivy League school – Cornell. It was a thrill for me to play there, but the "Big Red" won 84-70. Two nights later, we played in the Aud again vs. Northern Illinois. The result was no better – NIU 106-UB 86.

Next, we traveled to West Point to play a tough Army team. This was during a period of time between when Army's coaches were Bobby Knight and Mike Krzyzewski. It was an awesome experience to be on that campus, and to play in that field house, but we were now on a four game losing streak – Army 80-UB 74 in a close game.

Then came Niagara University in the Aud, and again, another loss – 96-76. Our next game was finally back at Clark Gym vs. Eastern Michigan. I was on the injured list with a sprained ankle suffered in the Niagara game, and could not play (this was the only game of the season I could not play.) It was especially disappointing because I would miss the opportunity to compete against EMU's All-American stud – George "the Iceman" Gervin. It was a "run and gun" affair with EMU winning 109-96. That was a rare loss for us in Clark Gym, but George Gervin was a rare player. He dropped 36 points on us, smooth as silk whether it was a 25' jumper or his patented "finger roll." Gervin averaged 30+ points per game that season, and four of his teammates averaged double figures as well. Later, Gervin was drafted, signed, and starred for the San Antonio Spurs, then of the ABA. The Spurs were one of a handful of ABA franchises which moved over to the NBA when the two leagues merged.

Our next opponent/game needs a little back story. During the late 60's, there was considerable student unrest at UB and many other college campuses around the country. In 1967, two standout basketball players from Elmira Free Academy came to UB – Ron Gilliam (5'9" Calvin Murphy-ish point guard) and Guy Vickers (a power forward.) Those two, along with my Kenmore West HS idol, Steve Waxman, formed the nucleus of an outstanding freshman team. As the story goes, those three were uncomfortable with the atmosphere on campus and, subsequently, Gilliam and Vickers transferred to Brockport State, where they sat out the 1968-69 season. The coach at Brockport then, Mario Panaggio, was formulating a star studded team, and by the time we played them at Brockport 2/11/72, they were loaded (especially for a small college team.) Gilliam and Vickers, particularly, had something to prove to UB. They both played like they were possessed. The lineup also included a 6'6" jumping jack – "Stormin'" Norman Bounds. Bounds was a JUCO transfer from Erie Community College. Norman's style of play was "unconventional" and with reckless abandon, but effective. Rounding out their starting lineup was 6'9" center John Collins, and the coach's son Mike Panaggio at the #2 guard. Still bothered by an ankle sprain, I saw limited playing time, not that it would have made a difference. We were a heavy favorite going into that game, but Brockport embarrassed us. They ran us right off the court with a 102-60 rout in front of an absolutely raucous full house.

"Stormin'" Norman, Gilliam, and Collins all had tryouts with the Buffalo Braves, and Bounds actually did very well against Bob McAdoo, but he was a little too unconventional to fit in with the NBA. Later, Coach Panaggio coached the Rochester Zeniths semi-pro team which featured Norman Bounds as its star player.

The good news was, that game marked the end of our seven game skid, with five games left to play. Those seven losses were tough, but they were all against very good teams and, believe it or not, we were starting to play some of our best basketball. Next, we would fly to Long Island to play Stony Brook. I was now back in the starting lineup, and we won 81-69. The University of Rochester would then come to Clark Gym. That was a particularly interesting game for me because their star player was none other than sophomore Fran Moulin (my former High School teammate at Kenmore West.) No one was more competitive than Fran, and he scored his team high 17 points, but we won 85-74. I was now getting back in the groove – 11 points on 7-for-7 free throws.

SIDE NOTE: I need to take a pause to give credit where credit is due. Curtis Blackmore was a beast for us all season long. He averaged 19 points and 17 rebounds per game, setting numerous school records. Curt was a powerful force to be reckoned with. Curt went on to be an NBA draft pick, and his jersey, #52, was the first to hang from the rafters at the beautiful Alumni Arena. He was truly a Bulls legend.

Albany State was our next victim – 76-67 – then a rout of Merrimack – 107-76 – both at Clark Gym. Our final game was vs. Buffalo State, which was originally scheduled to be played at the Aud, but for some reason was moved to Erie Community College. Again, there was an interesting factor for me because my Kenmore West HS teammate, Dave Casselman, played for Buffalo State. By the way, a year earlier, Buffalo State's all-time greatest player, Randy Smith, was their leader. By now, fortunately for us, Randy had moved on to play for the Buffalo Braves in the NBA. Buffalo State was tough, but we played one of our best games of the season with five players in double figures, including me with 16 (equaling my high of the season.) Bulls 93 – Buffalo State 75.

So, we finished the season 12W – 12L, with a five game winning streak and a feeling of optimism looking forward to next season. We would lose a part of our seven man rotation – Greg Bruce, Neil Langelier, and Eric Rasmussen.

GREG LAKER

K-West UB Cager Plays Reserve Role

Greg Laker, a 6-foot, 6-inch 1971-72 varsity letterman at the State University of Buffalo, will be seeing limited action Saturday at 8:30 P.M. as the UB Bulls host the Samford Bulldogs of Birmingham, Ala. in Clark Hall.

Laker, a 190-pound UB senior forward from Kenmore West, is recovering from a neck strain he suffered last week when the Bulls had morning and afternoon practices during the semester break.

Greg battled a virus in pre-season and was slow getting into the swing of the 72-73 season, serving in a reserve role capacity coming off the bench to relieve his teammates.

A transfer from Seward County Community, Laker had a brilliant JC career with ten school records such as most game and career points, most field goals and most rebounds. He led the UB Bulls a year ago with .85 at the free throw line, hitting 35 of 41.

Samford Coach Ron Harris has six lettermen among his Bulldogs for Saturday's battle. UB defeated the Bulldogs, 78-63, in their first game last year. Samford has played in fast company with wins over Abilene Christian, 81-73.

The UB Bulls are fresh from four straight victories after downing Farleigh Dickinson, 64-50, this past weekend on Capt. Bob Vartanian's best scoring night of the season, 20 points.

Horace Brawley, a transfer from Nassau Community College, posted 12 points with Jim Tribble collecting 11 and Al Denman 10. Tribble had 10 rebounds, high for both teams. The Bulls lost the boards, 52-45.

Leo Richardson will send his Baby Bulls against Canisius Saturday at 6:30 P.M. at Clark Hall in the varsity preliminary. Buffalo is led by 6-0 guard Ed Meltzer, who averages 17 points and 6-2 John Ruffino from Canisius High School.

THAT OLD LAKER HUSTLE

Gary Monahan
Greg Laker

UB forward sprawls for possession of ball

...C-E photo by Frank Schifferle

For the record, my final stat line, per game, for the season: 21 minutes, 4.1 rebounds, 7.3 points and 85% free throws.

The long season was now over, and unless you have been a college student athlete, it is hard to appreciate how demanding it is. Between practice, travel, and games, the time and energy spent is significant. On top of that, of course, are the academics… 16 credit hours of classes plus homework. So, now, with the season over, and without its formal structure, we had some time to decompress.

As I mentioned earlier, UB was huge (25,000 students) and made up of a wide cross section of matriculaters – not the least of who were full blown hippies. There were Hari-Krishnas, Araftafarians, and a lot of braless women dressed in tie-dye outfits as though they were on their way to a Grateful Dead concert. It was not unusual to walk the quad or the hallways of the dorms and catch the unmistakable odor of incense and marijuana. In my days in Liberal, KS, and even in Kenmore, to this point, I never had this type of exposure. As basketball players, we were fairly high profile (no pun intended) on campus and, for the most part, welcomed to various parties where pot might be smoked. It was very common, to say the least, and I had many opportunities to partake, but to this point I had resisted. At some point, though, soon after the season, I was at a party, somewhere in the Allenhurst apartments, with another (unnamed virgin) teammate and we were invited to an upstairs bedroom to smoke some pot. My curiosity finally got the best of me, and my (unnamed) teammate and I gave into the temptation. It all seemed quite covert, but interesting. That was my introduction to marijuana.

April 3rd (my father's 49th birthday), word came that my grandmother Marjory Laker (Nanny) had passed. She was just 71. My brother Jim, and sister Amy, made the trip to Indiana for the funeral.

On April 13th, the 63rd annual "Block B" banquet was held at the plush Hearthstone Manor in Amherst to award "Block B" letters to all of the UB varsity athletes who had earned them. It was a lavish affair attended by many Buffalo dignitaries, and to top it off, the key note speaker was none other than Howard Cosell – "Tell it like it is."

Howard was, then, in his prime, with ABC's Monday Night Football, and very entertaining. "Not just another pretty face."

Not long after the "Block B" banquet, we were on spring break, and I went home to 115 Warren to stay with the family. Out of the blue, a couple of days into the break, there was a knock at the door. It was my buddy, John Johnston, along with Kevin Munro and Tom Leistner. Leistner had a brand new pickup truck and they were headed to Florida. "Come on, Laker. Come on and go with us," they taunted.

It was in the evening, and there was still snow on the ground. John's mother's cousin had a bungalow in Lauderdale by the Sea, so we would have a place to stay. The plan was to drive straight through, rotating drivers. After a short period of contemplation, I was convinced it would be a good idea, and my parents put up very little protest. I literally packed a bag within 15 minutes, and we were on our way. I'm sure I had no more than $50 in my pocket. Since I was the odd man out, I was assigned to ride in the back of the truck for the first leg of the trip, while the other three were in the warm cab. The first leg was from Kenmore to Akron, Ohio (about 200 miles), and even though I was wearing layers of my warmest clothing and bundled up in my father's Army mummy bag, I still froze my ass off. It was now my turn to rotate into the cab as we followed a more southerly route which took us through Kentucky, Tennessee, and Georgia. We finally made it to the Florida border and the welcome sight of palm trees. However, if you have ever driven to south Florida, you know it's a long drive from the northern border to Lauderdale. It was a good 20+ hours by the time we arrived at Lauderdale by the Sea and Cousin George's abode. George was a construction worker, and quite a character, with a speckled history. However, he was quite hospitable, considering four strange 20-something guys were invading his space. George's bungalow was located within walking distance of the beach and the "downtown" area of LBTS, such as it was in those days. We spent much of our time at the beach, where we met a group of gals about our age. They were from Michigan, I think, and we kind of hung out with them that week. None of us thought anything about sun screen back then, and I got quite a sunburn. Ft. Lauderdale (proper) was about 5 miles south of LBTS. With no hesitation, we made the walk down the sidewalk of A1A to where the "action" was. There were hundreds, if not thousands, of other young people walking and cruising the strip. It was great people watching, and a lot of hootin' and hollerin'. Some beer was consumed.

> SIDE NOTE: While we were in south Florida, we lucked into seeing an ABA playoff basketball game. It turned out to be the very last game for the Floridian franchise with Mack Calvin (their star.) Because the Floridians were not expected to make the playoffs, their home court (the Miami Beach Convention Center) was booked. The game was moved to Miami-Dade Community College, where they played the top seeded Virginia Squires with, guess who – Dr. J. The place was jammed packed, and we were lucky to get in. Julius Erving and the Squires put on a show and pounded the Floridians. It was a real treat to get to see the Dr. operate.

The rest of the trip was kind of a blur. I think we spent about five nights there, and no doubt funds were running low. George, I'm sure, was not unhappy to see us go, but I give him a lot of credit for putting up with us. Of course, it was a long drive back to Kenmore, but certainly a memorable trip.

One of the really nice perks we had as UB basketball players were free tickets to the Buffalo Braves NBA basketball games at the Aud. By now, the Aud had been expanded (roof raised) to add several thousands of seats (the Orange section.) Paul Snyder, owner of the Braves and UB alumnus, would see to it a group of tickets was left at "will call" for us. The seats we had were in the "Gold" section – just above court level and close to the action. We saw many great teams and great players come in – but, to my delight, it was especially a thrill to see the L. A. Lakers team with Wilt Chamberlain, Jerry West, and Elgin Baylor. That team would win the 1971-72 NBA championship and, by the way, Pat Riley played on that team. Of course, Pat would go on to coach the "Show Time" Lakers with Magic Johnson and Kareem Abdul-Jabbar.

> SIDE NOTE: Unfortunately for us, the subway which now runs from the UB Main St campus directly to the Aud was only under construction at the time; would have been nice.

Meanwhile, we were only a month away from the end of the school year. One of those remaining weekends, I went down to visit Sue Ensminger at Alfred State College. We hung out and went to the Ratskeller. I think things were starting to fade for her and me.

As for a music reference – *Horse with No Name* by the group *America* was popular at the time. I also attended my first concert that Spring – Neil Young solo at the Aud. It was a packed house, so there were probably about 16,000 attendees. When the lights went down, the Bic lighters lit up, and the air was filled with that unmistakable odor. Neil put on a great show, and it inspired me to go to the student book store and buy the Crosby, Stills, Nash & Young album *Four Way Street*.

When Summer came, I was again a painter at UB. This time, I was strictly painting dorm rooms. My painting partner and I got quite the system going. We would go into a room – mask it off – then one of us would cut in while the other one rolled. We were quite efficient. On June 23rd, while painting in one of the dorms, it started raining cats & dogs and would not stop. It was the beginning of the iconic "flood of 1972." Buffalo took quite a hit, but it was nothing compared to the devastation on the southern tier of New York State. The flooding from Almond to Corning was of epic proportions. Human life and major property were lost. In Corning, water levels were up to the second floor of buildings on Market Street and other low lying areas. There were many millions of dollars in damage, and it took a very long time to recover. In Almond, a woman stepped off her back porch and was swept away by the raging waters.

Three days a week, before punching in at the paint shop, I had an early summer school class – Kinesiology. It was actually a pretty fun class, even though we were studying with the use of cadavers and dead cats. One of our projects was dissecting a dead cat to learn more about the muscular system. We paired up with a partner for this assignment, which was a weeklong project. To add a little fun to the exercise, my partner (I think he was a wrestler) and I decided to have a little fun with a pair of girls at an adjacent table. We got to the next class a little early equipped with a spool of thread. Before the girls got to class, we had tied thread around the paw of their cat and unrolled the thread over to our table – maybe 6 or 7 feet away. When the girls got down and ready to work on their cat, we gave the thread a little tug so as to make the paw give a little wave. The panicked screaming echoed through the lab, and we and the other classmates were hysterical laughing – our instructor, not so much.

Later that Summer, I was invited to be a counselor at Bob Kaufman's (Buffalo Brave – NBA All-Star) and NorbBaschnagel's (UB assistant basketball coach) basketball camp at the Kellogg-Clarke Estate on Lake Erie in Derby, NY. The days were filled with drills and coaching for the campers, but at the end of the day, there would be a scrimmage amongst the counselors – including Kaufman. Bob was a rugged 6'8" 235 lb. NBA All-Star power forward, and many times during these scrimmages, I would be matched up against him. Although I was no match for Kaufman, it was a great experience for me – including the bruises.

In the Fall, we were back to school, but this school year my roommates Bob Dickinson, Jim Tribble, Bob Vartanian, and I would be sharing a suite on campus at 811 Clement Hall. Clement Hall was located on the corner of Main St. and Bailey Ave. overlooking Grover Cleveland municipal golf course. It was much more convenient living on campus (compared to Allenhurst.) We didn't even have to leave the building to get to the dining hall. There was also much more opportunity for socializing.

Sometime early in the Fall, I had a bout with the flu. It was bad enough to land me in the campus infirmary for a few days. Because of my illness, I missed a number of classes and a week of basketball practices. When I did get back to basketball practice, it took me a while to get up to speed. As like every season, there was a turnover in the roster. Here is a summary of the UB Bulls 1972-73 team roster.

Bill Janicki	5'10" Jr guard via Erie Community College
Kenny Pope	5'10" Jr guard via Erie Community College
Otis Horne	6'3" So guard/forward – first year
Horace Brawley	6'3" Jr guard/forward via Nassau Community College
Rayfield Gauss	5'11" Jr guard via Oakfield (MI) Community College
Bob Dickinson	6'4" So guard Frosh star – Plainview LI, NY
Curt Blackmore	6'7" Sr center returning – Selkirk, NY
Jim Tribble	6'6" Sr forward returning – Cleveland, OH
Bob Vartanian	6'3" Sr C guard returning – Worchester, MA
Greg Laker	6'6" Sr forward returning – Kenmore, NY
Bill Stark	6'7" Sr center - last year off for studies
Al Delman	6'0" Sr guard – last year off for studies

With the nucleus of returners, and the addition of these other players, we were much stronger than the 1971-72 squad.

VARSITY BASKETBALL (16-8)
Coach: Ed Muto '50 3rd

L	71	Syracuse at ECC	83
L	70	at Illinois State	84
L	70	at Northern Illinois	89
L	55	at Northeastern	84
W	85	Georgia State	63

Gem City Classic

W	72	Lafayette	71
W	92	Gannon	87

W	64	at Fairleigh-Dickinson	50
W	73	Akron	71
W	86	Samford	81
W	72	at Cornell	69
W	98	Brown at ECC	87
L	77	Niagara at ECC	79
L	63	at Colgate	80
W	76	at SUNY/Albany	62
W	103	Stony Brook	63
L	64	at Maryland	93
W	67	Army (MA)	64
W	81	UT-Chattanooga	80
W	84	St. Francis (Pa.)	82
W	71	at LeMoyne (ot)	70
W	97	Oglethorpe	66
W	91	Rochester	90
L	84	Buffalo State (MA)	86

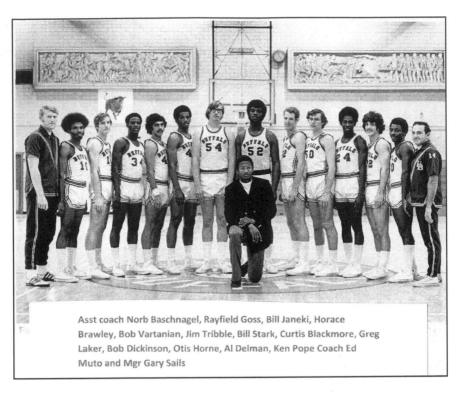

Asst coach Norb Baschnagel, Rayfield Goss, Bill Janeki, Horace Brawley, Bob Vartanian, Jim Tribble, Bill Stark, Curtis Blackmore, Greg Laker, Bob Dickinson, Otis Horne, Al Delman, Ken Pope Coach Ed Muto and Mgr Gary Sails

As mentioned earlier, living on campus in Clement Hall was much more convenient and enjoyable. It was nice to be able to go to the dining hall without even leaving the building (especially in the winter.) Clement was one of the twin tower dorms. The towers were joined by a common area including game rooms, a post office, and a huge dining hall. It wasn't long into the Fall when I started noticing a young co-ed who also lived in Clement. Some of the guys thought she resembled "Cher." Most of the time, my suite mates/teammates and I went to the dining hall as a group. The guys knew I liked this gal, and they were prodding me on to introduce myself. They thought she had a thing for me, too. For a couple of weeks, her group would pass my group in the corridors and exchange glances and smiles. It was kind of like the John Mayall lyric – "I was looking back to see if she was looking back to see if I was looking back at her."

Finally, I worked up the nerve to say hello and introduce myself to her. Fran Sichenze was an underclasswoman from Long, Island, NY. She was a sweet, unassuming gal, and we developed mutually fond feelings toward one another. Living in the same dorm made it quite easy to spend time together. Fran was a "down to earth" gal, and was very diligent about her school work and other responsibilities. We would do things like go to the library or to the movies or just hang out. She became good friends with my suite mates/teammates also. She and her group became great fans of Bulls basketball.

Our season opener was, again, against Syracuse, but this time on a neutral court at Erie Community College. This year, we made a better showing, but the Orange still prevailed 83-71. By the way, Jim Boeheim was still an assistant coach to Roy Danforth. Once again, I will try to hit only the highlights of the Bulls 1972-73 season, but for those interested in greater detail, they may refer to my Buffalo 1971-73 scrapbook.

It didn't help I was sick during the preseason, but in reality, I was facing much more competition for playing time on this much improved Bulls roster. Specifically, Horace Brawley was the other #3 forward, and he was a great player. Horace was a 6' 3" junior transfer from Nassau Community College, where he was a standout. He was very athletic and smart (basketball IQ.) He was quick, could jump, and he made our team better. Even though I always thought of myself as a "hustle" player, this inspired me to work even harder on the intangibles – scrapping, diving on the floor for loose balls, etc.

SIDE NOTE: During the summer of 1972, the Olympics were held in Munich, Germany. At that time, the USA men's basketball team was made up entirely of college players (no pros were eligible.) The USA men's basketball team had won 7 straight gold medals dating back to 1936 when the sport first began Olympic play. The Soviet team was made up of so called "soldiers" who had been playing together for years. The gold medal game pitted these two teams against each other. To make a long story short, the USA team came from double digits behind and, with the Soviets leading by one, USA guard, Doug Collins, was fouled hard while going to the basket with 3 seconds remaining in regulation. He missed the layup and was briefly knocked unconscious after crashing into the goal stanchion. A groggy Collins stepped to the line and calmly sank his first free throw. As he was attempting his second free throw, the buzzer at the scorer's table sounded. The second free throw went in and the USA led by one point. Meanwhile ,the Soviet coach was trying frantically to call a time out (which was against the rules in that situation, and worthy of a technical foul, which was not assessed.) Chaos ensued, and many irregularities worked against the USA team. The Soviets were given multiple chances in those final 3 seconds, and eventually connected on a full court pass for a layup to steal the game as time expired. Go to YOU TUBE and see for yourself how the Soviets were allowed to steal that game. The USA team, coached by Henry Iba, filed many protests, to no avail, and the USA team refused to accept their silver medals. By the way, Bill Walton declined to play on that team; they could have used him.

I offer this side note because, just a few months later, we traveled to Illinois State who featured Doug Collins, the 1972 Olympic star. Even though Curt Blackmore scored 27 points, ISU won 84 – 70. We also lost the next two games on the road to Northern

Illinois and Northeastern, so we were 0 – 4, a bad start, needless to say. Finally, we broke out of our skid with an 85 – 63 win over Georgia State at Clark Gym.

Leading up to the break, we traveled down I-90 to Erie, PA for the Gem City Holiday Tournament. The first night, we beat Lafayette in a close game 71 - 70. Then, in the finals, we beat host Gannon College in the final 92 – 87 to win the tournament. Little did I know in just a couple of years, I would be living and working in Erie.

Of course, I spent the Christmas break in Kenmore with the family and did the usual things – sleep, poker with the boys, pool at Bobby Cue, and a few trips to the Belmont YMCA.

Chapter Sixteen
1973

After the abbreviated Christmas break, we were again back at Clark Gym preparing for our next opponent – Farleigh Dickinson in Hackensack, NJ. Interestingly, another Kenmore native and Crosby Court regular, Mike Dyrek, played for FDU. Mike was a graduate of Cardinal O'Hara High School in Tonawanda, NY. We had no trouble with FDU, and we extended our win streak to four 64 – 50.

Back in Buffalo, our next game was versus a tough Akron team. Horace Brawley was now our leading scorer at 18.1 points per game ahead of Curt Blackmore's 14.5 PPG. We won that close game, 73 – 71, and our next vs Samford, 86 – 81. Because of an injury I suffered in practice before the Samford game, I had limited playing time. I strained my neck trying to leverage myself while attempting to guard my 260 lb. teammate, Curt Blackmore in the low post. Ouch!

Our following two games were against Ivy League teams – first vs the Cornell Red in Ithaca. That trip was memorable because we were treated like Royalty by the Cornell staff. Dressed in our red blazers, we were served a pregame steak dinner on china and linen with "real" silverware in one of their ivy covered castle like stone halls. We were waited on like dignitaries. To top it off, after dinner, we adjourned to an adjoining game room that featured a 9', turn of the century, Brunswick leather drop pocket pool table. By the time we had to head to the field house, there was no doubt who was the best pool player on the team. Cornell's field house was huge – similar to the one we played in at West Point the previous season – UB 72 – CU 69. Next was another Ivy League team – Brown. They came to Buffalo but, like many other opponents, declined to play us at Clark Gym. We played the game at Erie Community College. Bob Vartanian had a big night with 23 points, and we won 98 – 87. We were now on an eight game winning streak and playing with confidence.

Again, our next game was at ECC (for the same reason) vs the post "Calvin Murphy" Niagara Eagles. It was a hard fought and physical game. With 5:30 remaining, in a 2-point game, Niagara's Zeke Royster instigated a fight with Curt Blackmore. Both players were ejected. At that point, Curt had 16 points and 18 rebounds. We definitely missed Curt more than Niagara missed Royster… even Niagara's coach Frank Layden admitted that. With four seconds left, Niagara's Watson hit a jumper to make it 79 – 77 Niagara. Brawley got a jumper off from the top of the key that rattled in and out. Despite 29 points by Vartanian, it was a really painful loss.

Although I must take responsibility, looking back, I think I was a victim of poor counseling relating to my Physical Education major course planning. I should have been doing my student teaching in the second semester of my senior year, but because I lacked a certain required course (I think it was Physiology), I was ineligible to do so. At that point, of course, it was apparent I would not graduate. I was allowed to do a number of observations at some area schools (elementary and secondary), and assist in some instruction. As a result of my situation, I was in kind of a funk, wondering what I was going to do at the end of the school year with no diploma.

The basketball season went on. We lost to Colgate in Hamilton 80 – 63, then a win at SUNY Albany, 76 - 62. On Saturday, February 10th, Stony Brook came to Clark Gym and we blew them out, 103 – 63. We had little time to gloat, since we had to board a flight (in nasty weather), to Maryland Sunday morning for an afternoon game vs the 9th ranked Terrapins in front of 12,140 crazies. This year, they not only had their two All-Americans – Tom McMillan and Len Elmore, but a future All-American guard, John Lucas. All three would have NBA careers and, by the way, McMillan was on that 1972 Olympic team. After we jumped out to a 12 – 9 lead, it was all downhill – UM 93 – UB 64.

We got back to our winning ways with a win vs Army at the Aud, 67 -64, and then vs Tennessee-Chattanooga, 81 -80, at Clark Gym. Notably, there were three Buffalo Braves at Clark Gym that night – Dick Garrett, Bob McAdoo and Randy Smith. It must have inspired Curt Blackmore – he had a career high 37 points.

A few nights later, at Clark Gym, we defeated St. Francis, 84 – 82, at the buzzer; Curt Blackmore had 29 points and 23 rebounds. Lemoyne was the next casualty, 71 – 70, win in overtime and Oglethorpe, 97 – 66, both at Clark. Our last home game at Clark would come Saturday, March 4th vs the University of Rochester. Again, we would be facing my former Kenmore West High School teammate, Fran Moulin. It was a heated game, with a contentious finish in front of a packed house at Clark. Blackmore's offensive rebound and put back at the buzzer gave us the 91 – 90 win (our 6th in a row). At that point, we had high hopes we would be considered for an NIT (National Invitational Tournament) bid. We had one game remaining versus our cross town rival, Buffalo State, to be played at the Aud. Again, we would be facing one of my Kenmore West High School teammates – this time, my buddy Dave Casselman. It was another close game which came down to the wire, and Buffalo State played one of their best games to prevail 86 - 84. Cass had a career game with 24 points. The loss all but squashed any hope for a post season tournament bid for us. Despite it all though, we finished with 16 wins and 8 losses, which was one of UB'S best basketball seasons to date. Curt Blackmore finished his career as the school's all-time leading rebounder, and in the top 10 of scoring leaders. Blackmore became the first UB Bull to have his jersey hung in the rafters at the beautiful Alumni Arena. Bob Vartanian became UB's 10th leading scorer ,albeit in only two years as a JUCO transfer.

In summary of my college basketball career at UB, I reached my goal of playing at the highest level of competition I was capable of. Yes, my junior year I got more playing time, but in my senior year we were a much better team. The bottom line is I got to see and play against a lot of great teams and players while earning my way through two more years of college.

Back at Clement Hall, I was still seeing a lot of Fran Sichenze. She even made a couple of trips with me to visit with my parents and Wende in Kenmore.

When the basketball season was over, I had a lot more free time. A couple of things stick out to me from that Spring. I had a part time job umpiring intramural softball (a thankless job) and I threw my arm out playing catch with a baseball because I did not properly warm up. Since then, I have never really been able to throw hard overhand. One of the benefits of working out of the intramural department was access to the "Watts" line. It was a phone line which enabled toll free calls throughout the USA.

So, I would call my brother Jim in Hornell, or my buddy Dale Reed down in Commerce, TX just to chat.

> SIDE NOTE: When the Phoenix Suns came to town that Spring, I made a point of going to the game to see if Paul Stovall was still with the Suns. Remember, Paul was a JUCO All-American at Pratt Community College I played against when I was at Seward County CC. He later went on to Arizona State. Paul got a few minutes in that night against the Braves, and after the game, I tried to make contact with him to no avail. Paul Stovall was one of the best players I played against in my career, whether it was JUCO or NCAA Division I. It put in perspective, for me, just how elite the players in the NBA are.

In a show of poor judgment, on my part, I yielded to the temptation of seeing another gal who also lived in Clement Hall. Ava Warren was a freshman who lived down the hall from our suite. Clement Hall was a co-ed dorm, with guys and gals living on the same floors. When the word got back to Fran I was seeing Ava, she was, rightfully, upset and disappointed with me. Realizing my poor judgment, I pleaded, unsuccessfully, for Fran's forgiveness. She would, again deservingly of me, have nothing to do with me. I was crushed, because I thought the world of Fran. It was now approaching the end of the school year, and I continued to see Ava.

On May 7, 1973 the 64th annual "Block B" banquet was, again, held at the prestigious Hearthstone Manor to honor all of the UB varsity "Block B" letter winners. Again, a well-known ABC commentator was the key note speaker. This time, it was Jim McKay. You remember Jim McKay for his coverage of many Olympic Games – especially the 1972 Olympics in Munich which were marred not only by the fiasco of the gold medal men's basketball game stolen by the Soviets, but tragically the murder of 11 members of the Israeli Olympic team by Arab terrorists. McKay was also well-known for his coverage with the award winning *ABC's Wide World of Sports* that opened each week with: "The joy of victory…and the agony of defeat".

When the school year ended, I was in limbo as to what the future would hold for me. My brother Jim pulled some strings for me at A. L. Blades & Sons, Inc. and got me a job there working construction for the summer. I packed up my gear and found an apartment in Hornell, NY (15 Maple St.). By this time, I had sold the maroon 1964 Chevy Impala SS and was now rolling in a, low mileage, blue 1961 Dodge Dart with push button automatic transmission and a crumpled up left front quarter panel. My father bought that car from a neighbor widow on Warren Ave. ALB (A. L. Blades & Sons, Inc.) placed me on a road job which ran from Arkport to Canaseraga – NYS Rte 961F. The job was about a 6 or 7 mile stretch of two-lane highway which involved prep and blacktop resurfacing. Obviously I had zero experience at road construction, and it showed to my co-workers who were seasoned construction workers. The pay was good - $12 per hour was pretty good iron, at that time. It was hard work, though, and I did everything from digging ditches, flagging, and operating small equipment to working behind a blistering hot blacktop paving machine. Some of the weeks were long, and the overtime at $18 per hour, which was great. On the other hand, rain days made for short weeks and smaller pay checks.

I think I paid about $25 a week for my small, but adequate, apartment at 15 Maple St. Most of my groceries came from the nearby ACME grocery store where the Steuben Trust Company now stands. My dinners mostly consisted of Dinty Moore beef stew and such. I packed several sandwiches and a large thermos of water for eating on the job. Occasionally, I would treat myself to breakfast at the "Texas" café, or dinner at McDonalds, which was then on Seneca St. and Bennett. Conveniently, for me, right around the corner on Seneca St. was Abby Joseph's pool hall. Abby was probably in his 70's then, and his pool room there on Seneca St. was a down size from his infamous (much larger) up-stairs pool room on Broadway in Hornell. As I remember ,Abby's pool hall on Seneca St. included three 9' Brunswick Anniversary tables, a 9' AMF table, and a 10' three cushion billiard table. It was a "no frills" operation, and Abby didn't put up with any non-sense. I would sometimes go there in the evenings, or on a rain-day from work. It was never a problem finding a game there.

Back at 15 Maple St., I would amuse myself with my growing collection of 33 LP vinyl platters (McCartney's *Red Rose Speedway* was my newest album) on my new stereo, or watching something on my portable black & white TV. That summer, I watched a lot of NY Mets baseball. Rusty Staub was their slugger, and Yogi Berra was the team manager. The other ongoing TV coverage that summer was of the Watergate hearings. It was easy to get hooked on that historic drama.

On the weekends, there were a couple of night spots I would patronize – Down by the Station on Loder St. in Hornell and Harvey's in Almond. Both places attracted a young crowd, and they both often featured bands.

> SIDE NOTE: Some things from that Summer would resurface in my later years. The biggest irony was my eventual wife, Shelley, lived with her parents Fred & Ann Adams in the very same apartment at 15 Maple St. in the early 1950's while Fred and his father, Herbert, were building a home at 29 Chestnut St. in Canisteo – quite a coincidence. Then, one night at Harvey's, I struck up a

conversation with a guy who was wearing an East Texas State T-shirt. Bob Miller was a track star there, and of course he was acquainted with my old roommate/teammate from Seward County Community College, Dale Reed, who had played basketball at ETSU. If that was not a coincidence enough, years later, I would learn Bob was from Canisteo, and he graduated with Shelley – small world. Shelley and I sometimes look back at the summer of 1973 and wonder if we may have crossed paths, even though we did not meet until 1979.

While working on the Arkport/Canaseraga back road job, I met a couple of interesting guys. Bobby Griswald was a Hornell guy, and the son of the iconic Hornell YMCA director, Robert Griswald. Bobby and I would car pool to and from the job. He was going to dental school and this was his summer job. Bobby was a very bright guy and he did go on to his own dental practice. Dick Young was another laborer on the job with me. He was from Scio and went on to a career in the highway construction industry. Eventually, Dick succeeded his father, Jim, as the Highway Superintendent and DPW director for Allegany County, NY. Later, when I sold International trucks for ALB, I did some business with Dick and Allegany County.

My brother Jim's brother-in-law, Brad, and I became good friends. We had family in common and we both liked to play pool, among other things. I had been in phone contact with Ava a couple of times since school was out, and she wanted me to come down to NYC for a visit, so Brad and I headed out on a road trip in the '61 Dodge Dart down to the "Big Apple." As I remember, Ava actually lived in Queens, and I don't think her mother was in favor of her seeing me, so I think it was on the sly. Brad and I took in a few NYC sights and I got to see a little of Ava, but when it was time to head back to Hornell, I was sure there was no future in a relationship between Ava and me.

Elden Miles (one of many Miles' who worked for ALB) was the superintendent for the Arkport/Canaseraga back road job and he was a little on the "snarly" side (at least to me.) He knew I was not cut out to be a career construction worker, and he would rag me hard for any little blunder I might make.

"You better go back to college," he would taunt me.

Of course, I knew I wanted/needed to go back to finish up my BS degree – but where? I remained in contact (still do) with Virgil Akins, my basketball coach at SCCC. Through his connections with head basketball coach, Bob Johnson, at Pittsburg State College (Kansas), Virgil was able to pave the way for me to become an undergraduate assistant basketball coach there. It was a sweet deal which included room, board, books, and tuition. However, there were more summer of ''73 events to report on before I packed up and headed back out to Kansas.

On July 23rd, my father was encouraged by Exxon to retire. He was 50 years old and had been with the company for 27 years. Although he got a decent severance from Exxon, his working days were not over, and he soon was in the job search mode.

My brother Jim and his wife, Barb, owned a small, self- contained, camping trailer suitable for 4 people and easily towed behind an International Travel-All (one of the early SUVs). On Saturday July 28th Jim, Barb, Brad, and I headed to Watkins Glen for the "Summer Jam." The "Summer Jam" was a highly anticipated two-day music festival featuring The Band, The Grateful Dead, and The Allman Brother's Band. When we got to Watkins Glen, the traffic was backed up for miles (a la Woodstock.) We inched along in bumper to bumper traffic to finally find a place to park the camper. By that time, festival goers were trampling down the surrounding fence – it was a hippie free for all. There was so much action, music, and partying – similar to what you've seen in documentaries of Woodstock. There were more than six hundred thousand people, and it was awesome to see and hear these iconic bands. Although these three bands were in the earlier stages of their careers, they all went on to stand the test of time. Since it was never checked or collected, I still have my full, unblemished $10 "Ticketron" ticket from the event.

The camping trailer would be called back into action in August. I can't quite remember how it all unfolded but Dad, Jim, and I decided to go on a camping trip to Darien Lake. We hadn't done anything like that in a long time (if ever.) We were semi roughing it, cooking on a camp fire and doing some good fathersons bonding. It's a good memory, but Jim and I didn't realize, at the time, how little time Dad had left.

Summer Jam - Grateful Dead, The Band & The Allman Brothers

Soon after, it was time to pack up all of my worldly possessions in the '61 Dodge Dart and head for Pittsburg, Kansas. Pittsburg, Kansas is located in the southeast corner of the state, approximately 400 miles straight east of Liberal (Seward County Community College.) I did the 1,000+ mile trip from Hornell to Pittsburg in three legs. When I arrived there in late August, I was surprised to see how green the area was – unlike the stark western Kansas terrain. The campus, of course, was much smaller than the University of Buffalo, but it was big enough. The enrollment then was about 7,000 students, and the population of Pittsburg was about 15,000 – so, the school was obviously a huge part of the college town. My room assignment was 517 Dellinger Hall, a graduate student dorm. The room was good sized with a view, and it easily accommodated all of my stuff. Remember, no cell phones or even a land line. (How did we ever survive?) As I was moving in, a guy pulled up to my car on his 10 speed bike and offered to give me a hand. He talked like a hippie and was built like an athlete. As it turns out, Tom Gordon was a graduate student from South Bend, Indiana, and a former football player. We became good friends from the start. Much of my fall course load was made up of electives, and I was able to establish a minor in Recreation. The athletic complex was beautiful. Built in 1971, the John Lance Arena included an indoor track, indoor archery range, aquatics center, wrestling gym, and tartan surface basketball court along with a state of the art weight room, training room, classrooms, and offices. All way better than the old Clark Gym at UB.

Since I was working construction all summer in Hornell, there was little time for basketball. It was the least summer basketball I had played in 7 years. I was out of basketball shape, and I needed to get back in the mode. Coach Robert Johnson welcomed me to the team warmly. He was well aware of my reputation in the junior college ranks in the state of Kansas. Eric Guenther was the graduate assistant coach. I had competed against Eric a few years back, when he played at Hutchinson Community College. The Pittsburg "Gorillas" basketball team was coming off a successful season, and had a solid nucleus returning. Coach Johnson had me running drills with the big men, among other things. These players didn't know me, so it was important I establish credibility with them. After participating in drills with them, I soon earned their respect. Pittsburg State College (PSC) sports teams participated in the NAIA, and they competed against schools from Kansas and Missouri in District 10. Socially, I was welcomed into the basketball players circle. After all, I was only slightly older than these guys. That was sometimes good, but sometimes not. There were no strict team training rules, so the guys would sometimes be found drinking beer at the off campus pubs and bars on the weekends. The beer of choice, in those days, was by far Coors Banquet. Coors Light did not yet exist, and Coors Banquet could be found only west of the Mississippi, back then. Football was huge at PSC, and there was great student body support. Most of the home games were on Friday nights under the lights. Invariably, there were after game house parties, which were a lot of fun, and a great place to meet people. These types of parties were not prevalent at either SCCC or UB.

Streaking was all the craze in 1973, and PSC had its fair share of streakers. You never knew when you might encounter a streaker being chased by campus security. One of our friends was a DJ at KSEK radio, so, one night, while he was on the air, a few of us streaked the studio. We were dying laughing. PSC sponsored many concerts in their performing arts center. I saw a few really good rock bands there and at a couple of local road houses. I also have a fuzzy recollection of a "purple passion" party. The party was out in the middle of nowhere, and party goers brought their own bottle of whatever to pour into an, on-site bath tub laden with grape kool-aid. There was 8 trac music emanating from the speakers of an automobile stereo System, and you could dip your plastic cup into the tub when you got thirsty. Mostly people crashed in their cars, and there were some hurtin' units when the sun came up.

Of course there was a pool hall in downtown Pittsburg. It was old school, with a barber chair, shoe shine, and cigar humidor. The tables were old but nice. Bob Williams, from nearby Parsons, Kansas, was a 6'7" forward for the Gorillas and he and I became buddies. I regularly schooled Bob on the finer points of 9 ball.

Somehow, I was invited to gatherings of a group of skydivers. They were a friendly bunch and going up in an airplane was not the only way they liked to get high. They invited me several times to go skydiving with them, but somehow I couldn't get past the fact they would be the ones packing my parachute.

During a Fall intramural touch football game, I was wearing a half worn out, UB basketball practice T shirt. There was a guy from New Hampshire on the opposing team, who was so enthralled with the T shirt, he had to have it. Negotiations ensued, and when it was over he had the T shirt, and I owned the double "Fillmore East" album by the Allman Brothers Band.

In October, I followed as Yogi Berra's NY Mets made an amazing late season pennant drive, beating the "Big Red Machine," Cincinnati Reds, before bowing to the Oakland A's 4 games to 3 in the World Series.

My "hippie" buddy Tom Gordon and I went on a few road trips in his 1950 something white Chevy panel truck named "Casper." One Saturday, he lined us up with a couple of gals who wanted to tour down to the University of Arkansas at Fayetteville. It was an all-day cruise and I was totally underwhelmed by the campus and the gals.

In one of my weaker moments, I agreed with Tom we should hop a freight train. (I must have been telling him some Bob Knight stories.) We ended up on a north bound train and it did not stop, or even slow down, until we reached Kansas City – 125 miles later. We had no luck catching a south bound train back to Pittsburg, and ended up spending the night in the ball room of a Hilton Hotel we snuck in to. The next morning, we hitchhiked back to Pittsburg. That was the end of my train hopping days.

Tom wanted me to go home with him to South Bend, Indiana for Thanksgiving break. We caught a ride with a group of students headed to Chicago. There were six of us in an old Ford station wagon. As we got further north, the weather got nasty and we went the last couple of hundred miles through a snow storm. Tom's father intercepted us somewhere around Gary, Indiana and took us to the Gordon's home in South Bend. Tom's parents, brothers, and Tom were all huge Notre Dame fans, and they had a block of four season tickets for football. The Gordon's hospitality was exceptional, including a lovely Thanksgiving dinner. They insisted I use one of the tickets for Saturday's game vs Air Force. On game day, they took me on campus to experience all of the pre-game pomp and circumstance. It was a crisp, clear day with blue skies – perfect for football. The most memorable part, for me, was watching and listening to the bagpipe marching band as they marched a certain route around campus and finally into the stadium. It was one of those spine tingling experiences. The team was led by legendary coach, Ara Parseghion, and they had no trouble handling Air Force. Little did I know, at the time, that the great ND football team would go on to complete an 11-0 season beating, none other than, Bear Bryant's Alabama Crimson Tide in the Sugar Bowl 24-23 for the National championship. My trip to South Bend could not have been cooler.

When the Pittsburg State College Gorilla basketball season began, I was in the unfamiliar role of being a bench coach. Since Eric and I were Coach Johnson's only assistants, he would actually welcome our observations and input. We were two more experienced pairs of eyes and ears, and it made me (us) feel like a significant part of the team. Since I don't have a scrap book, per say, for the 1973-74 PSC Gorilla basketball season, I am without a reference to add much detail. I can tell you about the nucleus of the team. My friend (junior) Bob Williams was our big man at 6'7" and leading rebounder; 6'4" Calvin Kinzer (junior) from Nashville was our leading scorer, and Barry Williamson (senior) from right there in Pittsburg was our 5'10" floor general. The other pieces were interchangeable, but these three were constants.

> SIDE NOTE: Calvin Kinzer was a smooth player and a smooth man. He drove a maroon 1950 Buick Special. It looked and sounded beautiful. I can still hear the sounds of *Marvin Gaye* music coming from his 8 track stereo. Every time I saw that car, I thought of Bob Knight's father Bill, who always drove one of those cool Buicks from that era.

Academically, I really worked hard. On my dorm room wall, I posted a sign that said "Get your ass out of bed!" It reminded me each morning why I was there. The hard work paid off. When report cards came out for the first semester, I had a 3.4 GPA, my best college semester to date.

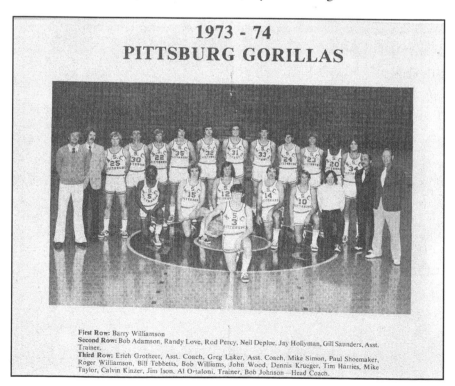

1973 - 74
PITTSBURG GORILLAS

First Row: Barry Williamson
Second Row: Bob Adamson, Randy Love, Rod Percy, Neil Deplue, Jay Hollyman, Gill Saunders, Asst. Trainer.
Third Row: Erich Grotheer, Asst. Coach, Greg Laker, Asst. Coach, Mike Simon, Paul Shoemaker, Roger Williamson, Biff Tebbetts, Bob Williams, John Wood, Dennis Krueger, Tim Harries, Mike Taylor, Calvin Kinzer, Jim Ison, Al Ortaloni, Trainer, Bob Johnson—Head Coach.

It was impractical for me to go home for Christmas this year, so I stayed on campus at 517 Dellinger. I pretty much had the place to myself, save for the couple who served as RAs, and a few others. There was a skeleton staff on campus including some cafeteria workers and maintenance people. Of course the basketball team came back early to practice, so it wasn't that long of a break for me.

Chapter Seventeen
1974

On Wednesday, January 16th, I reported to my student teaching assignment in Columbus, Kansas. I started at the elementary level (Physical Education.) I recall walking into a room with first graders doing gymnastics. My sponsor for elementary PE was Bobby Waggoner. He was probably in his late 20's and stood about 5'4". We hit it off immediately. He could not have been a more helpful and considerate mentor. For the first few weeks, I tried to make the 20+ mile commute from Pittsburg to Columbus. Finally, I was able to make a deal for an upstairs "no frills" studio apartment at 416 Kansas Ave. in Columbus. It was something like $25 per week, and I still had my room back on campus where I spent most weekends and nights when I had student teaching meetings and such. Bobby Waggoner was so generous to me – he would often invite me for lunch at his house where his wife, Donna, was looking after their young daughter Angie.

Since I have unearthed my diary from 1974, I may have the benefit of drawing from events of that year in a little more detail. Hopefully it won't sound too much like the bullet points format I used in that diary.

It wasn't long before Bobby recruited me to play on a men's traveling basketball team he was a part of. Somehow, they were sponsored by corporate Walmart. It was a great group of guys (older than me) with ample big men, which allowed me to play at my comfort position of small forward. They traveled a couple of nights a week, so I had a juggling act between that, coaching, and my student teaching prep responsibilities. We traveled to cities in Kansas, Oklahoma, and Missouri to play in tournaments. It was a tough brand of basketball and we were very good. Bobby was our "Mugssy Bogues" at the point... he could play. Next to the UB Bulls team, I played on, this Walmart team came next. When all the smoke settled at the end of the season, we were 35-1.

On the side, I was doing some reffing for men's and kid's basketball... $10 per game. There were a few more expenses that semester, and I am reminded from my diary my father procured a $2,000 loan for me at the Bank of Buffalo... on his signature alone. My sister Amy also loaned me $200. The only other loan I had throughout my college career was a $1,500 National defense loan back at SCCC. (Later, I would have my graduate work at Alfred University paid for while working as a graduate assistant basketball coach under Ron Frederes in the 1982-83 season.)

Walmart Team 1974

With Bobby Waggoner as my mentor, I got to teach K-6, including units which ranged from gymnastics to square dancing. Bobby was very engaged with his students, and they loved him. He was well respected by his peers, and I really felt fortunate he took me under his wing. Bobby introduced me to the close knit group of faculty. Eventually, I was welcomed into that circle and invited to dinners, parties, and other events outside of school hours. All and all, I don't think my elementary student teaching experience could have been better or more enjoyable.

Sometime in early spring, my father was offered a position in Erie, Pennsylvania. He would become the Manager of United Oil Refining there – a job which fit his resume perfectly. Erie, of course, is a port city on Lake Erie – one of the Great Lakes. Oil would come into Erie on huge tanker ships, pumped into mega oil tanks, and from there distributed by truck and trailer transports. Oil would also arrive in Erie via train. The Erie operation of United was huge, and it came with a lot of responsibility for the new manager. Soon after Dad took the new position, they were able to find a house there at 218 Maryland Ave. The house was a Cape Cod and was located just a stone's throw from the elite homes on South Shore drive overlooking the Erie Bay. Now, Mother had her dream home, and Dad had his dream job. We (the family) were extremely happy for them.

Because of my student teaching responsibilities and the logistics involved, I could not be on campus for every basketball practice, or be available for some road trips. That was just the way it was. It was now time for me to move up to the Columbus High School, where I would student teach secondary PE. Unlike my elementary PE experience, my stint at the high school was just OK. My mentor, Francis Siebuhr, was 55-ish, and biding his time until retirement. He was a nice enough guy, but he was the type to just roll out the balls for gym class. He wasn't big on discipline, and tended to look the other way when trouble was brewing with disobedient students. It made things tough as a young student teacher looking for direction on how to deal with such situations.

Meanwhile, at student teacher meetings with our advisor, we were busy preparing credentials and personal data sheets (resumes.) The placement office made us aware of job vacancies in our respective educational fields and we would follow up with applications, accordingly.

SIDE NOTE: On Friday March 8th I was invited by, a friend, Roger Allen, to do color commentary on radio for a high school basketball game. Roger was a DJ and a sports broadcaster for KSEK (yes, he was the same DJ my friends and I had streaked earlier.) The game was a 2A playoff game between Baldwin and Frontenac on a neutral floor – Chanute. Roger was able to tap into my vast basketball knowledge. It was a fun experience, but much more difficult and nerve wracking than I expected.

PERSONAL DATA SHEET

NAME: Mr. Gregory G. Laker   DATE: January 28, 1975

PERMANENT ADDRESS: 218 Maryland Ave., Erie, Pa. 16505

PHONE: (814) 459-6633

MAJOR: Physical Education   MINOR: Health Education

DEGREE: B.S. in Education   GRADUATION DATE: May 18, 1974

SUBJECTS PREPARED TO TEACH: Elementary and Secondary Physical Edu-
                           cation and Health Education

EMPLOYMENT: Substitute teacher, Erie School Dist., Erie, Pa., 1974-75
            Service station attend., United Oil, Erie, Pa., summer 74
            Construction worker, A.L. Blades, Hornell, N.Y., summer 73

HONORS AND OFFICES:

            Basketball Scholarship to Seward County Jr. College
                 Co-captain two years
                 Jayhawk Conference All-star 1969-70
                 Jayhawk Conference All-star 1970-71 (unanimus)
                 Region VI All-star 1970-71
            N.C.A.A. Basketball Scholarship to the University of
            Buffalo, New York
            Assistant Basketball Coach at Kansas State College of
            Pittsburg 1973-74

EXTRA-CURRICULAR ACTIVITIES CAN DIRECT:

            Basketball, Baseball, Intramurals, Letter Club

PRESENT INTRESTS: Sports, Music

STUDENT TEACHING:

            Unified School District 493 Columbus, Ks., Spring 1974
            Elementary and Secondary Health and Physical Education
            Cooperating Teachers: Robert Waggoner and Francis Siebuhr

My credentials are on file in the Career Planning and Placement
     Service, Kansas State College, Pittsburg, Ks. 66762

My buddy, and former roommate/teammate and co-captain back at SCCC, Dale Reed was now a married man with his first daughter, Andi. His first wife, Chris, was a Liberal, KS gal he met when we were in school there. Dale was now teaching and coaching in a small Kansas community, Kinsley, and I was overdue to visit them. It was Thursday, April 11, leading up to Easter Sunday. I left Columbus early AM and made the 250+ mile trip to Kinsley. Among the items I had noted in my diary for the visit were that: we ate catfish, I helped Dale organize his Kinsley basketball equipment, he sold me $10 worth of used tires, and I kicked his ass playing one on one! The Reeds lived in a basement apartment complete with kitchenette and all of the necessities. While at Dale's, we called our old SCCC coach, Virgil Akins, and he encouraged me to extend my trip out to Liberal to see the new campus. By the way, just as a point of interest, there were gas wars going on, and there were lines at the pump to buy gas for as low as 46 cents per gallon. So, on Easter Sunday, I continued on to Liberal. The new campus was freshly built and beautiful. (It would have been so nice to have been able to enjoy it). Dale Doll gave me the tour. Dale was another of a long line of players to come to SCCC from Little River. I had first met Dale Doll when I visited Little River with Dale Reed on spring break 1970. Noteworthy enough, Dale Doll and his wife Tammy spent their professional careers at SCCC. It was great seeing the new campus (the fruit of our efforts) and, of course, Coach and Mrs. (Denise) Akins. Also, just finishing up his freshman year at SCCC was Tim Whitcomb from Cattaraugus, NY. While I was at UB, I went to the Aud to watch NYS Section VI high school playoffs. Tim impressed me as a player, and I subsequently arranged to go to the Whitcomb's home in Cattaraugus to meet with Tim and his parents. Ultimately, I sold Tim and his parents on the idea of going to play basketball for Coach Akins at SCCC.

It was a long trip back to Columbus after Easter. The whole round trip, according to my diary, was 833 miles at 15.6 miles per gallon. It was a memorable road trip, and well worth the time and money spent.

Jeff Helland was Bob Williams' roommate at PSC, and we also became good friends. Jeff invited me to come home with him to Overland Park (suburb of Kansas City) for a weekend. The Hellands lived in an upscale part of Overland Park and, again, I was treated like a special guest. I can remember playing a round of golf at the OP Country Club with Jeff and his father, then returning to the Helland's house for a steak BBQ. Later that night, Jeff and a buddy of his took me out for the evening to an area called River Keys. That was Saturday night. Sunday, April 28th, we went to a KC Royals baseball game vs the Red Sox at the almost brand new, Kauffman Stadium. The stadium was "state of the art" gorgeous – water fountains and beautiful landscaping; clean as a whistle. The game went 13 innings, with the Red Sox prevailing 5 -4. It was a long ride back to Pittsburg for Jeff, and Columbus for me, but another fun road trip.

May 10th was my last day of student teaching. All of my requirements for my BS degree were now fulfilled, but I was not going to stick around for the cap and gown ceremony. The last couple of weeks in Columbus were filled with invitations to dinners, picnics, and other social events from teachers and their families who had been so hospitable to me. I was servicing up the '61 Dodge Dart – making sure I had good enough tires to make it all the way back to Kenmore. After saying all of my goodbyes, I hit the road Tuesday, May 14th and made it as far as Indianapolis – about 600 miles. On Wednesday, I made it to Erie, PA and stayed two nights with my sister, Amy, and the Labie family. The Labie kids (my nieces and nephew) were growing right up. Caryn was 8 now, and the twins, Chris and Susan, were 2 ½ . Thursday night, Amy and Jerry took me to the theater to see the highly acclaimed movie *The Exorcist* starring Linda Blair. That was a scary movie! On Friday, I paid Amy back $100 of the $200 she had loaned me earlier, said my goodbyes, and made the final 95 mile leg of my trip back to Kenmore.

Notable Ticket stubs

Notre Dame vs. Air Force

My buddy, Dave Casselman, and I had been corresponding while I was out in Pittsburg. He now had a year of teaching elementary school in the Ken-Ton School District. Dave was the first friend I saw when I got home. We went to see the movie *The Sting* with Paul Newman and Robert Redford (one of my all-time favorite movies) and then out for some beers.

Even though my parents had made a deal on the house in Erie, it would still be a couple of months before the actual move. Dad was working in Erie, and commuting back to Kenmore on the weekends. There was a lot of preparation to be made leading up to the move.

I was spending a lot of time chasing down and filling out applications for Physical Education/basketball coaching openings around western NY and the southern tier. Ironically, I even applied for an opening at Canisteo, where I would eventually call home. There was an opening at Al Dectabrons for a sporting goods salesman, which I also applied for and got an interview. It was an extremely competitive market for PE teachers, at the time. In many instances, there were up to 50 applicants for PE teaching positions. The timing was working against me.

On the social side, I was going to some Kenmore West HS sporting events, visiting friends, playing basketball (at the Crosby courts), playing pool at Bobby Cue, and sometimes, at night, patronizing some of our favorite watering holes with the boys – The Locker Room, Cole's, The Masthead, etc.

On Thursday May 30th, I helped Bob Clark (Bobby Cue) move a 9' tournament pool table from his pool room to the Kenmore East HS gym to be set up for an exhibition the next day. That Friday, I took Cass, Gary Witter, and my younger sister, Wende, to see the exhibition put on by Steve "the Miz" Mizerak and Irving Crane – two of the greatest champions ever. The Miz got the best of Crane in their 9 ball match, but Crane turned the table in the straight pool match with a 100+ ball run. They did not disappoint.

Earlier in the week, Dad invited me to ride with him from Kenmore down to Warren, PA – the Corporate home of United Oil Refining and their major distribution center. The purpose of the trip was sort of an orientation for my father. He got to meet some of the top brass for the first time face-to-face and do all of the necessary paper work. Warren was about 110 miles south of Buffalo, so my father and I had plenty of time to visit. It was clear he was excited about and proud of his new position.

Although much of my weekly activities included pool, basketball, poker, and beer drinking – I was also helping my mother get organized for the move, including a yard sale of sorts. I was also mowing the lawn and keeping up with the swimming pool, not to mention making out job applications. For each job application, I had to get PSC involved with sending out my credentials (at a price.) It was time consuming and frustrating when you hit a brick wall.

Steve Witter (Gary and Greg's father) also made a career move that summer, which necessitated him and his wife, Yvonne, to relocate to the Binghamton, NY area. They bought a split level house on a hillside in Vestal (a Binghamton suburb.) When it came time for Gary and Greg to go down for a visit, they invited Cass and me to go with them. We made a pit stop in Geneseo, on our way down to Vestal, to see one of Gary's local buddies,Leo. Gary had just finished up his junior year at SUNY Geneseo, and Greg was in the class of 1973 there. When we arrived in Vestal, Mr. & Mrs. Witter spoiled us with a steak BBQ. Later that night, we found a couple of watering holes which catered to the younger crowd – Thirsty's and The Other Place. Both places were wall-to-wall with people our age, but we must not have hurt ourselves too bad, because we were able to play pickup basketball the next day at Harper College, and then return to Thirsty's that night.

SIDE NOTE: Knowing how crazy I was about pool, in late June, my parents decided to buy me a pool table as a graduation gift. In part, I think it may have been as an incentive for me to move to Erie with them. Anyway, they gave me a budget of $300 and turned me loose to see what I could find. I scoured the classified ads in both the Buffalo Evening News and the Courier Express – nothing. Finally, Bob Clark (Bobby Cue) heard news of a pool room in downtown Buffalo which was going out of business. Bob accompanied me downtown to Gerrand's, an upstairs pool room, to check it out. By now, all of the tables had been disassembled with the slates leaning up against the walls, and various other parts and accessories loaded in cardboard boxes. Bob took inventory, and determined, in his opinion, the best table was #10. Gerrand's #10 was a 9' Brunswick Anniversary Model produced in 1945, marking 100 years of Brunswick pool tables. I made a deal with the owner for $300, and gave him a deposit of $15 to hold the table until the next day when I would return with the balance. The next day, I returned with the cash and some muscle to help me move the disassembled table. 9' tables are made up of three, one inch thick slates which weighed about 250 lbs. each. Those slates, plus the heavy duty chassis which they attached to, and the other various components added up to a significant amount of weight. Not only are the slates heavy, but they are very fragile and awkward to move – especially when it involves stairs It's a two, three, or sometimes four man job to, carefully, move each slate up or down stairs. We, carefully, loaded the pool table parts into a pickup truck and moved them to the living room of 115 Warren Ave. where they would await the move to Erie a couple of weeks later. Over that period of time, I cleaned up the table components the best I could. I hired Bob Clark to replace and recover the cushions. He was aware of my master plan to set up the table in the basement of 218 Maryland Ave. in Erie. Bob was a very talented pool table mechanic and he turned around the cushion/rail job in one day. With that done, it was just a matter of waiting for moving day. I couldn't wait!

On Tuesday, July 9th, the moving company came to pack up the household at 115 Warren. It took them two days to pack. On Thursday, they loaded the moving van and drove to Erie. We all drove to Erie that night, as well, and stayed with the Labies. On Friday, they moved everything in (under my mother's supervision.) Luckily for me, it was the responsibility of the movers to maneuver the pool table components (especially the slates) down the tight basement stairs. The basement at 218 Maryland was large and divided into two rooms. One room was finished in knotty pine and included a wet bar. The other side was unfinished, but a great spot for the pool table.

While all of this Erie, PA moving business was going on, my brother Jim and his wife Barb were settling into a house they had bought on Freiner Hill Rd. just outside of Canaseraga, NY. The acreage included a large old country house, a barn, and a large pond. Barb was a horse lover so it was a great setting for that. Another rare feature of the house was an indoor swimming pool. It was a great place for Barb and Jim to entertain their many guests.

When the Erie move was complete, I spent time helping my mother get organized in the new house. There were two upstairs bedrooms, one for my almost 14-year-+old sister Wende, and one for me (now 23.) My room had some nice built-ins, with space for my extra-long queen bed, and a sitting area with a window overlooking Maryland Ave. I spent a lot of my leisure time there listening, mostly with head phones, to my 33LPs and cassettes on my growing stereo system. There was an FM station just across Lake Erie in London, Ontario I discovered which played good rock music. There was no cable, only a small antenna. Late at night, I could sometimes pick up old reruns of Groucho Marx's *You Bet Your Life*, or the crazy *Dr. Demento Show*.

Of course I was anxious to get my pool table set up. The idea was for me to do as much preparation for Bob Clark before he came to Erie to finish the job. I spent days doing as much prep as I could. I even walked the slates across the floor and leveraged them into place on the chassis frame.

Meanwhile, I was back and forth from Erie to Kenmore and Canaseraga/Hornell several times. On one of my trips to Kenmore, Gary Witter and I road with Cass out to Tom Basher's in West Seneca for a poker game. Remember, we (Kenmore West) spanked Tom's West Seneca basketball team in the quarter finals of the 1969 NYS Section VI AAA playoffs. Now, Tom and Gary had become good friends as teammates at SUNY Geneseo. Tom had a man cave set up in the loft of the barn of the Basher family homestead. It was a great place for a poker game. The game went late that night, and we were all weary. On our way back to Kenmore on I-190, we were pulled over by the NYS Troopers. They were suspicious we were doing 45 mph in a 55 mph zone. They separated the three of us for questioning while they thoroughly searched Cass' car. After being detained for about 20 minutes, they let us go on our way. That night, I stayed with Cass in his penthouse at 108 Argonne.

The very next day was a big one. I was scheduled to pick up Bob Clark and take him to Erie to finish up work on my pool table. When we got to Erie, Bob went straight to work – always with a Camel cigarette dangling from his lips, with ashes falling where they may. Bob worked diligently for about 8 hours – leveling, stretching out the new green cloth, assembling the rails, etc. He barely took time to wolf down sandwiches and soft drinks my mother had prepared. I was strictly Bob's gofer – handing him tools while he was "standing on his head" putting things together. It was a difficult job, and I was paying close attention. Little did I know then, I would duplicate this task five more times in the years to come. When the job was done, Bob left me with a handful of house sticks he had put new tips on. It had already been a long day, but I still needed to return Bob 95 miles to Kenmore, and return to Erie myself in order to be ready to start work at the United Oil warehouse the next morning. It was a long first day at the warehouse, unloading a tractor-trailer of cases and 55 gallon drums of motor oil, but I knew at the end of the day I could go home and shoot a few racks on my pool table.

Although I was still busy chasing down Physical Education job opportunities (including the Erie City School District), Dad had paved the way for me to work for United Oil. Keystone gas stations were under the umbrella of United Oil, so I could just about name my hours pumping gas. As I mentioned above, I also worked at the warehouse, loading and unloading motor oil by the case or 55 gallon drum for distribution to local Keystone gas stations. The hardest (and highest paying) job, though, was unloading oil tanker rail cars. It was a big responsibility and you never knew what time of the day or night you might be called.

During those early days in Erie, Cass and Gary Witter (LW) would come to visit and I would go back to Kenmore for visits. When they came to Erie, we would ride bikes or cruise around the area. Being adjacent to mansions lined up on South Shore Drive, there were many cool sights to be seen. One of the greatest spots in Erie, during the Summer, is Presque Isle State Park. Presque Isle is actually a peninsula which protrudes into Lake Erie from the west end of the city, in a semi-circle, to downtown forming the Erie Bay. The peninsula stretches about 7 miles, and the north side (facing Lake Erie) is lined with beaches – one after another. Some of the beaches are more family-friendly, and some are more suited for young adults. It's a great place to bike, cruise, and beach it. Two of the bars I remember taking the boys to were Fat Daddy's and 3Ds. On one occasion, while hiking with Cass, we stumbled upon a very old, overgrown fort overlooking the bay – that was quite the exploring adventure.

GERRANDS # 10

THIS 1945 BRUNSWICK "ANNIVERARY" MODEL POOL TABLE MARKS 100 YEARS OF BILLIARD TABLE PRODUCTION BY BRUNSWICK. THE TABLE WAS PURCHASED IN 1974, BY JAMES L. & AMY LAKER, AS A COLLEGE GRADUATION GIFT FOR THEIR SON GREG.

THE TABLE WAS ORIGINALLY IN GERRANDS POOL ROOM IN BUFFALO, NY WHERE IT WAS PLAYED ON BY THE LIKES OF LEGENDARY POOL PLAYER WILLIE MOSCONI

Late that Summer, Joe Notaro (Kenmore East – Crosby Court buddy), invited Cass, LW, Jack Kolbas, Mike Vaccaro, and I to his parent's cabin adjacent to Allegheny State Park. We were all arriving from different directions, and I was rolling in the 1967

gray Ford Fairlane. By now, my mother was in a nice fat 1972 Ford LTD, and Dad was in a new company car. Anyway, without the assistance of a GPS, we were all able to converge on the cabin in the dark of Friday the 13th of September for a weekend get together. Mass quantities of beer were consumed, and Joe was becoming concerned the excessive pissing in the side yard would cause swamping conditions, which would be telltale evidence to his father there had been a dreaded beer blast. We could not stop roaring with laughter at Joe's premise.

In September, I started getting calls from the Erie City School District to substitute teach. The subbing assignments were mostly elementary PE (which I liked), but also high school PE and classroom assignments all around the City. On average, I subbed twice a week up until 11/25 when the teachers went on strike. Aside from subbing, I was an assistant manager at a Keystone Station on Buffalo Road, way out on the East side of town. So, between subbing and Keystone, I was pretty much working 5 – 6 days a week. That Fall, Jerry Labie was transferred from Erie to Detroit (still with IBM.) This would be just the beginning of many moves the Labies would make with Jerry's work. According to my diary, the Labies bought a house in West Bloomfield (suburban Detroit) on 10/3, and actually sold their home in Erie the following week on 10/10. Of course, the tough part of the move was we had just moved to Erie, and the Labies were already leaving. In the big scheme of things, however, we all realized moves like this were just a product of Jerry's movement up the corporate ladder. By the way, Jerry's brother Eddie still lived in Erie. He was about the same age as me, and we would sometimes hang out. To me, Eddie (RIP) bore a close physical resemblance to Frank Zappa.

SIDE NOTE: We were all still huge Buffalo Bills fans. As I mentioned in earlier chapters, my father was a season ticket holder dating back to the old Rock Pile. In Erie, however, most pro football fans were either for the Cleveland Browns or the Pittsburgh Steelers – so the Bills were rarely on TV in Erie. My father would go to great lengths to see his beloved Bills on TV – like drive up the NYS Thruway to Westfield, NY and rent a motel room for a Sunday afternoon to be within range of the Buffalo broadcast. He would sometimes turn the TV audio down and tune the radio to WBEN so as to listen to Van Miller (play by play) and Stan Barron (color commentary.) O.J.Simpson was in his prime then, and this was the only year the Bills made it to the playoffs with O.J. They were promptly beat by the Steelers in the first round.

Barb and Jim came to Erie for Thanksgiving along with Barb's brother, Brad, and her mother, Bonnie Beeke. Even though there was now a pool table in the basement, Brad, Jim, and I were itching for the competition usually found in the local taverns. Jim and I had the reputation of sneaking away from family gatherings in search of a bar room with action on the pool table. Sometimes these excursions could take hours, and there would be hell to pay when we got home (rightfully.) By far, we were mostly successful, as a team, on these tavern bar boxes, and there would be many road trips with my brother Jim in the years ahead. Strangely, on Friday morning after Thanksgiving, we came outside to find that Bonnie's 1972 Cadillac had a broken driver's side window. Attempted burglary?

My mother became involved with the Church of the Covenant in Erie. She was part of some Bible Studies, and some other social groups, like bridge club. It was great for her, and she got to meet some very nice people there. During the Erie City School District strike, the church organized an emergency school and asked me to teach Physical Education for them. I did, but it was short lived as the strike was settled before the Christmas break. By the way, my 14-year-old sister Wende was unaffected by the strike since she was enrolled in the 8th grade at the private Erie Day School.

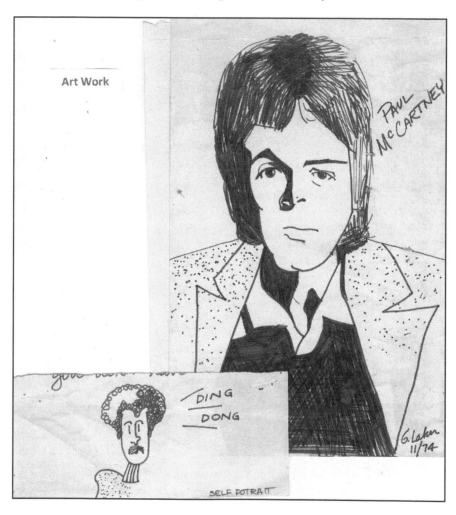

Art Work

The Church of the Covenant had a men's basketball team and of course they recruited me to play for them. Frankly, I was not excited because the level of play was, well, not very competitive. To appease my mother and some nice people at the church, I agreed to play. The games were played at the Erie YMCA and a few other church gyms. This may sound very condescending, but I dominated the league. Our record was 13-1 (I was not there for the only loss.) It was like Kareem playing against a bunch of 8th graders!

On Tuesday, December 10th I got a call from Steve Witter (Gary's father). He wondered if I could procure tickets for a basketball game the next night – SUNY Geneseo at Gannon College in Erie. I was able to get a block of tickets and, of course, I wanted to go to the game myself. Before the game, I met the Witters and divvied up the tickets. It was a hard fought game, but Gannon had the home court advantage and won 74-69. After the game, I got to visit briefly with Gary and Ed Robota.

The subbing jobs were coming more regularly now, in part, I think, because I rarely turned down an opportunity. Usually I would get called the night before, but sometimes I would get called at 6:30 AM and have to be at some city school at 8:00 AM. Finally, I got a great, long-term subbing opportunity at Tech Memorial High School (inner city – Erie). The position was for grades 9-12 Physical Education. I was filling in for a male teacher who was going to be gone for the rest of the school year while convalescing from surgery. Tech Memorial High School was huge. As a matter of fact, there were so many students, they had to split them into two sessions – Monday, Tuesday, Wednesday and Thursday, Friday, Saturday. The 9 hour days were long, but only teaching 3 days a week was great. My assignment started early February and ran through mid- June. That was a great Christmas present.

My long weekends allowed me to make regular trips to Canaseraga to visit Jim, and to Kenmore to visit Casselman and other friends. Cass made several trips to Erie, as well. While in Kemore, of course, I would always stop into Bobby Cue and visit with my friend Bob Clark. Bob was always full of stories about his colorful clientele.

Chapter Eighteen
1975

On one of my trips back to Kenmore, I went to the Eastern Hills Mall (for reasons unknown.) Out of the blue, I ran into my old Kenmore West flame – Anne McGuire. We visited and actually made a date (of sorts) to go to Coles Pub that night. It was all quite surreal, and I have very little recollection of our get together. To make things more bizarre, that night, I ran into my old elementary Physical Education teacher from Washington School – Duane Alt. He looked great and fit; he still had the curly gold hair, but now with a goatee. Somehow, now that I towered over him, he didn't seem quite as daunting to me as when I was in the 4th grade. It was great to talk with him, and he was pleased I was following in his footsteps as an aspiring PE teacher.

Sometime late in January, Cass and I made a trip to Geneseo to visit LW. If memory serves, I think we watched a Geneseo vs. UB basketball game. I can't remember how that game turned out, but my old UB roommate, Bob Dickinson, was now a junior on that team. I wish I could remember more about that game. Anyway, Cass and I stayed over that night at the Sig Tau fraternity house. We were just becoming acquainted with Gary's, unruly, roommate, J.B. Kolbas III (Curly), from Hamburg.

Curly had a pension for practical jokes and crazy pranks – sticking his wet finger in your ear or shit like that. While waiting for Gary and Curly to go out that night, Cass and I toured ourselves around the house. In the large dining room, the walls were lined with composite group portraits of the brothers through the years – dating back decades. As we looked closer, we noticed almost every brother had a nickname. Some of the nicknames were hysterical – Barfo, Potato Head, etc. Cass and I got on one of our laughing jags and we couldn't stop. We were in tears.

Among other places we stopped that night was the on campus ratskellar. Remember, 18 was the legal drinking age at the time. The crowd at the ratskellar went into a frenzy when Buzzo and his band came on stage. Buzzo was only a little older than most of the students, then. He was a little crusty looking, and loved to entertain in his "trademark" bath robe and unmatched socks. Buzzo was a bearded, long-haired, trumpet playing hippie with wire rimmed glasses – he kind of reminded me of Jerry Garcia. We roared with our approval, as he and his band entertained us. Buzzo came to SUNY Geneseo from the NYC area and never left. To this day, he still entertains, and still owns and operates a music store on Main St. in Geneseo. You are likely to see a "BUZZO" bumper sticker anywhere in the USA or beyond. He has truly become a legendary icon.

Back in Erie, I was ready to start my long term subbing assignment at Tech Memorial High School. It was a tough school, and it took me a while to get into the flow. I think I had seven 50 minute periods each school day. When you factor in the time for gym goers to dress for class, and then shower and dress after class – you were lucky to have 35 minutes of activity. Invariably, there were students who were unprepared for gym, or simply did not want to be there. It was an ongoing battle. The support for discipline from the front office was lacking. They didn't want me to send every kid with an attitude down to the principal's office every time there was a problem. The kids knew I was a "young sub," and they tested me. I did the best I could, and cherished the fact I was well-paid and had a 4-day weekend every week. Soon, I was welcomed into the inner sanctum teacher's lounge by some of the more established teachers – that felt good. By the way, there was no such thing as a NON SMOKING teacher's lounge back then. During the lunch hour, I had a 30 minute assignment to monitor one particular boys' lavatory. The boys would crowd into this particular lav to smoke. I once made the mistake of going into this lav and trying to stop them from smoking. That was a joke, and I realized it was a lost cause. From then on, I simply tried to keep the peace and roll with it. Oh, by the way, there was more than cigarette smoke emanating from the area!

Eventually, the "older" teachers invited me to their weekly happy hour, which was always held at a nearby "Polack" bar. Every 6 weeks, the schedule was flipped - six weeks of Monday, Tuesday, Wednesday, then six weeks of Thursday, Friday, Saturday – whatever the case. The standard fare at the bar was $1.50 pitchers of beer and peanuts in shells. After a couple of pitchers, the teacher gossip really started to flow.

As an investment, Amy & Jerry Labie bought a condo/villa in Kings Point, Florida and arranged for Jerry's mother, Sylvia, to reside there. Over the spring break of 1975, we (my father, mother, Wende and I), drove to Florida primarily to visit (the only one-year-old) Disney World and stay at Kings Point with Sylvia. It was the first time for all of us to visit any Disney facility, and we were not disappointed. We first rode the monorail, then the train, right into the Magic Kingdom. We enjoyed many rides and attractions but, for me, my favorite was Space Mountain – which I road several times. As the day wore on, I couldn't help but notice Dad was taking several opportunities to stop and rest.

He would sit on a bench while the rest of us were enjoying various amusements.

The condo/villa at Kings Point was very nice, but a little cramped with all of us Lakers and Sylvia. One night, I decided to go out by myself. My mother did not want me to go. It was about a 20 mile drive down to Hollywood, where I first went to the dog races and then to watch jai alai. The greyhounds were unbelievably fast and fun to watch, but I was an inexperienced better, so I contributed a few bucks to the cause The jai alai was also very fast. The ball was whipped at very high speeds, and the players were very athletic. All-and-all, it was a very entertaining night, and I'm glad I went. Of course, dog racing is no longer legal.

Back in Erie, after spring break, the weather was warming up and I was able to take my Tech Memorial PE classes outside. This really helped the situation. One of my favorite activities with my classes was softball. The kids liked being outdoors, and I liked running the show as the all-time pitcher.

> SIDE NOTE: As I mentioned earlier, my mother was becoming more and more involved at the Church of the Covenant in Erie and meeting new friends. Not too long ago, in real time, I came across a letter written to my mother (back then) from one of these new friends - Margorie "Gar" Richardson. Come to find out, much later, the Richardson's lived in a country home in Millcreek, just outside of Erie. The extreme irony of the story is Gar was the aunt of my future wife, Shelley. The letter was written several years before I would even meet Shelley – another "small world" coincidence.

My buddy Gary Witter and some of his SUNY Geneseo college friends had a master plan after graduation. There was a building adjacent to the campus, in the heart of downtown Geneseo. The building was formerly a laundry/cleaners, and it was for sale. Gary and his friends Frank Adonnino, Tom Basher, and Dave Silliman were hatching plans to buy the building and turn it into a bar which would appeal to the college crowd. They were all gung ho but, of course, they needed the financing. Gary's parents were dead set against his participation, and Dave Silliman (a basketball teammate) was also unable to make it happen. They were both highly disappointed. Tom Basher and Frank Adonnino dove in head first, and the *In Between* bar was born.

For me, the school year at Tech Memorial was coming to an end, and the thought of going back to pumping gas didn't thrill me. I didn't want to miss out on what was going on with my friends in Kenmore – Summer stuff, Crosby Courts, and especially the night life. To make a long story short, Gary, Cass, and I decided to get a place together. My brother Jim's longtime friend, Jack Quinlan, was getting involved with real estate, and he had a house for rent at 34 Knowlton Ave. (Kenmore) right next to the Washington School playground. It was only four doors down from 52 Knowlton where the Laker family had lived in the early '60s. Thirty-four Knowlton was a typical two-story, 1920's vintage house with a front porch, living room, dining room, and kitchen on the first floor. There were two bedrooms and a bathroom on the second floor, and in the attic there was a finished room with a front window overlooking Knowlton Ave. below. After a card game to determine choices of bedrooms, I ended up with the attic room – my second penthouse on Knowlton Ave. Remember, I had a similar attic room just down the street at 52 when I was 9-12 years old.

Needless to say, I was familiar with the neighborhood. Up until this point, Cass had lived only with his parents at 108 Argonne just a couple of blocks away. He had commuted his four years at Buffalo State. Cass was teaching in the Ken-Ton School District now, and working on his Masters. Gary's only experience away from home was his four years at SUNY Geneseo. He still had a chip on his shoulder about not being a part of the *In Between* and he was ready for some independence. We had a fourth house-mate, as well. Jake was Gary's dog, who came into the picture back at Geneseo. Jake went EVERYWHERE with Gary. He was driving a puke orange 1970 Ford Mustang, which he and Jake abused. Cass was driving a brand new 1975 copper colored Chevy Camaro, and I was still rolling in the '69 Ford Fairlane.

A lot would happen that Summer while we were living at 34 Knowlton Ave. Our landlord, Jack Quinlan, and his partner hired Gary to paint some of his rental properties. Joe Czop (salt of the earth, RIP) and I became employees of Gary. Of course, I had two summers worth of painting experience at UB. One house in North Buffalo sticks out in my memory. The house was huge and had dormers at the attic level, which needed painting. The dormers were way up there and required some tricky ladder placement and climbing. I got up to the dormer and painted it all right, but climbing down freaked me out. I do not like heights, so it took a lot of concentration to work up the nerve to climb down. That was the end of any high ladder work for me. I'm pretty sure Gary was uninsured, and of course, there was no thought of safety harnesses. There were a couple of days I slept-in and showed up to work late, so Gary fired me. Then, when he couldn't keep up with the work load, he begged me to come back. Another special paint job which sticks out was a cottage on Lake Erie in Canada, near Crystal Beach. Joe Czop was in on that one, too. The cottage was owned by Vince Daigler (a friend of Gary's dad Steve Witter.) The job took us a few days and required a cou-ple of overnight stays. Much Canadian beer was consumed.

Back at 34 Knowlton, the 3rd floor penthouse proved to be

where visitors wanted to hang out. We could often be found in a circle of bean bag chairs, listening to music, and shootin' the shit. I can't remember having a TV, but we did have a wall mounted telephone in the kitchen. Guys would bring over 33LP vinyl or cassette tapes and listen to what is now referred to as classic rock. The regulars, besides the three of us, were Curly (Jack Kolbas), Mike Vaccaro, and Tauro (Joe Tauriello.) We were listening to Pink Floyd *Dark Side of the Moon*, Rolling Stones, The Marshall Tucker Band, Neil Young, and The Allman Brother's Band, just to name a few. When things got too boring, we would revert to our adolescence and break out our pea shooters. From the attic window, we had a clear shot at passers-by, kids, mostly, coming from the Washington School playground. They wouldn't know what hit them and, of course, we were rolling on the floor in hysterical laughter.

On a serious note, though, you remember Gary's Geneseo basketball teammate, Dave Silliman, who was also unable to participate in the *In Between* bar deal. Dave got involved with some serious drugs and became distraught. He was experiencing delusions and apparitions which caused behavior that landed him in the Buffalo Psychiatric Center on Forrest Ave. There he was, kept on a close suicide watch – it was scary. Gary talked to Dave on the phone at the facility and things were not right with him. His behavior was strange. One storming, rainy day the telephone rang and I was the only one home. It was Dave Silliman calling for Gary. I told him Gary was not home, but he wanted to come to the house anyway to wait for Gary. I was only casually acquainted with Dave from my visits to Geneseo, and I was nervous (actually scared) not knowing what to expect if he came to the house. Although I was expecting Gary to return, there was no way for me to contact him (remember, no cell phones back then). So, there I was, alone at 34 Knowlton in a thunder and lightning storm with pouring rain. The doorbell rang and it was Dave Silliman – soaking wet. I let him in. His eyes were glazed over and he was chilled to the bone. Not knowing what else to do, I drew a hot tub of water for Dave and gave him some dry clothes. Gary finally arrived home and eventually coaxed Dave into returning to the facility.

Sadly, things did not get better for Dave. The following Winter, we got the news Dave had jumped from a bridge through ice to his death near his home in Baldwinsville, NY.

On a much lighter note, we were all still going to the Crosby Courts, occasionally. We were now the old guys. One evening, after basketball at The Courts, a discussion arose as to who could eat Big Macs the fastest. This led to a challenge between Gary and our good friend Charlie Forness (Chucky Wow). Charlie was a little older than us, and as I mentioned earlier in this book, he was a former college football player, and signed at Marshall University (post airplane crash) and a Crosby Courts regular. Charlie and Gary were both big eaters, and after some negotiations, a contest was set. A group of us made our way to a McDonalds on Hertle Ave. near Elmwood. Gary and Charlie each bought three Big Macs. The Big Macs were placed (fully wrapped) on the trunk of Charlie's Chrysler Imperial at the very rear of the parking lot, about 40 yards from Hertle Ave. The two contestants set up in three point stances at the curb of Hertle Ave. waiting for the GO command.

"On your mark, get set – GO!"

They sprinted up the driveway to the Big Macs – wrappers and coleslaw was flying, and major mauwing was under way. The loser would have to reimburse the winner for the Big Macs. In less than two minutes Chucky Wow had polished off his three Big Macs while Gary was just starting his second. Charlie was the undisputed Big Mac eating champion.

This is a good time to note, Charlie also introduced us to "moron" milkshakes at the Avenue soda bar on Delaware Ave. in North Buffalo. The proprietor would mix up gallon sized milkshakes and serve them up in large flower vases. You really had to be craving a milkshake to finish off one of those babies!

We had several night spots we liked to frequent, in those days. Most of them were in or near the "Elmwood" area, adjacent to Buffalo State College. These bars were so popular with the 20-somethings, many times you had to stand in line and wait for someone, or a group, to exit before the bouncer would allow you to enter. The *Locker Room* on Delaware near Forest was a great place. My buddy, Mike Vaccaro, tended bar there. The bartenders were way busy with patrons three deep at the bar. You had to be ready with your order. There was no time for lollygagging. We would sometimes go there during the day, when it was not so busy, and get a beef on weck – best in the city. Coles on Elmwood was also one of our favorite spots. Coles and the Locker Room were both set up so the flow of the crowd traveled in a circular pattern. It could take an hour to squeeze your way around one lap – or longer if you ran into someone interesting. The music was loud, so conversations were sometimes more like shouting matches. There were several other fun and interesting bars in the "Elmwood" scene.

Mulligan's was a name associated with several locations. They had an upscale club on Hertle Ave., and a Summer spot out on Lake Erie near Sunset Beach. Then, there was Mulligan's Brick Bar located in Allentown (the artsy section of the city.) Early that Summer, I made my first trip to the Brick Bar with the boys. Same scenario – stand in line to get into a wall-to-wall sea of humanity. No circular pattern – you were just looking for a place to stand. On this particular night, a group of us were stationed in an area at the rear of the room, a good distance from the bar.

Since it was next to impossible to get to the bar, we would relay money and an order for a case of beer to the bartender. So, the cash would make its way to the bar with instructions for a tip and in this instance (I think it was Rolling Rock splits night) a case of splits, smothered with ice, would be passed/relayed overhead back to the area we had staked out. Again, it was loud and hard to carry on a conversation. With my height 6'6", it was always a challenge to talk with people in that situation – especially shorter gals. The good news, though, my height allowed me to see over crowds. That night, I was introduced to a gal I could talk to face-to-face.

Donna DeGlopper was introduced to me by her cousin, Ellen DeGlopper. Ellen and I had gone through K-12 together, so we were well acquainted. Donna and I had quite a chat that night. We hit it off well, and she gave me her phone number. I can't remember how long it took me to work up the nerve to call her. After all, what if it had just been the beer talking that night at the Brick Bar, and she regretted giving me her phone number. Maybe a week went by, and I called her. It was a little awkward, but I think we arranged to meet out somewhere her group and my group, respectively, were going to be. Soon after that Donna and I started dating. She had a real appreciation for music and she was a musician herself. We had some unconventional dates. I wish I could remember the name of the old theater she took me to see a pipe organ concert. I think it was in North Tonawanda somewhere. I know I was quite reluctant to go, but she encouraged me and I ended up being quite impressed. Sometimes we would just hangout and listen to music. She turned me on to Frank Zappa and Stevie Wonder, who I now have on my Pandora list. Donna also introduced me to roller skating. Yes – roller skating! My recollection of the roller skating rink we went to was disco music and lighting. It was a lot of fun and a great workout.

Donna's parents were the "salt of the earth" type. Mr. De-Glopper (Harold) didn't mind having a beer or two, and he could often be found in his garage tinkering on one of his Chris-Craft wood boats. Most of his boating, I think, was done on the nearby Niagara River. Cass told me Harold was the regular bus driver for the Buffalo State basketball team. Cass always had nice things to say about Harold.

Donna was also a seamstress, and she made some of her own clothes. She was very frugal. I remember her saving towards a new car, which she eventually bought – a 1975 AMC Pacer, as I recall.

August 8th 1975 was a very memorable date. The Rolling Stones were at Rich Stadium. There was a group of us who had tix. We rendezvoused at Jack Kolbas' house in Hamburg. From there, we were able to walk to the stadium. Our seats were on about the 20 yard line (on the field), and the stage was about in the end zone at the tunnel end of the stadium. They were great seats – especially considering this was before the days of Jumbotrons and such. It was a sell-out – even the upper decks were filled. Although I don't remember clearly – I believe The Outlaws were the opening band. It didn't matter. Everyone was psyched for the Stones. The place was bedlam, and Mick and the boys did not disappoint. Although I cannot verify it, Mick appeared to be tugging on a bottle of Jack Daniels. As you can imagine, there were a lot of characters in the crowd, and it was an "anything goes" atmosphere. At one point, all heads turned toward the opposite end of the stadium. You know the cable that stretches from one upper deck to the other? The one that supports the net which catches extra-point kicks and field goals? Well, some idiot made his way from the upper deck and did a "monkey crawl" out on to that cable. There he was, hanging by his hands and feet, high above the stadium floor. I can't remember how they got the guy down; maybe he fell. We were more interested in seeing the concert. Buffalo was the last stop of their "Tour of the Americas."

> SIDE NOTE: In all, I have been to four Rolling Stones concerts in four different decades. The other three were:
>
> - 1989 "Steel Wheels" with my wife Shelley at the Sky Dome in Toronto.
> - 1997 "Bridges to Babylon" with Shelley at Rich Stadium in Orchard Park.
> - 2003 "Forty Licks" with my daughter, Kaitlin, at the Mellon Center AKA the Igloo in Pittsburgh

All in all, it was an eventful summer at 34 Knowlton, and I have only hit on some of the highlights. We did have a few poker games there in the dining room. The last one, in particular, was in the early Fall and it stands out to me because two memorable attendees were present – Bob Olson (RIP) and my good buddy, John Johnston. Olson was known for his crazy talk and gibberish. At one point, Bob just stared out the window in the direction of the Kenmore business district and blurted out "Bank of Buffalo!" Only those who knew Bob Olson could appreciate that tidbit.

Gary's parents, Steve and Yvonne (still living in Vestal), were in the market for a house in Tonawanda as an investment, and possible retirement home. They found a place at 257 Puritan Rd. in the Town of Tonawanda near Brighton and Colvin. The Witters allowed us (Cass, myself, Gary, and Jake) to live there for the same amount of rent, as we were paying at 34 Knowlton. It was an upgrade for us, and it helped pay the mortgage for them. 257 Puritan was a post-World War II ranch house which featured three bedrooms, a kitchen, a living room, and a dining area. It also had a full semi-finished basement, garage, and in-ground swimming pool. We moved to 257 Puritan in the fall of 1975. Although we did nothing to hurt 34 Knowlton, I think we took extra good care of 257 Puritan, knowing Gary's parents were our land lords. By the way, if my chronology is correct, Gary's older brother, Greg (Big Witt), was well-established with General Motors, and sharing a condo with his good buddy, Billy McLean, at nearby and upscale Rain Tree Island. Big Witt was a regular visitor to 257 Puritan, as were several other close friends.

By this time, my finances were becoming an issue. With the house painting season over, I had no steady job (not that the house painting was steady.) For a short period of time, I was a door to door Electrolux vacuum cleaner salesman. I did a lot of demos, but sold none. To this day, though, Electrolux is still my favorite brand of vacuum cleaner. Steve Witter's good friend, Vince Daigler (whose cottage we painted in Canada), put me to work as a moving man at his Mayflower moving business. I learned some neat packing and moving skills there, but the work was sporadic. Needless to say, I was just squeaking by.

We did have a few parties at 257 Puritan – nothing too crazy, no loss of life or limb. In the Summers to follow, it was nice to be able to entertain at the pool. There were two stag parties I can remember there – Curly's and Cass'. Yes, we called them stag parties back then, not bachelor parties. None of my buddies back then could even think about going to Vegas for a bachelor party or anything like that. Mostly though, it would just be a few guys (maybe gals – I was still seeing Donna then) just stopping by with a six pack to watch a ball game.

Most of the "post college" basketball players who were worth their salt played in the Eldridge Club league in Tonawanda. It was definitely the best brand of "post college" basketball played in the greater Buffalo area, and players came from all over Western New York to compete. The Eldridge Bicycle Club is a unique old building with a unique old basketball court. There was a bar similar to what you might find at an Elks Club or an American Legion. The court was less than full size, which lent itself to a physical style of play when playing 5-on-5. It was a little like playing at an old YMCA. Of course, this was way before the 3 point arc. Our team was sponsored by the Locker Room bar (Mike Vaccaro's employer). On our roster, I think, were Mike, LW, Cass, Joe DePriest, Tom Basher, Bump Haskell, Ken Spencer, Dave Cownie, and myself. Again, I'm drawing from memory, and a little help from my friends. You needed that many on your roster to hope you would have at least seven guys show up on any given night.

Because I was financially embarrassed, I had to give serious thought to my future employment options. Unfortunately, I was not having good luck with my prospects for a full time PE teaching and basketball coaching position – my number one choice. The timing was very poor for that. I could always go back to Erie to sub or pump gas and live with my parents, but I needed my independence. While visiting in Erie one weekend, my father told me about an opportunity with United Oil which may be presenting itself. He would soon know the inside scoop.

SIDE NOTE: Our next door neighbors in Erie were the Hawns. Mr. Hawn was a very meticulous guy, and an engineer for General Electric. (GE was a major employer in Erie, then.) To give you an idea – Mr. Hawn would use a toothbrush to detail out the grill of his Mercedes Benz. He was also a big fan of classical music, which he played on his "state of the art" stereo system. As a hobby, Mr. Hawn dabbled in photography. My mother had become friends with Mrs. Hawn, who was a sweet lady, and my sister, Wende, was friends with their daughter. Their son, Ben, was about six years younger than me, but we also became friends. He was an extremely bright guy, and he was in defiance of his father. Ben (6'5") and I would shoot hoops, play Frisbee (he was a master at that), and listen to rock music. When his father wasn't home, we would sneak into the stereo area and play some of our own 33 LPs on the forbidden stereo system. Anyway, my mother, through Mrs. Hawn, arranged for Mr. Hawn to come to our house and take some family portraits while everyone was home for Thanksgiving. The portraits turned out great, and they are definitely a cherished part of the family archives.

Jerry, Amy, Dad with Chris, Mom, Jim, Greg, Wende, Caryn, Susan & Barb

Chapter Nineteen
1976

The opportunity with United Oil my father had told me about came to be. If I wanted to, I could become the operator of a Keystone gas station/general store in Lowville, PA. Lowville is a very small berg in northwestern Pennsylvania (PA Routes 8 & 89) about 15 miles southeast of Erie, and only a couple of miles north of Wattsburg (a slightly larger community – approximately 350 population). The Keystone facilities consisted of one large building with one pump island on a lot which was about 300' x 150'. The building was about 35' x 75', of which was 1/3 store area and 2/3 living area. The store area included display cases, coolers, store room, public bathroom, cash register, safe, etc. – everything needed to run a mini-mart type store. This was before the days of 7/11 or convenient. My deal with United was I could sell mini-mart type items (except for alcohol and tobacco products) as I saw fit, and I would get X number of cents on every gallon of gasoline and diesel fuel I sold. The deal included rent and utilities free of charge. The attached residence featured four bedrooms, bathroom, open kitchen/living area, and a large bonus room which would be perfect for my pool table and stereo system if I decided to proceed.

My father was very enthusiastic about the opportunity. I think he wished he had that type of opportunity when he was my age. Sometime in late Winter, he took me to the vacant facility to show me around. He had a lot of ideas for me, including, for instance, producing "LAKER'S OIL." He was quite the "promo" man, with a lot of experience in the gas station business. He convinced me this would be a good deal for me, and there were no strings attached. If I came up with something better, I could always just walk away.

In the early Spring of 1976, I moved into "Laker's Keystone" and opened for business. I immediately noticed there was a trailer court within walking distance of my store, so I inventoried all of the staples: milk, bread, eggs, canned food, paper products, candy, etc. - stuff which turned over quickly. Like Dad suggested, I started filling one gallon jugs with 30 weight oil from 55 gallon drums – labeled "LAKER'S OIL." That was a popular item, priced right and with a great mark up.

When I pumped gas for a customer, I always cleaned their windshield and offered to check under the hood. Truck traffic was scarce, but when they did pull in, they were usually good for 100 gallons of diesel fuel at a pop.

Soon, I realized I was going to need some help if I was going to establish regular hours – 7 AM to 7 PM. I was now getting to know more of the locals – especially the younger ones. After a while, I recognized certain guys by the cars they drove. The young local guys would drive "the loop" - Wattsburg to Lowville. Laker's Keystone was the turnaround spot on the Lowville end. Some of those young guys would stop for gas or a bottle of pop, and that would lead to conversations. It didn't take long (in this small community) to learn who was who. A couple of guys, Jesse and Pete, expressed an interest in going to work for me, and I agreed to try them out part-time. They were motor head types in their late teens. A system was in place for inventory control, such as it was, but there were a few questionable shift shortages. Nothing real serious, though. The pros of the part timers outweighed the cons. I now had some breathing room to take care of the significant paper work and the, much needed, leisure time.

When the weather got nicer, I started getting company from my friends in Kenmore. I had all kinds of room there if you didn't mind crashing on a mattress in one of the bedrooms. Donna made a few trips to Lowville (now in her new AMC Pacer) and she never came empty handed. She would always bring some kind of culinary treat. When my other buddies showed up, it was usually with beer.

One of the more popular activities, in Lowville, the guys and I really enjoyed was par 3 golf. The locals had steered us to one particular par 3 course out in the boonies. The course was carved into the woods – very scenic and private. We loved going there. It was well kept, very casual, and the price was right. You didn't need to carry many clubs – maybe a 7 iron, pitching wedge, and a putter. It was so casual, as a matter of fact, we sometimes played barefoot. After a round of par 3 golf, our favorite place to go was the Wattsburg Hotel. It was THE place to go for the locals. They had great food, a busy bar, rockin' juke box, and a pool table. One of their specialties was a meatball sub – that was very popular with the guys. I can remember doing very well on that pool table. The local game was bank the 8 ball. This, of course, favored the better players. From the Wattsburg Hotel, we would retire to the comfortable confines of my residence at Laker's Keystone. My living quarters there were very roomy and Bohemian. One of the four bedrooms served as an office, so there were actually two guest rooms besides my own. Like I mentioned earlier, the "bonus" room was perfect for my pool table, and the whole place was wired for music. Somewhere along the way, I acquired a 25" color console TV and, of course, I had a telephone. As the evenings unwound, the guys would get hungry. It became common place for them to raid the mini-mart – Stewart sandwiches, pastries, chips, pretzels, ice cream, candy, etc. They all felt they were entitled, but the truth be told, I was just happy to have the company. I don't think there was a visitor to Laker's Keystone who didn't enjoy themselves. If they didn't, it was their own fault.

> SIDE NOTE: May 21, 1976 – my sister Amy gave birth to her 4th child, Jennifer – another beautiful and welcome addition.

One of my brother Jim's duties at A.L. Blades & Sons, Inc., besides managing their International Harvester truck business, was purchasing vehicles at Tracey's weekly auto auction in Dansville. Mostly, the automobiles he purchased there were for company employees. At the time, I was still rolling in my (rough) 1969 Ford Fairlane and a 1960 red Chevy pickup truck which was only reliable for local use. I needed an upgrade, and I wanted a "fat ride." Jim knew what my budget restrictions were, but for $500, he was able to come up with a 1970 "sky blue" Chrysler Imperial with a white vinyl roof – loaded. The car was perfect, and it made my trips to Erie and Kenmore much more enjoyable.

Dad would occasionally make the trip out to Lowville from Erie. It was now clear he was not well. He had lost significant weight and he had a chronic cough. On July 4th 1976, he was admitted to the Erie Veteran's Hospital. The news was not good. He was diagnosed with terminal lung cancer. Although he was weak, he continued to work. Mom and Dad had previously invited their Lafayette Presbyterian Church couples club "gang" for an overnight visit at 218 Maryland in August. Because Dad was not up to it, the event had to be postponed. Postponed turned out to be wishful thinking.

In August, Cass, Joe Tauriello, Big Witt, and I took a road trip in the Chrysler Imperial to Detroit. The trip was two-fold. First of all, the Labie family, now with their 3 month old daughter,

Jennifer, in the mix, resided in West Bloomfield, a suburb of Detroit. Secondly, Gary Witter now lived in Detroit and worked at the GMC/Chevy plant there. In a strange twist I had introduced Gary to Bob Williams (former basketball player at Pittsburg State College - KS where I had coached him.) The Labies, very hospitably, put us all up. I think Amy was actually tickled to have us. Two activities I remember quite well were playing golf and going to a Detroit Tigers baseball game. While Gary and Bob were working, the four of us – Cass, Big W, Tauro, and I went golfing. On the golf course, we happened to be following a foursome of "older" gentlemen – probably in their 60s. We noticed they were not hitting their tee shots very far – but straight. From there, the term "old man's golf" was coined, I think by Cass, and it has remained in our verbal repertoire ever since. The sad thing is, now we are the "old men," and we don't always hit our balls straight! The second activity of note was all of us going to a Detroit Tigers baseball game at the, now gone, iconic Tiger stadium vs. the Texas Rangers. Pitching for Detroit was Mark "Bird" Fidrych – rookie sensation and All-Star. Fidrych went through all sorts of antics on the mound – talking to the ball, etc. He was very entertaining and effective. In those days, it was not uncommon to have an usher escort your group to better seats if they were available. Of course, they expected a gratuity for such a favor but, at the time, we were too naïve or cheap to accommodate our usher for delivering our group to box seats right behind first base. He was giving us the "hairy eyeball" the rest of the game, and cursed us on the way out. The finish was great, though. Tiger's slugger Willie Horton hit a walk off home run off of Hall of Famer Gaylord Perry to get the win for Fidrych.

On October 11, 1976, all of the Labies and the Lakers traveled to Akron, Ohio for a family reunion to celebrate Uncle Carl and Aunt Mary Jane's 50th wedding anniversary – all but Dad, that is.

He was just unable to make the trip. It was a wonderful get together, and we got to see extended family we hadn't seen in years. It was a big disappointment for us Dad could not be there, but even more of a disappointment for him.

Halloween in Lowville

The biggest event during my time at Laker's Keystone was, by far, Halloween. The guests arrived in waves and from many different directions. The early arrivers were Donna, Joe Tauriello, Casselman, my brother Jim, and his wife Barb. They all helped with party preparations including pumpkin carving – which we decided to make into a contest. Each of us would, simultaneously and independently, carve our pumpkins into Jack-O-Lanterns, and then wait for the final reveal. There was much anticipation, as the time came to expose our work. When the Jack-O Lanterns were unveiled, most were very nice and carefully thought out carvings – but when Joe Tauriello revealed his work, there was thunderous laughter. (I'm laughing right now as I write this.) Joe's pumpkin looked like the work of Jack the Ripper – all chopped up and disfigured. We were all rolling on the floor, roaring in laughter – including Joe. The party was a kegger + BYOB, I wish I could remember more of the costumes. Jim and Barb were Mr. & Mrs. Potato Head. I was doing my best Bill Walton with my hippie hair and beard, but the most memorable costume of all was Joe Tauriello's. After the Jack-O-Lantern carving, Joe disappeared for a while. When he returned, he was dressed in a white sheet sandwiched by two large, brown, round pieces of cardboard. On the front large, brown piece of cardboard, a message read: "I am an Oreo Cookie." On the back large, brown piece of cardboard, the message read: "Waiting to be eaten". Again, Joe had us all laughing with tears running down our faces.

Like I said, party goers (maybe 25 or so) were arriving from all directions and in waves. Of course there was a large contingent from Kenmore. There was a late arriving van full from Detroit (260 miles each way) which livened up the party. We later discovered, however, one of the passengers fell asleep on the way to Lowville. He slept through the party without even leaving the van, and never regained consciousness until sometime late that night, on the trip back to Detroit. Another guest came knocking on the door late. It was a masked man with a half empty, bottle of Jack Daniels in his hand. None of us could figure out who this man was. He called himself "Hugo." Finally, "Hugo" removed his mask to expose his real identity. It was, my friend, Bob Blades. Hugo had driven the 120 miles from Hornell to join the party. The party was a great success, but if I had to name an MVP, it would have to be Joe T.

Another unforgettable evening in Lowville – which I'm not particularly proud of, but it happened – came in the late fall when Cass and, our friend, Joe Notaro came for an overnight. My younger sister Wende also happened to be visiting that night. Cass and Joe were now housemates in a nice old house they were renting on East Hazeltine in Kenmore. Joe, among other things, was known for his "gator" move. Sometimes, out of the blue when he was partying, Joe would drop to the floor – belly up – and kick his feet and hands like a flopped gator. We all had been drinking beer while playing pool and listening to music. Suddenly, Joe went down for one of his familiar "gators." In his haste, he miscalculated his descent to the floor and clipped the side of the unforgiving pool table with his head. Ouch! We soon discovered Joe had a gash in his head (under his hair) which was bleeding, and it was apparent it was going to need stitches. Like I said, we had been drinking, but Joe needed medical attention. We all loaded into the Chrysler Imperial and headed to the nearest hospital, which was about 12 miles away in Union City. When we got to the hospital, Joe was loaded onto a gurney and was waiting to be treated. We were all in a silly mood and we started rolling Joe around the hospital – Three Stooges style. The staff at the hospital was not amused, but Joe got his stitches and we returned to Lowville and resumed our partying.

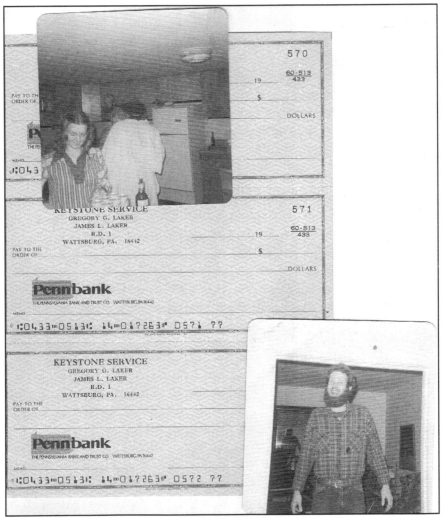

Halloween 1976 at Laker's Keystone - Lowville, PA

Sometime late in 1976, when I was visiting my friends in Kenmore, we were out making some stops at our favorite places on Elmwood. The last stop was at Coles. I can remember standing at the rear of the bar when I was approached by a cute young gal. She struck up a conversation with me and said something like, "You're Greg Laker, aren't you? And you played basketball at the University of Buffalo, didn't you?"

Of course, I was very impressed and flattered. Her name was Mary Ellen Lonergan – about 5'4" with short brown hair and from South Buffalo. We had quite a visit and, by the end of the night, she had given me her phone number and asked me to call her. This presented a girlfriend quandary. Although there was nothing binding in my relationship with Donna, I felt some discomfort about calling Mary Ellen. The temptation finally became too great, and I broke down and called Mary Ellen for a date. Some of my guy and gal friends showed their disappointment in, what they thought was, my poor judgment, and that hurt. I was torn.

Chapter Twenty
1977

In those days, when I went to visit my friends in Kenmore, I would stay with Cass and Joe Notaro at the house they were renting on East Hazeltine. The two-story 20s vintage house was furnished and decorated like your typical Gramma and Grampa house – quite formal but cozy. There was a sunroom at the front of the house on the first floor, with a day bed that served as a guest room.

Mary Ellen and I were now seeing each other regularly. Since I was still living in Lowville, at Laker's Keystone, the relationship was long distance (as it was with Donna.) Mary Ellen was a couple of years younger than me, and she lived with her Irish family in a typical South Buffalo neighborhood not far from Cazenovia Park. If my memory serves, she was in a nursing program at Mercy Hospital. Eventually, I got to meet the family. They were very kind and accepting to me. She called her father by his first name, Pete. One night, when we were looking for something to do, her mother suggested we go to "such and such" local tavern for chicken wings. Believe it or not, this was the first time I ever had wings.

Some of the nights with Mary Ellen got to be quite late, and I remember having a hard time staying awake on my way back to Kenmore.

The grind at Laker's Keystone was getting tiresome, and I was anxious to move on to something different. Oh, by the way, I had adopted two female gray tiger kittens. Gladys and Gertrude were now full grown.

My father was getting weaker, and working only sporadically. It was a terrible feeling of helplessness, knowing there was nothing we could do for him. My mother had her hands full looking after Dad, keeping up with the house, and overseeing my sister Wende, who was now 16. Mother was still healthy at this point, and she was getting good moral support from her friends at the Church of the Covenant and her group in Buffalo.

> SIDE NOTE: Significantly, the Blizzard of 1977 hit Buffalo with a vengeance, January 28th through February 1st. There was accumulation of up to 100" of snow, and winds up to 69 mph, causing drifts up as high as the street lights. Buffalo was at a standstill.

Around this time, my brother Jim broached the idea of hiring me at A. L. Blades & Sons, Inc. to sell International Harvester trucks. Although I had zero experience with trucks or sales, the challenge and opportunity to work with my brother was very appealing. After some negotiations between Jim and the Blades, it was set – I would start my sales job at Blades February 21st. My starting salary was $125 a week, and I had the use of a company car – a 1973 silver Chevy Monte Carlo, previously driven by Robert U. Blades Sr. (VP), plus gas at the company truck pump.

The timing of the new job allowed me to give ample notice to United Oil. Barb and Jim graciously offered to let me stay at their house in Canaseraga TEMPORARILY until I found an apartment. In one of my last conversations I had with my father, he emphasized to me my stay with Barb and Jim should be temporary, and I shouldn't be a divider. I agreed and promised.

Over the next month, while still taking care of business at Laker's Keystone, I gradually moved my stuff to Canaseraga – including my pool table. Brad Beeke was a big help in the moving. Barb and Jim had a nice room in their basement which provided a great spot for the pool table (it's 3rd home under my watch). I was also able to sell my 1970 Chrysler Imperial and my 1960 Chevy pickup. The 1960 Chevy pickup went to Charlie Forness (he loved it.)

So, on February 21st I went to work for A. L. Blades & Sons, Inc., and moved in with Barb and Jim. Jim already had enjoyed success selling trucks at Blades. After all, Jim is a born salesman – he has a way with people. He had learned a lot about trucks since taking the job seven years prior. It was now time for Jim to impart that knowledge to me. There were stacks of truck data and pricing books to digest, and I needed to get out into my new territory to introduce myself to my prospective customers. Bear in mind, Blades was primarily a construction company. They were now in their 3rd generation, stretching back to post World War I when Archie Lee Blades started the company. They became an International Harvester truck dealership in the 40s, primarily to support their own fleet of trucks. Additional truck sales now would be a bonus.

My truck sales territory (area of responsibility – AOR) was basically Allegany and Steuben counties, with parts of Livingston and Yates counties mixed in. The Blades name was very well known and respected in that area, but more for road construction and blacktop than for IH trucks sales. By far, most of Blades' construction work and asphalt products were sold to municipalities – towns, counties, and NY State. Jim had previously been out in the territory and paved the way for me.

The strategy of selling trucks (or any product) to municipalities was to have the bid specifications favor your truck. Bids were submitted in sealed envelopes which included written specifications and price. The bid opening would be advertised for a certain date, time, and place. If you met all of the specifications and you were the low bidder, you would normally get the award. If you were the low bidder, but didn't meet the specifications, the municipalities' officials had the right to accept or reject your bid at their discretion. That's basically how it worked.

On some of the weekends, I was traveling to Buffalo (in my 1973 Monte Carlo) to visit Mary Ellen. Things were going well between us – I really thought a lot of her.

The inevitable came to be Sunday, March 20th when my father passed away. He spent the few preceding days in the Veterans Hospital in Erie, so we all got to spend time with him then. The gravity of my father's loss did not hit me right away. Of course, I knew he was gone, but it took me years to understand how distressing it was to lose him at age 53, and how much I missed him. My daughters would never know their grandfather Laker, and he would never know the joy of knowing them. Having grandchildren, now, puts it all into perspective. It makes my time spent with my daughters and grandchildren that much more precious.

Many of my close friends came to Erie for Dad's calling hours, including Mary Ellen AND Donna. That was a little awkward for them and me, but I give Donna a lot of credit for her show of compassion.

There was a nice service for my father on Wednesday the 23rd at the Church of the Covenant, and we eventually laid his ashes to rest in a Smith (Mother's family) plot at Forest Lawn in Buffalo.

SIDE NOTE: Forest Lawn and hundreds of acres of land stretching to the Niagara River were once owned by my great, great, great grandfather (and namesake) Erastus Granger. He was commissioned by Thomas Jefferson to be the first Post Master of Buffalo and a liaison to Chief Red Jacket.

Soon after my father's passing, I moved to a newly renovated apartment at the top of Crosby Creek Road above Alfred Station with Gladys and Gertrude. I kept my promise to my father to live with Barb and Jim only temporarily. Before long, for reasons unknown to me, Mary Ellen ceased to return my many phone calls. That's all still a mystery to me. I guess it was now my turn to feel the pain.

So, as not to end this Volume 1 on an unhappy note, please be assured after re-reading the preceding 250+ pages, I realize how lucky I was to that point in my life, and how lucky I will be to, someday, share the next number of great years of my life in Volume 2.

JAMES L. LAKER

UNITED REFINING CO.   2ND & CASCADE STS.
MANAGER   ERIE, PA. 16512
ERIE WHOLESALE   TELEPHONE 814 / 456-7516

APPENDIX

MISCELLANEOUS

GL EMPLOYMENT HISTORY

1963 -	Assist paperboy for John Johnston, - Exxon Tiger - Kenmore
1965 -	Stock boy RX store - Kenmore
1967-68 -	Pump gas Exxon – T/O Tonawanda
1969 -	Janitor @ SCCC, Brown's furniture store deliveries etc. – Liberal, KS
1970 -	Janitor Hoover Junior High School, garden shop worker – T/O Tonawanda
1970-71 -	Basketball team laundry @ SCCC – Liberal, KS
1971-72 -	Painter SUNY Buffalo
1973 -	Construction @ A L Blades - Hornell
1973-74 -	Under graduate assistant basketball coach @ Pittsburg State University - KS
1974-75 -	Substitute Phys Ed teacher – Erie, PA school district, Assistant manager Keystone gas stations, unload fuel tank train cars United Oil - Erie
1975-76 -	Painter for Gary Witter, Moving man, auto parts press mfg, Electrolux sales – Buffalo area
1976-77 -	Laker's Keystone Lowville, Pa
1977-92 -	A L Blades International Truck sales, high school basketball official - Hornell
1982-83 -	Graduate assistant basketball coach @ Alfred University, NY
1992-2013 –	Truck equipment sales – CYNCON EQUIPMENT – Rush, NY

GL RESIDENCES

1951-60 199 Parkwood Ave	Kenmore, NY
1960-63 52 Knowlton Ave	Kenmore, NY
1963-64 213 East Steuben St	Bath, NY
1964-66 160 Knowlton Ave	Kenmore, NY
1966-69 51 McKinley Ave	Kenmore, NY
1969-70 203 W. Walnut St	Liberal, KS
1970-74 115 Warren Ave	Kenmore, NY
1970-71 1142 N. Jordan Ave	Liberal, KS
1971-72 23A Yale Ave (Allenhurst)	Eggertsville, NY
1972-73 811 Clement Hall	Buffalo, NY
1973 15 Maple St	Hornell, NY
1973 517 Dellinger Hall	Pittsburg, KS
1974 416 East Kansas Ave	Columbus, KS
1974 218 Maryland Ave	Erie, PA
1975 34 Knowlton Ave	Kenmore, NY
1975-76 257 Puritan Rd . . . . . T/O	Tonawanda, NY
1976-77 Routes 8 & 89	Lowville, PA
1977 Friener Hill Rd	Canaseraga, NY
1977 Crosby Creek Rd	Alfred Station, NY
1977-78 254 Walnut St	Hornell, NY
1978-79 Old Almond Rd	Hornell, NY
1979-89 43 Third St	Canisteo, NY
1989-90 35 ½ Elm St	Hornell, NY
1990-91 31 Collier St	Hornell, NY
1991-now 8 Buffalo St	Canisteo, NY

Gerrands' #10

HOLE	1	2	3	4	5	6	7	8	9	GROSS	H'CAP	NET
H'CAP	6	9	7	2	3	1	8	4	5			
PAR	4	5	4	3	4	5	4	4	3.	36		

DATE   /   /

SCORER

ATTEST

LOCAL RULES

1. USGL Rules will govern except as modified by local rules.
2. Tee off behind head spot/diamonds.
3. Any scratch is penalty stroke.
4. Ball off fairway is penalty stroke.
5. Allow faster players to play through.

LOCAL RULES

6. Object balls stay in cup in case of scratch.
7. Cue ball in hand in case of scratch.
8. Repair all ball marks.
9. APPROPRIATE ATTIRE REQUIRED.

ENJOY YOUR DAY!

BASEMENT BLUES......For your entertainment

THE TUNAGE YOU WILL HEAR TONIGHT IS A MIX PULLED FROM THE
VAULTS OF "BASEMENT BLUES". WE HAVE BLUES, CLASSIC ROCK,

CONTEMPORARY AND COUNTRY ROCK. SOME OF THE GROUPS WE HAVE,

FOR EXAMPLE, ARE:

ROBERT CRAY

BB KING

KENTUCKY HEADHUNTERS

LED ZEPPELIN

ZZ TOP

CCR

BROOKS & DUNN

BUDDY GUY

BOB MARLEY

STEVIE RAY VAUGHAN

HANK WILLIAMS, JR

THE BEATLES

THE ALLMAN BROS BAND

AND MANY MORE........

MUDDY WATERS

JOHN LEE HOOKER

THE DOORS

SANTANA

JIMI HENDRIX

DUKE ROBILLARD

GLENN MILLER

TRAVIS TRITT

STEELY DAN

DON HENLEY

THE ROLLING STONES

JOHN MAYAL

CHARLIE MUSSELWHITE

SIT BACK AND ENJOY....BETTER YET GET UP AND DANCE

DON'T BE AFRAID TO MAKE A REQUEST !

Greg Laker

8 Buffalo St
Canisteo, NY 14823

(607) 698-9161 Office
(585) 703-1713 Cell
grangerlaker@yahoo.com

EDUCATION

Alfred University, Alfred, NY (1982-83)
- Graduate School: Athletic Administration
- Assistant Head Basketball Coach

Pittsburg State University, Pittsburg, KS (1973-74)
Obtained B.S. Degree in Education
- Certified Physical Education K-12
- Assistant Head Basketball Coach

University of Buffalo, Buffalo, NY (1971-73)
- Undergraduate work toward B.S. in Education
- 2 years NCAA Men's Basketball Scholarship

Seward County Community College, Liberal, KS (1969-71)
- A.A. degree
- 2 years NJCAA Men's Basketball Scholarship

Kenmore West High School, Kenmore, NY (Graduated 1969)
- General Studies
- 2 years Varsity Basketball

EMPLOYMENT

CYNCON Equipment Inc., Rush, NY (1992-present)
Truck and Municipal Equipment Dealer:
- Sales Coordinator for 8 county territory

A. L. Blades & Sons, Inc., Hornell, NY (1977-92)
Navistar International Truck Dealer:
- Truck Sales Manager
- Manage International truck sales for 5 county territory